The Potentials of Spaces
The Theory and Practice of Scenography & Performance

By Alison Oddey
and Christine White

'Oddey and White's book is a must for anyone engaging in areas of performance and scenography, immensely readable and profound. This international collection of scholarly chapters gives readers the latest thinking, practice and research in this subject.'

— Professor Lawrence Wallen, School of Art and Design, Zurich

'A significant text, a highly informative and at times provocative synthesis — with a welcome global dimension to the exciting examples of interdependencies in performance and scenography.'

— Professor Eric Prince, Colorado State University

The Potentials of Spaces

The Theory and Practice of Scenography & Performance

By Alison Oddey
and Christine White

intellect
Bristol, UK
Portland, OR, USA

First Published in the UK in 2006 by
Intellect Books, PO Box 862, Bristol BS99 1DE, UK

First published in the USA in 2006 by
Intellect Books, ISBS, 920 NE 58th Ave. Suite 300, Portland, Oregon
97213-3786, USA

A catalogue record for this book is available from the British Library

Cover Design: Gabriel Solomons
Copy Editor: Holly Spradling
Typesetting: Mac Style, Nafferton, E. Yorkshire

ISBN 1-84150-137-9

Printed and bound in Great Britain by 4edge Ltd.

CONTENTS

ACKNOWLEDGEMENTS

We would like to acknowledge the assistance we have received in compiling this book, and the intellectual generosity of all the contributors. We also extend our thanks to colleagues who expressed a strong interest in contributing to this volume but, for various reasons, could not do so.

We would like to thank the Arts and Humanities Research Council and the Higher Education Funding Council for England in the Science Research Initiative Funded schemes for their financial support. We would like to thank all the photographers who have provided their images for this volume.

We would like to acknowledge how Scenography and its links to Performance have become an area of intense study for academics and practitioners, and, in particular, the research undertaken through the Scenography Research Group of the International Federation for Theatre Research. The discussions on offer in this volume testify to the immense activity both within and outside of the academy in terms of both theory and practice.

Lastly, we gratefully acknowledge the advisory board of Scenography International for all their contributions and comments.

LIST OF ILLUSTRATIONS

INTRODUCTION
THE POTENTIALS OF SPACES

Alison Oddey and Christine White

This book is developed from the diverse and international research being undertaken in the areas of Scenography and Performance. The diversity of approaches has necessitated new methods of working, requiring artists to interrogate new media, and to develop a theory of making performance for differing spaces. Our research questions for this project were developed from the changed and changing practices of artists, academics and practitioner-researchers, who were engaged with making performance, positioning their own work within contemporary practice, historical precedent and across disciplines. What interested us and provoked this investigation related to a central enquiry as to what it was that practitioners and academics want to place in space as Scenography and as Performance. How does the space change and develop the project? How do these spaces simply allow us to be and to indulge in a process of reverie, memory and nostalgia? What are the problems of liveness in multimedia work and how do you create a sense of presence in the virtual space? We also wanted to look at the playing and rehearsal space, the dialectics of those spaces, using the imagination, technology and the notion of being transported in space, potentially transformed to a point where it becomes impossible to articulate a level of unconscious responses to the work we experience. The chapters contained in the book develop these theoretical discussions and cross boundaries of diverse performance companies and individual artists' work.

We began this research by asking, what is the relationship of Scenography and Performance with regard to the potentials and poetics of spaces? In attempting to answer this we have referred to Jerzy Grotowski who in *The Theatre's New Testament* writes of the arguments for and against the confrontation of design and literature:

In practice the most original stage-designers suggest a confrontation between the text and a plastic vision which surpasses and reveals the playwright's imagination. It is probably no coincidence that the Polish designers are often the pioneers in our country's theatre. They exploited the numerous possibilities offered by the revolutionary development of the plastic arts in the twentieth century which, to a lesser degree, inspired playwrights and producers.[1]

Therefore, the book attempts to show the interdependence and relationship between experiments, which see the potentials of Scenography and Performance and demonstrates the multiple narratives of Scenography and Performance as experiential communication. The primacy of the text has been the underlying assumption of much of western dramatic theory; however, in his *Poetics* Aristotle noted the non-literary aspects of drama, as spectacle and music. We have, therefore, selected work for this volume, which explores the use of the scenic, music and text, in focussing the developments of new performance potentials.

Our intention is that this work will be used by undergraduates and postgraduates, and as a useful collection of international academics' and practitioners' responses to the changed environment of theatre-making, performance, theatre design and scenography. It is a unique volume in this regard for its coverage and readership, and for its application across the boundaries of what is defined as and understood as Scenography and Performance.

Since its inception in 2000 the *Different Directions* series of Symposia has developed groupings of researchers and practitioners who have discussed working practices and developments that have crossed boundaries between theatre, performance, visual art, multimedia and computers, alongside pure research. *Different Directions* was conceived as a brand name, deliberately ambiguous, and suitable for encompassing any number of diverse and evolving interests. We have divided the research from our first investigation of Scenography and Performance into three parts: 'Different Beginnings', which looks at the beginnings of the work; 'Performance Potentials', which looks at the potentials of new media and 'Aesthetic Visions', which demonstrates combinations of Scenography and Performance. These categories holistically reflect a fascinating diversity of insights into practice and research being undertaken in and across the interdisciplinary areas of scenographic and performative work. Scenography explores time and space performatively. Space has become practice, a practice of space rather than a presentation of space. The Scenography becomes the Performance, and the experience of the space for the spectator is integral to the performance experience.

HISTORICAL CONTEXT

Scenography and Performance have frequently been discussed by practitioners and academics, in practice and through theory since the Renaissance, not necessarily using these terms and often not recognising them as symbiotic partners working towards the same ends. These debates have also varied in their context and veracity. The battle between literary and visual texts is documented in a number of forums, for example, Ben Jonson and Inigo Jones' arguments about the body of theatre as related to spectacle and the visual; and the soul of theatre being Jonson's poetry and prose, the latter according to Jonson being disrupted by Inigo Jones' lavish spectacles particularly of the Court Masques. However, all this really achieves is a diversion from the crux of the activity, which occurs on stage – that is performance. What all the chapters presented here recognise is that any performance that occurs is a visual experience, and it encompasses three dimensions, which reflects the cultural identity of the society who are watching it.

The need for a distinction of the acting or performance space from the audience environment has also been continually debated over the centuries. The requirement that a performance space should be in front of the scenic space, is set down unequivocally by the author of Europe's first treatise on theatre architecture in 1767, Francesco Algarotti.[2] The debates about space are, therefore, covered in a number of different essays and across a variety of cultures and centuries. However, Colley Cibber, the English actor and playwright concluded that, "this extraordinary and superfluous space occasions such an undulating from the voice of the actor generally [that] what they said sounded like the gabbling of so many people in the lofty yarns of the cathedral."[3] By 1740, when Cibber condemned Vanbrugh's attempt to create a playhouse, the Kings Theatre had already become an opera house. Even then its large size and awkward shape were among the reasons which led the composer Handel in 1734, to transfer allegiance to the smaller and more intensely focused first Covent Garden, which moreover was equally effective as a playhouse. Thus, spaces, which have been built for a specific purpose, have often been found to be less than satisfactory, therefore, the changing of space and the ways in which spaces have been used, has also developed our sense of what makes for a 'good' space for performance.

Theatre practitioners of the modern movement developed technical innovations in playhouses, in an attempt to try and present more naturalistic settings, which were becoming fashionable towards the end of the nineteenth century in England and America. In addition, in Germany and in Austria, new technologies such as a revolve, the use of hydraulics, of lifts and flying systems, and other labour-saving devices were developed. However, the innovative scenographic ideas of Adolphe Appia and Edward Gordon Craig were given little credence in popular theatre. The pivotal shift from conventional realism towards symbolism and other modernist trends was further enhanced in the production of stylised performances by Meyerhold and Tairov, which were later to be called constructivist. These experiments explored the nature of the stage space as visceral visual performance, with the talents of women designers Liubov Popova and Varvara Stepanova.[4] For Meyerhold's production of The Magnanimous Cuckold in 1922, Popova did not paint a set in a pictorial sense but built a construction, an autonomous installation that could function anywhere, in the street or within a building. It was a spatial formula. The energy of the construction is said to have pulsed along the beams and meant that the performances were stimulated by the beams and cross-beams of the set, and the plastic movements of the performers exposed the dynamic of the stage space. The architectural lines of the space, therefore, met the visual interaction of the performers' action. In performance, action and construction, Scenography and Performance were inseparable. The Scenography, which had been produced by Popova, however, was the space that was being sought by theatre practitioners around the world, "not a painterly representation of an object but the very materiality of these objects."[5] The development of quite distinctive stage spaces during the twentieth century from Guthrie's thrust stage to Terence Gray's proposed Festival Theatre in Cambridge, to the Olivier Theatre, by Dennis

Lasdun, for the Royal National Theatre in London; Mariano Fortuny's experiments with lighting, along with George Izenour's books on *Theatre Design* and *Theatre Technology* all extended the scope of what should or could be a performance space. They were all wrestling with the volume of the stage, not as a void but as a substance to be worked with. What has developed is an interest in the potentials of the poetics of stage space, "Of course, the naturalist theatre had no need for such development of the stage area, for in real life all normal people walk on a level floor, and those who all of a sudden decide to climb over chairs and tables are put in a lunatic asylum."[6] In 1989, Ariane Mnouchkine interviewed by Gaelle Breton and published in *Theatres*,[7] made the case for 'found' space. The preference for found space was to many theatre architects incomprehensible; however, to the experimental and avant-garde artists, found space clearly advertises that the theatre played there is different from that which was or is played in the traditional theatre buildings.

THE CREATIVE SPACE

What this development of the use of found space did show was that buildings and spaces had existing character, ambience and dramatic potential, which were and are exciting, offering a creative space very different from that of the traditional theatre building. It is also worth considering that found space directly involves Scenography and Performance, where the skills of theatre artists are provoked to envisage what is possible. There is a poetic intention alongside the practical, where the spirit of the space develops alongside the nature of the performance. In 1976, the French stage designer Pierre Chaix wrote, "the spectacle should no longer be confined to the stage, but should invade the entire space."[8] The development of such an invasion of Scenography in performance can be seen in the work of William Dudley and Bill Bryden in the United Kingdom with their production of *The Ship* in Glasgow in 1990, which was rooted in a variety of historical heritages. Bill Bryden's dream was that:

> ...we build the ship-the liner-in fact, and at the end of the evening. It is launched...In the engine shed of shipbuilders Harland and Wolff Dudley created, in steel, a liner that was launched into an infinity of smoke at the end of the slipway once that half of the audience seated in three galleries formed by the steel ribs of the hull had left to help remove the timber supports prior to the launching. This ship/theatre, long and narrow with opportunities for staging the length of the vessel, held 550 seated and 350 promenading....[9]

This structure became almost a theatre building in its own right, a crucible of Scenography for performance. In his book *The Empty Space*, 1968, Peter Brook wrote "the science of theatre building must come from studying what it is that brings about the most vivid relationship between people and this is best served by asymmetry, even by disorder? If so, what can be the rule of this disorder?"[10]

PERFORMING SPACE

In her book *Space in Performance: making meaning in the theatre*, Gay McAuley states that:

> A theatrical performance, whatever its genre, is a physical event occupying a certain space and a certain duration...A traditional theatrical performance creates and presents a fictional world

or worlds and a series of events occurring in this fictional worlds, or the series of actions presented, is also segmented, as the word 'series' in both phrases indicates, and it is therefore itself necessarily structured.[11]

However:

> To claim that performance segmentation occurs on two levels, the presentational and the fictional is doubtless to invite the objection that not all theatre creates a fictional world, and it must certainly be recognized that in the performance practices of the avant-garde from Dada onward, the notion of fiction, and particularly narrative fiction, has been under attack. The experience of fiction is always precarious in the theatre due to the complexity and power of the stage reality and the fascination exercised by the presentational system…the theatre also functions very powerfully to fictionalise whatever it presents.[12]

In this respect theatre is a place where fiction and reality come together to promote each other, "What is presented in performance is always both real and not real, and there is constantly interplay between the two potentialities, neither of which is ever completely realized. The tension between the two is always present, and, indeed, it can be argued that it is precisely the dual presence of the real and not real, that is a constitutive of theatre."[13]

The potentials of spaces for performance are necessarily spaces where the reality and illusion are both a simulation of the material world but also, and simultaneously, real. Therefore, there is a combination and interaction of fictional events, actions, all global utterances and presentational means that construct and present these two senses of reality, and which mark the segmentation process at all levels. Subsequently, it is this interplay between language, space and scenography which is then activated. What remains meaningful and global to some extent (in terms of the event's communication), is made significant within the space, which has been explored in the work of artists like Richard Foreman. In Foreman's work, units of action are built up in different ways and spectators must work from the detail of the micro-levels from which the physical material and vocal construct operate. The process by which Scenography in performance makes meaning, however, has referents to the real world and the combination and recognition of Scenography in performance as a part of contemporary performance practice, holds both concepts of the fictional and presentational intention, one and the other, at the same time. For Artaud such tensions of objects were important, "No décor. Hieroglyphic characters, ritual costume, 30 ft. high effigies of King Lear's beard in the storm, musical instruments as tall as men, objects of unknown form and purpose are enough to fill this function."[14] The rupture of the real world, and the inability to ascribe particular functions of a utilitarian nature to Scenography, and the realisation that the object can be neither understood nor can it be controlled, has produced a stage space of objects and images which have a surreal power, and this is discussed in the chapters concerned with the work of Foreman by Neal Swettenham and Michael Levine's Scenography discussed by Natalie Rewa.

INTERDISCIPLINARY SPACE
In her essay, *Directing and Producing Theatre with the help of Virtual Reality*, Joanne Tompkins identifies the difficulty of accessing theatre spaces, both from the point of view of practitioners and

researchers of theatre, exploring the possibilities of virtual reality as a means for the development of ideas for performance. Studies of space and, "the reflected meanings of spatiality",[15] have provided a crucial interdisciplinary focus on space, where the particular theories of the practicalities of theatre combine with theories of geography, philosophy and politics. In Edward Soja's reading of Foucault he suggested that space is determined by its relationship to sites.[16] Soja is looking at a critical human geography, and what we are concerned with here is a cultural geography, provoked by the need to interpret space and review the nature of spatial imagination for performance. Soja suggests that biography is used to express and, "to gain knowledge, that is useful and beneficial, if not emancipatory, in its cumulative effect."[17] The ontology of human existence is being debated, therefore, in a variety of forums, "the inherent and encompassing speciality of being and becoming is beginning to be more forcefully recognised than ever before."[18] It is with this in mind that we embarked on collaborative research, which directly developed from the two discrete strands of study of Scenography and Performance, and it was with a view to not privileging either research study area over another, our intention was to make historical and practical sense of these research areas within spatial perspectives. In this sense, we want to provoke a look at imagination, perceived space, and the potentials of space that are part of theatre makers and theatre practitioners' modus operandi. This might be seen as a transcendental pursuit but the climb upwards here is looking towards a Kantian sense of creating, making and producing work which has no definite rule, "hence originality must be its first property," but also where there is a place for tradition which can form an example to be followed, "whom it wakens to a feeling of his own originality."[19]

The research contained within the chapters of this book is dependent on the approaches of artists, practitioners and academics and has led directly from an experienced world of theatre making, which the practitioners and academics have been exploring. We know from theatre practice, and from critical analysis of how space works in an architectural form, that it can powerfully control the way we think. The material and objective, the ideal and the subjective, are not opposite poles in its practice, but rather this bicameral view enables the potential of spaces. This also enables the shifts of rhythm from a linear or diachronic sequencing to the development of simultaneous experiences and synchronies, which are contained in many of the chapters of the book. Perhaps what are most pertinent to Scenography in Performance are the words of bell hook's, *Yearning: Race, Gender and Cultural Politics*, "spaces can be real and imagined. Spaces can tell stories and unfold histories. Spaces can be interpreted, appropriated, and transformed through artistic and literary practice."[20] All of the work contained within this book is open to interpretation, exercising the imagination within the gymnasium of the brain, and thus contributing to the experiences provoked in an audience.

In contrast to this, we must also recognise the world of the production of performance, "In the culture industry the individual is an illusion not merely because of the standardization of the means of production. He is tolerated only so long as his complete identification with the generality is unquestioned...What is individual is no more than the generality's power to stamp the accidental detail so firmly that it is accepted as such."[21] This fear that Adorno and Horkeimer proposed in the 1960s must be dispersed by an understanding of the geographic imagination that the potentials of spaces can achieve an understanding of production and reception. We can coalesce in these spaces using new technologies and modes of production, which can equally set up radical and resistance histories, be re-invigorated by the potentials of spatial relationships to biographical and autobiographical material, whether that be by the use of virtual reality, motion capture, or visual design. Contrary to Adorno and Horkheimer, this can support the individual in the pursuance of creativity, rather than corrupt or diminish creative activity.[22] This is explored in the chapters by Scott Palmer, Katie Whitlock and Lesley Ferris.

WRITING SPACE

The involvement and interactivity of the audience is primary to the success of Scenography in Performance, where most importantly "actor and audiences employ the same space."[23] Culturally we learn to read the messages of theatre spaces, locations, and decoration, as we do any related architectural and urban codes and by this reading we intellectually structure our environment. However, never before in history has a public had available for its consideration, paintings, music, or drama, from so wide a range of cultures and historical periods. The collective system of responses characterizes the physical spaces in which theatre today may be presented. As Marvin Carlson writes:

> This vast array of possibilities in performance spaces has clearly heightened the awareness of producers of performance concerning the semiotic potential of such places... In this way, the theoretical self-consciousness, so typical of modern life in all its aspects has entered this area of the theatre experience; ...our traditional emphasis upon the dramatic text, both written and performed, has often led us to neglect the other conditioning elements of the theatre event.[24]

The Writing Space of the performance has, therefore, been extended from the literary text, and memory has formed a potent source of material for performance. Whilst nostalgia might be defined as the postmodern response to the human condition, nostalgia has always been fundamental to the making of performance. The difficulty for academics is how such nostalgia can be or should be interpreted. Wendy Wheeler suggests that, "Nostalgia ...turns us towards the idea of the individual as non-alienated, as knowing and being known by others in, the commonality of the community which is identified as 'home'."[25] This has become a very potent force within the work of contemporary practitioners where biography and autobiography have been fore-grounded as the material for performance. Autobiography, biography and performance blend without erasing the distinction and as such resurrect real life as an aesthetic appeal for an appointed audience. The autobiographical performer fixes on the importance of individuality, where as George Lukács suggests "character becomes much more important, and at the same time, much less important...the drama comes to be built upon mathematics a complicated web of abstractions, and in this perspective character achieved significance, merely as an intersection."[26] Contributions from Alison Oddey, Lesley Ferris and Johan Callens revisit the use of biography and autobiography as lived experience in the scenographic and performance spaces. Oddey's writing for self-representation negotiates subjectivity; multiple definitions of identity in the self as 'Other' and as the 'I' performer, who sees herself seeing herself in performance. Biography in Ferris's chapter is fundamental to the approach she undertook with her team to present the performance, and the use of environmental Scenography, which was produced through digital media and was used to add a reflective sense of the biography being played out, in a play, which is deeply autobiographical. Naturally, to theorize the autobiographical we need an adequate critical vocabulary for describing, "how the components of subjectivity are implicated in self-presentational acts…[W]e have defined five constitutive processes of autobiographical subjectivity: memory, experience, identity, embodiment, and agency."[27] The notion of the autobiographical and biography are resonant in the works by Oddey and Callens, as they both present a sense of the creation of performance as a reliance on the stimulus of the artists from their own real world situations.

ARCHITECTURAL SPACE

In the work of Bernard Tschumi, as a practising architect and in his research, we can see his interest in new technologies and an explanation of how technology is inextricably linked to our contemporary condition, which further refutes Adorno and Horkeimer's belief that society is now about media and mediation, and not a lived, even spiritual experience that might or can be enhanced by technologies and new performance spaces. The direction taken by technology is less the domination of nature, or ourselves through technology, but the development of information, the construction of the world, the stage world and visual performance as a set of images, which technology and new technologies of editing and projection enable. In performance, we are continually playing with familiarity and familiarisation as part of the aesthetic experience of performance. It is this very significant importance of the image, which has destabilised the hierarchy of literary texts over image, which we believe has been important to interrogate through the chapters and research contained in the book. Scenography is no longer ornamentation, but rather the body, which is intrinsic to the media of theatre culture. The different realities that can persist within the simultaneity of performance are explored in the work of Ferris, Katie Whitlock and Thea Brejzek, all of whom challenge a single interpretation and categorisation of play, film, piece of architecture or exhibition.

In the chapters by Oddey, Scott Palmer and Christine White, the research is as much about the event that takes place as it is about the space it takes place in and space itself as a communicative tool. This research looks at the non-hierarchical concept and experience of space and use, which is, of course, influenced by the situationists' discourse of the last century. In this respect, a questioning of the organisation of performance-making and the assumptions through which performance can occur, ultimately changes the nature of the event. Jacques Derrida expanded on the definition of 'event', calling it, "the emergence of the disparate multiplicity."[28] He also suggested that the worthy event shared its roots with the word 'invention', and in our research 'event' and 'invention' are related to new technologies and different beginnings, which can be created for performance through image. It is interesting to note that Bernard Tschumi suggests that architects in their practice are, "the only discipline that by definition combines concept and experience, image and use, image and structure."[29] However, in the chapters by Swettenham, Rewa, Callens and Brejzek the work discussed is clearly enabled by such combinations, though unlike Tschumi, the intention here is to explore the human condition and create a resonant performance for our cultural imaginations.

Performance requires the live presence of both performer and spectator; and in one sense, space and the potentials of space is the medium of theatre, the organisation of the fictional worlds created, or the extended meaning of what space actually refers to, all of which is also interrogated in this book. The energy of the performance and the notion of presence, which can be achieved within the space, are disturbed by the notion of the real and not real. As more and more media and multimedia technologies impinge on the litheness and presence of the performing body of the actor, and if the highest expression of, "appropriated space is the work of art",[30] where dominated space is transformed and mediated by technology and controlled by the institutions of political power, then appropriated space is modified to serve the needs and possibilities of a particular group in society. This notion creates difficulty for the development of new media technologies for performance.[31] This does not take into account, as McAuley points out that, "the current generation must go to a rock concert or a football final to experience the kind of performance energy Kierkegaard found at the Königstädter Theater in Berlin."[32] This anti-technology attack does not recognise how appropriated digital technologies have become for both the current generation and for a variety of entertainment platforms. Indeed, in many ways, the Internet has become a very revolutionary tool. It is potentially a re-appropriation of space, which Lefebvre would have approved of, where the spectator is not dis-empowered. The study of presence in relation to mutation, psychology, cognitive science, computer science, engineering, philosophy and the arts has uncovered a new media richness, which has been measured by the capacity for interactivity and impact on the number of senses involved, as such a medium which is high in presence and allows interactions to adjust the overall level of intimacy. With regard to digital media, notions of presence are problematic. When we reflect on ideas of realism, that is the closeness to real life, which can be achieved, we can see the duality that lies in perception. Whilst for perception, realism is clear. For example, in terms of science fiction, science fiction is unreal; however, certain events that can be perceived, to be plausible in this context and believed to be possible, make a significant change to our perception of what is real. There is confusion within realism and presence, which is precipitated by and through digital media, involving the transportation and participation of the spectator, and can be both effective and a potent part of performance. This is evidenced in the experience of the operator and performer in the research conducted by Palmer. Where television has used a sense of presence in an environment that is computer-generated, this sense can disturb live performance. Some researchers believe this can be the result of a form of out-of-body experience,[33] which in the work of Ferris and Whitlock developed a sense of participation from the audience in the performance environment and a sense of involvement as spectators were engaged with seeing a diversity of media, and therefore experiencing a variety of levels of presence.

PRESENCE IN SPACE

The research in live performance, which has interrogated this sense of presence, has suggested that the larger the image, which is projected or transmitted, the greater the presence responses from the spectator. Therefore, a large high-definition digital television which could be hung on the wall, begins to look like a window, giving a particular visual field and viewing angle, and again plays with the notion of presence and subjective camera shots, which encourage the viewer to participate.[34] The relationship of presence and interactivity are explored in Roma Patel's chapter, where the user influences both the form and the content of the performance piece.

The fictional realities referred to earlier, which have been outlined by McAuley, are deeply problematic to our understanding of Scenography and Performance, as Scenography expands and develops a digital identity, potentially in virtual space. The human perspective within space and 'points of view' are referred to again in the work of Michael Levine by Rewa, but notions of cyberspace challenge the very meaning of space. Cyberspace presents the interaction of digital codes and human desire and it is entirely dependent on technological equipment, a performance alliance of digital technologies, which enables the expansion of potential space as well as geometric space and can alter the dimension of time or the duration of the performance. Cyberspace very concretely creates a new spatiality, through the Scenography of this media and mediated space. The environments, worlds and architectures are all spaces of potential performance. Again, the spaces of the sites that are real and the speed of communication in a live performance arena becomes part of that aesthetic, not simply a way the future is celebrated but in the way it conditions and it pursues the aesthetics of disappearance and reappearance:

> no need any longer for preliminary exposition of facts and places, so important in theatrical work…with accelaration, to travel is like filming, not so much producing images as new mnemonic traces, unlikely, supernatural…train, car, jet, telephone, television…our whole life passes by the prostheses of accelerated voyages, of which we are no longer even conscious…the need for peregrination has led to the establishment in displacement itself of the very fixity of life.[35]

The subjectivity of the eye can create images that are absolute, but which are respectful of the individual's perception. Scenography and Performance play with the real and the representation. The appearance and the disappearance; new technologies and performance raise ever fascinating questions about truth and illusion, pragmatism and idealism, the real and the unreal. The imaginary places of events for performance have been expanded to ever wider dimensions by new technologies. In our research we are looking at the subject of Scenography and Performance and the subsequent emphasis and shift of how audience perception is organised, modes of spectating and the spectators' sense of time and space, which becomes the foregrounded research content for enquiry.

The interconnectedness of Scenography and Performance allows for adjustments of particular details, "to the choice of objects, to the lighting and the atmosphere, all in order to attain the desired degree of vagueness.[36] However, unlike Italo Calvino's sense of exactitude for this quality of suggestiveness in the real, exactitude and particularity have to be practised with, "the poet of exactitude, who is able to grasp the subtlest sensations with eyes and ears and quick, unerring hands."[37] This is especially important as Calvino defines exactitude as three things: one, "a well defined and well calculated plan for the work in question", two, "an evocation of clear, incisive, memorable visual images", three, "language as precise as possible, both in choice of words and in expression of the subtleties of thought and imagination."[38] This definition seems most apt to us for the framing of these debates and the selected chapters involved here about Scenography and Performance.

Notes

1. Grotowski, J., 'The Theatre's New Testament', translated by Jorgen Andersen and Judy Barba, in Grotowski, J., *Towards a Poor Theatre*, London: Methuen, 1969, pp.27–53.
2. Algarotti, Count F., *An Essay on the Opera*, 1767, London.
3. Mackintosh, I., *Architecture Actor & Audience*, Theatre Concepts, London: Routledge, p.29.
4. *Russian Women Artists of the Avantgarde 1910–1930*, exhibition catalogue, Cologne: Galerie Gmurzynska, 1979.
5. Efros, A., 'The Artist and the Stage' (Khudozhniki stsena), *Kultura teatra*, no.1:11, 1921.
6. Tairov, A., 'Stage Ambience (Stsenicheskaia atmosfera), 1921 in Markov, P., (ed.), *T.Y. Tairov*, Moscow: VTO, 1970, pp.160–161.
7. Breton, G., *Theatres, Theaters*, 1989, Paris.
8. Mackintosh, I., *Architecture, Actor & Audience*, Theatre Concepts, London: Routledge, 1993, p.100.
9. Ibid.
10. Brook, P., *The Empty Space*, London, 1968, p.168.
11. McAuley, G., *Space in Performance, making meaning in the theatre*, Ann Arbor: University of Michigan Press, 1999, p.126.
12. Ibid. p.127.
13. McAuley, G., *Space in Performance, making meaning in the theatre*, Ann Arbor: University of Michigan Press, 1999, p.127.
14. Artaud, A., 1970, *The Theatre and its Double*, translated by Victor Corti, London: John Calder, p.76.
15. Tompkins, J., 'Directing And Producing Theatre with the help of virtual reality', in 'Digital Modernisms', White, C., (ed.), *Scenography International*, 2004.
16. Soja, E. W., 'Thirdspace: expanding the scope of the geographical imagination', in *Architecturally Speaking: practices of art, architecture and the everyday*, Read, A., (ed.), London New York: Routledge, 2000, pp.13–30.
17. Soja in Read, p.14.
18. Soja in Read, p.14.
19. Kant, E., *Critique of Judgement*, translated by Bernard, J. H., New York, 1951, paragraph 49.
20. bell hook's, *Yearning: Race, Gender And Cultural Politics*, 1990, p.152.
21. Adorno and Horkeimer in *Cultural Studies Reader*, During, S., (ed.), London: Routledge, 1993, p.40.
22. Adorno, T. W., *The Culture Industry: Selected Essays on Mass Culture*, editor, Berstein, J. M., London Routledge, 1991.
23. Schechner, R., '6 axioms for environmental theatre', The Drama Review, 12, spring, 1968, p.43.
24. Carlson, M., *Places of Performance*, Cornell University Press, 1989, pp.207–208.
25. Wheeler, W., 'nostalgia isn't nasty – the post modernising of parliamentary democracy', in Perryman, M., (ed.), *Altered States: postmodernism, politics, culture*, London: Lawrence and Wishart, 1994.
26. Lukács, G., 'The Sociology Of Modern Drama', in *Sociology of Literature and Drama*, Burns, E. and T., (eds.), (Harmondsworth: Penguin, 1973), pp.435–436.
27. Smith, S., and Watson, J., *Reading Autobiography: A Guide for Interpreting Life Narratives*, Minneapolis, The University of Minnesota Press, 2001, p.9.
28. Tschumi, B., 'Six Concepts', in Read, A., (Ed.), *Architecturally Speaking: practices of art and architecture and the everyday*, p.175.
29. Tschumi, B., 'Six Concepts', in Read, A., (ed.), *Architecturally Speaking: practices of art and architecture and the everyday*, p.176.
30. Lefebvre, H., translated by Nicholson Smith, D., *The Production Of Space*, Oxford-Blackwell, 1991, p.165.
31. Ibid. p.26
32. McAuley, G., *Space in Performance: making meaning in theatre*, Ann Arbor, University of Michigan Press, 1999, p.281.
33. Rheingold, H., *Virtual Reality*, New York: Summit Books, 1991, p.256.
34. Utley, G., *HDTV: New TV, but not just digital*, (CNN/Interactive, 1997), 3rd April 1997.
35. Virilio, P., *The Aesthetics Of Disappearance*, translated by Philip Beitchman, New York: Semiotext(e), 1991, pp.59–60.
36. Calvino, I., *Six Memos For The Next Millennium*, Cambridge: Harvard University Press, 1988, p.55-56.
37. Ibid.
38. Ibid.

PART I: Different Beginnings

DIRECTORS AND DESIGNERS

IS THERE A DIFFERENT DIRECTION?

Pamela Howard

The visionary architect Adolphe Appia saw that 'creation' meant the synthesis of space, light and performance achieved by one total personal vision. Diaghilev introduced the painter to the theatre and artisan scene painters such as Vladimir Polunin, previously a bespoke decorator, became an interpreter. In 1935 Robert Edmond Jones observed, "the excitement that should be in theatres is found only in baseball parks, arenas, stadiums and racecourses." In the twentieth century and twenty-first century the move out of playhouses into new spaces demands an exploitation of the architecture before relying on design. Logically this results in the work of designer and director merging to become a single and unique creator of text and vision.

In reality the collaboration between directors and designers is often uneasy. In 1988 at a conference organised by The Society of British Theatre Designers on this subject at Riverside Studios, an entire panel of invited directors declared that they never had 'any trouble' collaborating with designers, and described a life of sweetness and light with ideas flowing freely back and forth culminating in, as they saw it, riveting and groundbreaking productions. A packed house, mostly of designers listened thoughtfully, their minds focussing on the panel of designers who would soon be asked to respond. Many designers had refused to be on such a panel, fearing that were they to voice their views on the director/designer relationship truthfully, they would probably never work again. However, there were some senior designers willing to be on that panel with a large enough reputation to make them able to speak out, and voice the thoughts of many of their more vulnerable colleagues. What emerged were two very different views of the same experience. When a director felt that there was a good 'shorthand' with the designer, the designer often had taken the easiest way out just to avoid conflict. 'Designer speak' and intricate subterfuge was quickly revealed. When a designer saw that the agreed space could be better used, the suggestion to the director had to be framed within a question, "Do YOU think it would be a good idea if...." Above all, it emerged, a designer had to be like a wife – supportive, a friend and a partner, ready to co-operate at all times and on all occasions, good with money, decorative, good sense of humour, and accepting that no relationship is finite and when someone else came along, you would be passed over.

At this time there were hardly any designers who were also directors – the one exception being Philip Prowse at the Glasgow Citizens Theatre. Prowse was part of a triumvirate with Giles Havergal and Robert David MacDonald who teamed up in the early 1960s at the Palace Theatre, Watford. They worked on the principle that the most important thing was to be able to do the plays they were passionate about. Their passion would communicate directly to the audience. From 1978 to 1985, they produced plays that could not be seen anywhere else in Britain, and confounding all box office myths, they played to capacity audiences.[1] They educated themselves as well as the audiences, exploring drama, and playing out their individual passions – each of the three making work in their own visual language. They created a generation of daring actors, and used young designers straight out of college that they thought could add to their stable. But Philip Prowse had a very clear individual vision, and at this famous meeting at Riverside Studios he was able to state that, "the best conversation I ever had with a director was with myself in bed at night". In fact Philip Prowse was not really interested in the concept of 'designing'. He did not do elaborate drawings or renderings, rarely made scale models, but created around him a team of interpreters who understood his visual vocabulary which, used similar elements over and over again in different combinations. He was only interested in how to stage plays that he was able to choose himself, and he was prepared to take full responsibility for success or failure. The most original of the Glasgow Citizens' productions, and in particular Philip Prowse's, were usually reviewed as being 'European' and that became the euphemism for designers who dared to break out of their boxes.

In retrospect, it can be seen that Philip Prowse was doing no more than following a vision presented by the visionary architect and theatre-maker Adolphe Appia at the turn of the century. Appia saw that 'creation' meant the synthesis of space, light and performance achieved by one personal vision. The Czech architect and scenographer Josef Svoboda (1920–2002) used exactly the same words in 1973 to define his own works.[2] Although the obituaries carefully used the word 'co-operated' rather than 'collaborate', Svoboda worked with several directors, notably Alfred Radok, but his true contribution to the advance of theatre-making was in his self-authored productions. Here, in total control, he was able to combine direction and design in one creative statement. Working autonomously, he invented and patented lighting and projection techniques that sculpted the dark void of the stage space where creation always meant starting from zero. "Scenery", Svoboda said, "is not an end in itself, but a logical component of the complementary arts of the stage. The scenic artist collaborates on equal terms with the author and the director."[3]

In his note to the third edition of *The Development of the Theatre*, Allardyce Nicholl describes his," belief that we stand in an age where there is urgent need of a boldly fresh orientation toward stage form, involving an abandonment of worn out devices, and the creation of new theatrical concepts."[4] In the preface he draws attention to the American stage pioneers Lee Simonson, Donald Oenslager, Jo Mielziner and Robert Edmond Jones, crediting the American public as being, "specially sensitive to visual appeal." Nicholl's readers are directed to read the visionary lectures of Robert Edmund Jones, who, in Theatre Arts Monthly of 1941, warned of the imminent death of the realistic theatre stating, "...the best thing that could happen to our theatre at this very moment would be for playwrights and actors and directors to be handed a bare stage on which no scenery would be placed, and then told they must write and act and direct for this stage. In no time we should have the most exciting theatre in the world." As a further warning, Jones observed, "the excitement that should be found in theatres is only found in baseball parks, arenas, stadiums and racecourses" – a view many people hold today. However, a deep division had already happened with the evolution of two distinct creative pathways – the director and the designer. Way back in 1911, while Appia was experimenting with space and light and human form at Hellerau in Germany, Diaghilev, the impresario extraordinaire, was inviting painters to create scenery and costumes for the theatre, and creating an incredible synthesis of colour, music and movement that enthused the world. Masked balls were held with the 'Ballets Russes' theme, and fashion designers such as Patou and Chanel were inspired to use the bold patterns and colours that were seen on stage. The word 'theatrical' became descriptive of expressive and individualistic dressing and decoration, and the concept of 'stage décor' was born.

These artistic collaborations between composers, painters and choreographers naturally brought together the primary artists commissioned to create new work that had a sensual non-verbal impact on the spectators. The parallel stream of Drama that used words and therefore actors, while creating new works with writers, also took the responsibility to re-create the dramatic repertoire, and needed a manager of the stage at the very least to make sure the actors went in the right doors and did not crash into each other. Producers, who financed and planned productions, devolved this responsibility to a new breed of people known as Stage Directors. These Stage Directors were charged to realise the Producer's wishes, and over the course of the century have developed into 'signature' performers in their own right. The rise of the Stage Director meant that the artisan scene painters who had previously provided stock scenery to suit all needs, found themselves working with a specified designer who provided drawings and even models for made-to-measure scenery. Thus, these two interpretive professions evolved, and before long had become accepted as the way things worked, for better or for worse. But this was never, from the beginning an equal or balanced relationship. Crucially, it meant that designers, or visual theatre artists could only, and more or less can still only, work through the directors. The designers cannot choose the play they really want to do and then hire the director they would like to work with. A Designer may long to work on a particular drama or opera, but the likelihood that a director's choices will coincide with the designer's dreams is remote. Paradoxically, at the turn of the century it was normal for visual artists to initiate productions and add to their theatre work, writing, graphics, interior design and architecture. Vladimir Mayakovsky, and the Czech scenographer/director Frantisek Zelenka (1904–1944) are just two examples. These cross-disciplinary artists also extended their vision to embrace the new arts of film-making and projections, using them creatively as an integral part of the staging. However, by 1972 despite the exhortations of Robert Edmond Jones, the American lighting designer and scenic pioneer Joe Mielziner was telling design students at Yale University that, "the designers never precede the dauphin in the theatre. They are hardworking worms."[5] The accepted role of the designer became not only the logical mission to serve the play, but also to be the servant of the director. And just like in novels, the more obedient and obsequious the servant, the more the master classes believed they were good and enlightened employers, enjoying a unique and trusting relationship. In theatre terms this led to the illusion that the ideal collaboration involved artistic shorthand where the designer was so tuned in to the director that he, or sometimes she, could interpret what was in the director's head and produce it on the stage without prolonged discussion. Ralph Koltai defined and refined this as the art of, "giving directors something they have never envisaged."[6]

Custom and practice is an insidious thing. In a very short time, it seems impossible to remember that things can and often were done differently, for on the whole it is often easier not to upset the applecart, but to find devious methods of operating within the system. In many ways the theatre hierarchy replicates the architectural structures in which they operate. Producers and management offices are usually on the upper floors of the building in good light with perspective views, while the theatre artisans are usually located in basement workshops along with the heating plant and boiler room and no natural light. The axis of staging goes through the centre of the building from the stage to the director, who in rehearsal sits behind a production desk in the centre of the auditorium, much as a monarch sat in the Royal Box in earlier days. As the playhouse has developed in the twentieth century the degrees of separation have become intensified, so that once the pre-production collaboration with the Director and Designer has been completed, the model agreed between them, the designer continues to work with the interpreters, while the director attends to the actors. Of course the designer is always welcome to rehearsals, and usually finds a chair free at the back of the room. A designer in rehearsal is like a bag person carrying bits of models, portfolios, bags of fabric samples, reference books, and art materials from place to place, for there is never a dedicated space allocated for designers to put their things.

What is now needed is to find a different direction for directors. To end once and for all the master servant relationship, euphemism for collaboration and to develop real working practices which are appropriate for the theatre of today. It is clear that some people are born with spatial imaginations and some people are born with literary imaginations and in theatre terms, these have become translated into two separate strands called Director and Designer. Sometimes it works and sometimes it does not. Even the great and famous partnerships have their flaws. The Italian painter architect and scenographer Luciano Damiani who created so many memorable productions of incomparable beauty with the late director Giorgio Strehler, observed that the disposition of the scenic space dictated the structure and organisation of the productions, and this did not always create a space in which the dialectics of the drama could be played out. Damiani first created an entirely new playing space in Trieste, and later, at his home and studio on the Testaccio Hill in Rome. His *Teatro Di Documenti* consists of a series of carefully constructed inter-locking polyvalent spaces that can be used individually or in series.[7] The spaces possess an empty beauty, painted a uniform patina antique cream. The large ideas he developed in staging with Strehler, Ronconi and later Roger Planchon, can be seen in close up in this theatre of memory. Each tiny object perfectly

Figure 1. The scenography for "La Celestina" is part of a series of productions that sets out to explore the possibilities of re-using the theatre space itself, rather than building expensive scenery. It is site-specific to the Theatre, and starts from considering the audiences' experience from the moment of arrival at the theatre building. Space is not just where you go to, but where you walk through!

made and placed in the spaces accumulates layers of unspoken poetic meaning, and conjures up the entire world of the play. Ariane Mnouchkine at her Théâtre du Soleil collaborates creatively with the architect scenographer Guy-Claude François to alter the vast playing space at the old Cartoucherie in the Bois de Vincennes in Paris. Each time the audience enters the building they find a different configuration re-designed to suit the needs of the production. The decisions about the form of the production evolved after many months of research, study and development. The spectator's experience begins as soon as they enter the building from the street. They confront the world of the play, through the research pictures on the wall of the foyer café and the menu that changes in harmony with the production. In *The Open Circle* by architect and scenographer Jean-Guy Lecat,[8] he describes his search with Peter Brook to find how to create the best relationship in the space between the performer and spectator at the Bouffes du Nord Theatre in Paris, and then how to recreate that relationship in the many different spaces Brook has used. In a career of sixty years, and after his debut productions in the boulevard theatre of post-war Britain, Peter Brook has used very few stage designers. Brook has often 'designed' his productions himself even from the early days, and recognised the value of collaborating with architects who respond to the quality of the playing space before imposing scenic solutions. There are many instances of directors taking total charge of all aspects of the production, particularly in opera, as well as actors, and writers 'becoming' directors. There are comparatively few instances of designers crossing those boundaries, except for a few male designers in opera. There are hardly any women designers who have been able to do this, though several have tried. In an exhibition at the Prague Quadriennal in 1999, the Berlin-based artist, teacher and creator Achim Freyer showed his creations for Mozart operas, remarking that no director would have had the courage to even try the ideas he so successfully demonstrated through drawings and production videos.

These few examples, and there are many more, point to a different direction, in which 'designers' become architects of the space and the space itself becomes a major player in the production. The moment it is decided to move a production out of the theatre building or where a decision has been made to re-evaluate how the theatre building is to be used – the collaborative structure has to change. Firstly, the designer can no longer be a decorator of directorial concepts, but has to be an architect of the imagination, looking for all the spatial possibilities to exploit. This demands a real rigorous understanding of the needs of the text, ignoring spurious and artificial divisions between text-based and physical theatre. All that matters is that a harmonious creative language is invented for the production. As theatre moves forward, either textually or physically, there is little doubt that the actor/performer becomes the primary visual element to be enhanced with light, sound and movement, rather than constructed illusions. Thus, the director has to work in partnership with the movement director who becomes almost a co-director and the scenographer – the writer of the stage space – who becomes a visual director. This then allows the scenographer to collaborate with a team of other interpretive artists – sound artists, light artists, object makers, textile artists, costume makers, who should be part of the creative rehearsal process, and can see what is needed to make a moment in performance clearer to the spectator. In other words, a lateral collaboration rather than the more common vertical or linear management structure is needed.

Working in this way makes demands on all parties to rethink their method of working, and their 'custom and practice'. It also has profound economic implications. Instead of spending money on un-recyclable artefacts that get thrown away at the end of the production, for scenery costs too much money to store, and can rarely be used again, budgets could concentrate on paying people for their talents to exploit and enhance the newly discovered spaces. The German sound artist turned director, or as he more accurately describes himself, Creator, Heiner Goebbels, personifies this new thinking. In his productions, he works creatively with performers in the space to tell stories of pain and beauty that communicate across language and nationality.

At the Royal Society of Arts debate as part of their 2004 manifesto that includes 'encouraging enterprise' as one of its aims, the historian and thinker Dr Theodore Zeldin tackles this subject in describing his foundation, 'The Oxford Muse', as an effort to "bring together people who want inspiration to think more imaginatively, to cultivate their emotions through practice of the arts, to understand the past better and to have a clearer vision of the future."[9] This is exactly what theatre-makers can do, and so often do not do. Theodore Zeldin echoes the mantra that so many theatre designers have been saying for so many years, "Let us therefore move away from the labels, stereotypes and definitions and focus our attention on what we can do, individually, on the ground." That would be one way for theatre creation to move in a different direction.

NOTES

1. *The Citizens' Company 1979–1985*, Glasgow Citizens Theatre.
2. Ursic, G. U., *Josef Svoboda*, Union des Théâtres d'Europe, 1998, p.22.
3. Martin, D., *New York Times*, Monday April 22nd 2002.
4. Nicholl, A., *The Development of the Theatre*, Harrap, 3rd Edition, 1946, p.225.
5. Henderson, M. C., *Mielziner: Master of Modern Stage Design*, Back Stage Books, 2001, p.301.
6. Howard, P., *What is Scenography?*, Routledge, 2002, p.xvi
7. Ursic, G. U., *Luciano Damiani*, Unione dei Teatri d'Europa, 1998, p.88.
8. Todd, A., and Lecat, J-G., *The Open Circle: Peter Brook's Theatre Environments*, Faber and Faber, 2003.
9. *Royal Society of Arts Journal*, July 2004, p.39 http://www.the/RSA.org/events

DIFFERENT DIRECTIONS
THE POTENTIALS OF AUTOBIOGRAPHICAL SPACE

Alison Oddey

"Woman must write herself: must write about women to writing, from which they have been driven away as violently as from their bodies."

"Censor the body and you censor breath and speech at the same time. Woman must put herself into the text – as into the world and into history – by her own movement."

The performative strategies employed for the performance of self-identity are storytelling, the body and technology. However, they are often inseparable, appearing to have a single voice within which different discourses and practices are articulated. The fragments, stories or moments are used to signpost or direct the performer's persona, (who is directing the work), although the persona is not always present. The content is autobiographical in experience, which is embodied by the performers and re-processed in order to create the performance. The autobiography is the means of self-identity production, which is the making of the identity of the self, the 'I' in the performance, and contributes to the self-construction of the performer's persona. This enables the performer to speak about creativity, freedom and aspects of herself both as artist and academic. The autobiographical material, gathered from everyday life experiences, develops collective strands of meaning throughout the work and this is expressed in the performance *Nurturing Creativity*.

Jo Shapcott refers to her work as, "my poems are more like arguments with the original", and she says that the poet Basil Bunting's, "word for it was 'overdrafts'".[2] I relate to this. *Nurturing Creativity* and my other performed writings, for example, *Meditation Station* or *Points of Departure*, are all overdrafts to an original. These forms of writing are forms of art, too. Shapcott is fascinated by "identities" and argues that, "the act of writing makes identity fall away in fragments".[3] Different modes of multi-layered discourse are contained within my autobiographical performance. For Shapcott the question, "is how to put more of my best self into this writing just as I put it into poems", which I identify with given that "We are all many things to each other at the same time...I love being all of them."[4]

In the performance *Nurturing Creativity and/or What shall I do with my Inspiron 3700?* I explore the performer's identity through the act and textual space of writing for performance, the potentials of autobiographical space and the act of performing in the theatrical performance space. This is a space to express and assert the desires, thinking and discourse of the woman academic and her multiple identities within the context of the end of the twentieth century and the beginning of the millennium. The means of self-presentation is via the autobiographical impulse and shared spectatorship of the work. The audience is invited to spectate, to 'read' and to 'view' the performance text, creating a relationship with the performer, to explore the potentials of the work.

The physical writing of the fragments of text becomes part of the performative narrative. The framing, construction and interpretation of the 'bio' via acts of writing (as well as acts of photographing the visual experience), describes a self-narrating process. "The life at any moment is the casual consequence of what has transpired earlier...[and] since the life to be lived has also to be *told*, its meaning is seen as something that unfolds through the events."[5] The 'bio' is the performed life.

In the telling of past memories or moments, the performer constructs the meaning of the next moment or memory. Both performing and performance reveal the individuality of the writer through the spoken text, whilst also exposing the fragmentation and divisibility of the self, as one might expect of a poet. The textual mediations contribute to the performer's self-construction as to who she is and how she negotiates the continual shifting divisions between her private, public and unconscious selves.

The subject of this discourse is my life at a particular 'moment'. Fragments of autobiographical discourse are communicated as the performative experiencing self encounters the narrative self in performance and tries to document it. This self-expressive discourse is both a source and site of knowledge, a means to keep a record of my own time and thinking, as well as being a space to inscribe my experiences, views and thoughts. The performed autobiography, as opposed to the literary autobiography, is a representation of life, and the problematics of self-representation involving concurrently ideas of obscuration, alienation, reduction and self-modification. The complexity of self-definition is concerned with authorial presence and absence in the very act of performance. I am the performing protagonist, narrator and author. I am simultaneously dealing with history, the story of my life, and representation, my life as a performance text. As Derrida suggests, I am "put[ting] one's name on the line."[6] Implicit in my autobiographical performance are concepts of history, fiction and temporality.

I cling to the 'moment' and a particular idea. I glimpse into my life. The performance shifts between memoir and diary; the 'I' is questioned and the performer's identity is recreated. A transformative process is inherent in the recollection and representation of the life, for example, what is being spoken about the Professor's identity whilst the performer is physically and visually changing to an object, a cake with a star on top of it.

WOMAN: WRITING HERSELF

The textuality of the performance has inculcated within it inscribed cultural meanings represented scenographically and visually in the photographs of the city of Perth as the performer speaks, and in the writing 'performed'.

"I'm sitting here (totally in the moment) in 44 King Street, listening to some laid-back, yet energising music, waiting for my meal that I've ordered Kervella Goats Cheese, Roasted Capsicum & Black Olive Pizza. I'm about to sip my glass of South Australian Grosset Semillon Sauvignon Blanc 1999, having read that it has, 'voluminous perfumes of fresh gooseberries, mid-palate softness, vibrant guava with underlying hints of grassiness. There is gulpable juiciness, wonderful intensity and a crisp, dry zippy finish. This is as good as it gets…' – sounds like me right now. The wind blows gently in through the opened window – I stare out at the street. I let the wine flow round inside my mouth before swallowing it. Slightly acidy…I'm no expert, but it isn't quite integrated. It's not quite as described on the 'Guest Wines' list.

Five young singalese girls pass by on the street. This reminds me of my close friend Susan Leong, singalese born in Liverpool, brought up in Birmingham, who died of lymphatic cancer on August 14th, 1993.

Figure 2. Perth City

Figure 3. 'I' with her glass of wine

I finish my meal with a cappuccino and a date & macademia cake. I'm valuing the moment of being with my self right now, happy and content. Time to reflect, contemplate, think, pause – stop. I let my mind wander freely in the space. I am connecting to the city space."[7]

In this fragment of eating, drinking, fashion and everyday Perth, I am the text to be read and viewed. I am the editor of that text. The photograph of 'I' with her glass of wine constructs its own self-narrative, resorting, "to mnemonic places and images to invent their textual space."[8] The photograph uncovers and brings together both the mnemonic power of the visual image and the fragmentary texts of the script. The image in the photograph and the process of remembering in the live performing of the written fragments, inscribe the memory, both of which are intrinsic to this autobiographical performance. The photograph reflects a copy and a likeness of a realised self-identity, marking the place from which the potentials of the autobiographical space came. The performer's body invites the spectator to visualise the past, to engage, interpret, analyse and understand this representation of my self in the everyday, which simultaneously is a theatrical rendition of fragments of my daily life, performed.

I am performing a sense of otherness, which can happen in any place and at any time. At a particular moment, I adopt roles, both conscious and unconscious, that are appropriate to my situation, and watch myself being watched, for example, in the 'Dialogue with my soul' fragment of script set at St. Pancras Station with the young man opposite Simon Jones. This experience can be expressed as, "some audience that recognises and validates it as performance even when, as is occasionally the case, that audience is the self."[9] This sense of the mingled past and present within the context of the autobiographical self can be found in *if nobody speaks of remarkable things*, "…and she feels only a kind of sweet nostalgia. She wonders if you can feel nostalgic for something before it's in the past, she wonders if perhaps her vocabulary is too small or if her chemical intake has corroded it and the music goes doowoah doo-woah."[10]

In modern art, the preoccupation with memory and loss, is evident in the crossover of theatre, art and installation, exemplified in Deborah Warner's *Tower Project*, 1999, which invites us to look at London from the top of Euston Tower and observe what we see, how we feel and think at the turn of the century. The solo spectator's journey through London's Euston Tower, a project commissioned by the London International Festival of Theatre (LIFT), raises questions about what the text is, who is the performer, and the shifting roles of spectator as both performer and writer. Euston Tower, the building as silent text, "was the closest to working on a new play, because one was working on an undeclared, very complex silent text."[11] Warner was looking to discover ways of releasing what was latent within these buildings, working with them as though they were actors: "One had a tricky little actor called the building."[12] Warner began to invent the notion of offering a solo walk and it prompted self-doubt, "How can I call myself a director if all I am offering them is a walk?"[13]

The 'Fragments' in my autobiography *Nurturing Creativity* are competing memories and histories of the same events. In the Fragment, 'Faxed but not read…' the building of Euston Tower becomes the site of the performance, created and chosen by Warner to elicit a certain response from the spectator. This place is the performance space, where the narrative is played out, but quite what the narrative is, is left for the 'spectator-protagonist' to decide. The architecture of Euston Tower encourages a certain performance narrative with a particular reading of the past and a representation of history, which is subject to bias, assumption and judgement. Memories are performed and re-presented, but there are always gaps and elisions within the performed narratives, and an inadequate uncovering of the 'truth'. The spectator has the choice to follow the 'truth' of the performance or to resist and create an alternative 'reading' of the work.

"The twentieth century is about to pass us by and with it, the old, original computers piled high against a wall in one of those empty rooms, the broken office furniture and the redundant filing cabinets. Or, are they redundant? They're filled with musical instruments – that aren't those of

Figure 4. Angel Project, *Perth*

angels – but of children learning to play. There is a melancholy somehow about those rooms that explore the imagery of childhood and memory. Prolific images of black and white photographs, an old battered telephone toy alone on the carpet, with everything appearing very ordered and in the right place.

Is this what we learnt as children? A childhood view of the world is symbolised by a pair of black ballet shoes hanging from the wall.

I am attracted to a larger empty room with a fax machine spewing out rolls of white paper, creating a sculptural work of art in itself. I am fascinated and intrigued. What is being faxed? It is Milton's 'Paradise Lost', which I've never read. I roar with laughter and delight in the visual imagery, as it feeds in to my fragmentary experience of this site-specific performance so far.

…This space, this journey that I am on, is a metaphor for my life at this particular moment. Space to breathe, to reflect and to consider my position in this individual's digital, technological based world at present.

…I am connecting to 'being in the moment' and to the importance of 'dream-time'…I feel delight to be 'freed up' by being in this huge, open space, constantly surrounded by the panoramic view of London, stretched out from every window as far as the eye can see. This forms the canvas against which I can devise and play with my own self-created poetic narrative."[14]

The place of Perth in Western Australia is the performance site in Warner's *Angel Project*, which refers particularly to thirteen buildings in the city. Architects and management have designed and created representations of spaces, which demand a subjective response from the spectator. These architectural spaces encourage a certain spectatorial gaze through the skilled presentations we see, so that everything seen is a production by somebody. However, there is a contradiction of what we are seemingly observing at the same time as our own personal and often, difficult engagement with what we are 'seeing'. Perth, the city, is a pre-scripted performance of interpretation. The space · offers sites for multiple performances of interpretation that makes the spectator the subject of that space, "stories thus carry out a labour that constantly transforms places into spaces or spaces into places."[15] The concept of de Certeauian place is to think of place as space, so that the space becomes a site for multiple performances by spectators. The thirteen buildings are performative spaces, producing multifarious narratives of interpretation and creation by the spectator, which are not 'narrativised' in advance, as they are the result of a unique relationship between spectator and the silent text of the building.

Both the place of the city of Edinburgh and the space of the room I am performing *Nurturing Creativity* in, construct me as subject, performer and spectator. It is in the double consciousness of performing previous and present texts of walking through Euston Tower, or across the thirteen buildings of Perth, that I discover in both past and real-time present, what being a spectator means. I am spectating and I recognise that I too am part of the performance. I am in the event and the spectating becomes performative. I am performing too. I performatively enact the trajectory of memory in relation to the objects seen in the space, such as, the ornate gold mirror or the lilies in the bath. These objects help me to, "restage and restate the effort to remember what is lost."[16]

THE BODY: BREATHING AND SPEAKING

"Man thinks with his whole body."[17] It is the presence of the performer, via the body and their persona that stimulates and stirs systems of visual, vocal, spatial and fictional meanings, which contribute to the signification and identity of the performance space. The embodied reality of the performer and her relationship to that space is at the heart of the 'performing', the focus of the performance and the core of theatrical semiosis. The performer creates from her 'being', drawing on memories of previous 'being' in past spaces, fictions and narrative worlds, and in relation to the proxemics of the performance space. The writing of texts by the performer are inscribed in the body and articulated through voice, gesture, movement and facial expression. The body of the performer is both subject and object of contemporary performance.

Contemporary performance has a complex genealogy, originating in both visual arts and theatre practices, which are currently expressed as Live Arts:

> The process of devising is about the fragmentary experience of understanding ourselves, our culture, and the world we inhabit. The process reflects a multi-vision made up of each group member's individual perception of that world as received in a series of images, then interpreted and defined as a product…A devised theatre product is work that has emerged from and been generated by a group of people working in collaboration.[18]

In the twenty-first century, devising is a mainstream tool used in other art forms, crossing over and in-between, creating inter-textual forms of theatrical performance. This is clearly seen from the diversity of work from companies, whose work I wrote about in the 1990s, such as IOU or Forced Entertainment, who continue to tell stories through the weaving of the inter-textuality of installation, music, video, performance, film and art. The devising process still enables the telling of stories through the crossover of art forms, and thus, the director of the creative process has shifted direction, dependent on the hybrid form created and the nature of collaboration with other artists.

In the context of my original performed auto-bio-graphy *Nurturing Creativity*, it could be argued that the use of music and objects functioned primarily in relation to the performer. The objects, for example, the electronic plant, became meaningful when the performer handled and referred to it, whilst speaking the text with regard to Belbin[19] and the characterisation of selves. The performer brings the complexity of meanings about the plant to the audience's attention by gestural reference in relation to tonal, vocal delivery and the expression of text. Likewise, the music makes up a whole, sculptural narrative in its own right, but at the same time activates further fictional domains other than the dramatic fiction of the space, writing and body of the performer. For example, Vaughan Williams *Skylark* in relation to the text of 'Faxed but not read…', where we see the performer speaking her 'spectator-protagonist' perspective and encounter of Warner's *Tower Project* installation encouraging the audience to listen and dream within and between the two narratives.

PUTTING MYSELF INTO THE TEXT…BY MY OWN MOVEMENT

This is much more complicated in the example of the 'I' performer, still, standing against the breeze block wall of the Edinburgh performance space, listening to a tape recording of the 'live moment' of herself as spectator/performer at the *Angel Project* in Perth. For the audience, the immobile body of the 'I' performer, exerts its own fascination, as defined and determined by its relationship to stillness. "The stillness thus draws the move to the attention of the spectator, it brings it into existence as a completed entity within the flux of being, and calls for some effort either of aesthetic appreciation or interpretation on the part of the spectator."[20]

As the 'I' performer responds to the recording of herself 'live in the moment', she is responding and performing to the performing of herself, in the *Angel Project* that she is both spectator and performer of, and at the time. The audience of *Nurturing Creativity* simultaneously hear the Mozart music in relation to the recorded 'live' reaction of the performer in Perth, Australia, as the performer/spectator would also have then encountered the music, space and objects. The audience watches her move in response to this in the actual performance playing space in present time. It is this physical interface between the memory of a past time and now, through the moving body and gesture of the performer that actualises and endows the relationship of all the various fictions. The energy from the physical reality of the performer's body fires the liveness of presence between performer and spectators in the same space. "The body is, after all, the most readily available territory of expression."[21]

Theatrical communication takes place between the performer and spectator via the emotional and imaginative exchange of body and voice of performer. This interchange is captured in a temporal moment of engagement. The performer's presence, in the vocalised, moving body, energises that moment and process of time, space and audience reception, giving both meaning and making to the 'performing' theatrical moment. It is a collaborative experience. The performer's movement is a key signifier in relation to the vocal quality of text spoken, articulated and constructed as discourse. The visual, the moving and the emotional subtext of thinking with their body too, in response to what is seen, heard and imagined, fascinate the spectator.

The performer's bodily action in space, movement within the space, positioning with regard to direction and orientation, gesture, entry and exit to and from the space, focuses and re-identifies the performance space. For example, in seemingly vacating the performing space to lean against the wall. The emphasis is on the moving body, fragments of movement, which are used to deconstruct spoken, visual or spatial texts. The purpose of the bodily presence of the performer dictates and draws the attention of the spectator, giving meaning to the spatial relationship of performer and object or simply structuring the performance continuum. The body displays a fictional world and is integral to the creation of theatrical meaning. As Elam states:

"…predetermining the configurations of bodies onstage both to create visual patterns and to emblemize relationships."[22]

The orientation of the performer's body can signify the performer's attitude to her environment; for example, the performing Professor in her papier mâché cake costume is dressed by the lecturer/lighting designer and technical tutor/costume designer, signifying the politics of both theatre and academic study. Connections are apparent for both academics and artists in the audience, with regard to all the performers' 'roles'. The sound operator is visible, integral to and part of the whole performance. This woman academic is a performing technician performing the role of technical support, whilst performing for the audience the disinterested technician, who is serving the performance, but reading about research and teaching in *The Times Higher* newspaper. This 'role' raises questions about the status and hierarchy of the Professor, the Performer and the Technician in both the academy and higher education programmes of study of Drama, Theatre Studies and Performance.

TECHNOLOGY

In contemporary performance with the use of new technologies, within the blurring of boundaries of various art forms, and in the cross-fertilization of a developing new art stage platform (theatre, installation and performance technology), is an exploration and experimentation with trying to find the margins and limits of new forms, the interaction of scenography and performance. The use of technology in this performance is located in the opening relationship of performer, screen and the operation of the first projected image. The focus is in that relationship of performer and new technologies, and is key to the reception of meaning in this autobiographical work.

The performer's creative function in *Nurturing Creativity and/or What shall I do with my Inspiron 3700?* is 'to be' and to express that 'being', which as a composition of sound, text and image is selected, edited and interpreted in an individual, unique way by each spectator present. Depending on the performer's dominance of the presentational space, a powerful, emotional meaning may be conveyed simply in other signifying systems of the gaze, feeling, silence and presence of the performance text, activating and enabling new meanings to emerge and re-focussing the attention of the audience. As a visual signifier, facial expression is a strong part of the performer's bodily expressivity with each 'look' being a spatial act, "it directs the spectator's attention within the space and is one of the performer's most powerful stratagems in activating the whole space."[23] These simultaneous elements create a complexity of layers of 'performing', signified by the person of the performer, who is present in the space, simply 'being'. At the same time, the imaginative construct by the audience of 'the performer' playing in the space, and the physical creation of the 'persona', constructed by the performer via the moving body and the use of costume, contributes to several levels of semiotic function in relation to space, place, fiction and time. The performer is offering her presence and, "the making of meaning is subordinated to the experience of the present moment"[24]

How is that 'moment' conveyed to the spectator? The act of change is multi-layered and expressed via a whole range of practice, which includes the performance, digitised image-making, installation, photography and other forms of expressive media. When exampled in autobiographical work, what occurs is a belief in the reality of the performed 'role' and a realisation on the part of the spectator that this is a performed role. The performed text uses intonation, diction and the pictorial writing of the text, the scenography of the projected photographic texts, energised and full of imagery, to produce the autobiography. Linda Rugg states that, "the presence of photographs in autobiography…offers a visualization of the decentred, culturally constructed self; and it asserts the presence of a living body through the power of photographic referentiality."[25] In creating and composing the photographic image of a specific feminine identity of the self, such as the 'I' with her glass of wine, I am both revealing and questioning one way in which the body can be culturally contextualised and constructed through the image.

A 'MOMENT' IN THE CITY
"And this is a pause worth savouring, because the world will soon be complicated again."[26]

The scenography of the city has a fascination for artists, whether it is in the writing of the novel, *if nobody speaks of remarkable things*, by Jon McGregor, 2002, or the creation of a virtual reality installation, *The Living Image*, 2004, a project by theatre designer Roma Patel, installation and new media artist Graham Nicholls and site- specific artist Trudi Entwistle, described as exploring, "a technoetic approach to art",[27] which explores the concept of urban London through both memories and fantasies of city life, a fifteen-minute 'silent' journeying experience for the single audience member viewed through 3-D spectacles and the use of a remote handset, which, "blurs distinctions between what is real and what is computer generated."[28] The spectator is alone and able to explore the in-between darker places of the city at night, in a different way to the theatre-making crossover with installation art of Warner's new art form of the 'walk', *Angel Project*, in the Australian city of Perth, 2000, or in the American city of New York in 2003.

Graeme Miller's *Linked*, 2003, is a, "landmark in sound, an invisible artwork, a walk"[29] across the East London landscape of the M11, and Talking Birds' *Wanderlust*, 2002, a performance installation, described by *Live Art Magazine* as, "a bona fide example of a multi-media art event", with the company transforming the site of an underground car park in Scarborough, a non-traditional venue of performance – an in-between place of the city – into an art exhibition, an installation, and a performance of twenty minutes for fifteen people.[30]

It is the dark spaces of the city, those found non-theatre spaces of the underground car park, those in-between spaces that audiences pass through. There is a sense of journeying, travel, city noise, whether it is in the liveness of walking the *Angel Project* in Perth or New York, or of playing with technology in the multi-sensory interactive virtual space of *The Living Image*, the solo spectator wearing stereoscopic glasses and manoeuvring the remote control, as opposed to wearing the theatrical costume of the headset in Miller's *Linked* in the real landscape of the East End of London. The essential links between these 'walks' is in the experiential nature of past, memory and meditation. The desire for contemplative space and nostalgia, for the pre-M11 place and memories of the East London landscape in Miller's *Linked*, or for the creation of the spectator's

Figure 5. Linked M11 *roadway*

own cinematic masterpiece as the protagonist in Janet Cardiff's *The Missing Voice in Whitechapel, London in 1999*. The theatrical costume for the spectator of Miller's *Linked* is the headset and for the spectator of Cardiff's *The Missing Voice* is the Walkman, both interrogating how sound affects our visual perceptions and the inter-textuality of texts of the everyday city. However, in Miller or Cardiff's 'walk' there are no prescriptions to be silent or alone as the spectator experiences the environment, events and everyday living. The nature of listening, however, to the Walkman or the headset requires a theatrical engagement that is different to listening to a live performer, encouraging an integral solitude and silence without prescription. In Warner's *Angel Project*, however, the solo, silence of the 'walk' is requested from the spectator and an essential requirement of the 'walk'.

'I', the spectator, make choices all the time in these works, where to walk, who and what to interact with, where to turn my attention to; it is all about ME and my relationship to the spatial landscape, the place, the potentials of autobiographical space and my own 'willingness to be silent'. The real-time thrills, dangers or not of the city at night, in the virtual space of London, one version of a metropolis, is part of young people's lives, popular culture, a skateboarding game for youth, but is it art? I am watching a cinematic screen, which does not immerse me and I have no desire to move. However, in Perth, at night, as a woman alone walking the *Angel Project* in the non-theatre space of the city, I create and compose my own text to meet the half-narratives of real life around me. This experience is then performed in my autobiographical performance *Nurturing Creativity*.

CONTEMPLATIVE AND MEDITATIVE SPACES

The city has taken over from the garden, from the natural landscape, to become the new meditative and contemplative space. The trees and plants of parks and public gardens in both Perth and New York are still symbols within urbanity of time passing, of paradise and of a celebratory wilderness. The universal theology is of the sacred space of the city itself, of the 'remarkable things' of McGregor's novel, of everyday living, of a space for renewal, to recover, for reflection; a place to meander, to breathe and to be. It is the notion of space for ourselves; the ability for the soul to retreat into the sacred. The spectator, the viewer and the listener is spiritually consoled through these works, and it is in the sacred space of the empty concrete breeze-block room of Kingsgate in Perth that I self-compose the poetics of my text as spectator, performer and writer all at the same time. It is this space, which invites me to the possibilities of an imaginative space too. The solitude of walking in the in-between journeying space of thirteen buildings invites me to play and interact with the outside, real world. The nature of the solitary journey in these in-between spaces is entirely dependent on each spectator and is wholly dependent on each audience member's own story, agenda at the time and their developing relationship with the texts and performers of the thirteen cited spaces of the project. It is also about kindling the audience member's imagination towards their own creativity and poetics, so that one becomes the spectator, writer and performer by the end of the journey, having played with these different roles in an unusual order and relationship to each other.

In this way, Warner's *Angel Project* is a meditation in that the form of the journey, the walk, is a spectator's communion with the self, thus creating a relationship with the architectural, performance space of the city via the structured, guided walk.

The diversity and variety of spectator response to the last step of the journey in Kingsgate is indicative of the power of this new art form and how it works. The combination of the carefully chosen objects with the music, Mozart's *Ave Verum*, within the dynamics of a space where the light changes throughout the day, enables a multiple turning point possibility for the spectator to become the performer. The spectator is doing it alone and for his or her own self, and the turning point seems to occur whilst the music draws you in as you climb the stairs. There is no doubt that it is a film moment. It is almost as if you are 'on camera', in shot, and you are suddenly the protagonist, no longer watching but performing your own self-composed text. It is interesting how the transition from spectator to performer happens, and the fact that there is a duality of roles at the same time. Warner describes it as conjuring with elements, arguing that: "You do, suddenly, become a major performer. Nor do you step outside of yourself, not at all. I don't think you're conscious of being looked at in that moment, it's quite private there. You're very in it."[31]

The autobiographical performance of *Nurturing Creativity* is both an act of representation and an act of being. It provides access to the woman's lived experience, the 'I' of, "the new identity of a

Figure 6. Bill Viola in St. George's Cathedral

female academic in the age of computerized communication",[32] and as Liz Stanley argues, it also offers, "accounts of other lives influence how we see and understand our own and that our understandings of our own lives will impact on how we interpret other lives."[33] The autobiographical self is therefore a construction, "autobiographical selves are constructed through the process of writing and therefore cannot reproduce exactly the selves who lived".[34] They are chimera, which are shape-shifting and illuminating, true and lived experiences, which are also wholly mediated and as a form might even nurture creativity.

"I am all alone here in the Cathedral watching this amazing video installation of Bill Viola,[35] an American Artist, under water – a naked body transforming into a shape and then rising to the surface to take a breath of air. A gentle breeze wafts over me as I write; it feels calm and peaceful in this space. The soundtrack is of water flowing – the breath of life.

As his face comes up for air – it is life – the new-born gasping for breath – letting out a cry. The breath…breathing is so simple, and yet it gets lost in all the hubbub and bustle of the city.
Is this the space to place this installation?
In many ways, it feels exactly right."[36]

These journeys all return to, 'a willingness to be silent', as they are places of contemplation and places of space. They are also the places of the potentials of autobiographical space. What is interesting, leaving aside the ritualistic visiting of the church space as a place to be silent, to pray and to contemplate, is that the origins of theatre as a ritual place have moved to a place of polemic to make the audience think. It is not that these works are not polemical; they enable the audience to interpret and draw their own meanings, composing or completing their own narratives. In one sense this is to make the art form banal, returning to a twentieth-century need for contemplative space, however, it has developed into a twenty-first-century cross-art form, which is the contemplative space of the 'spectator-viewer protagonist performer'. The spectator is the celebrity, the focus and at the centre of the artwork, witnessing the process of the performance, the journeying, writing their own experimental, experiential, everyday life 'performative' texts, the imaginings, inventions and composition of made-up meta-narratives. It is in these narratives, that the spectator's attention stops, and shifts to the in-between fragmentary moments of ordinary living.

A WILLINGNESS TO BE SILENT
"and it stops
in some rare and sacred dead time, sandwiched between the late sleepers and the early risers, there is a miracle of silence.
Everything has stopped."[37]

As in Jon McGregor's novel, *if nobody speaks of remarkable things*, the focus of the passers-by is on the detail and banality of everyday living. The theatricality of the spectator's 'walk' is in the 'sited' buildings and the real world possibilities of the in-between journeying spaces of the city. The spectator imbibes the history, the memories, the visual imagery, and the city's soundscape, as she walks in the moment of past association, present living and future life. The public space of seemingly unmoving city buildings, which are solid, stable and secure, emanate and evoke past

Figure 7. Graffiti from Linked

memories, engaging and accessing energies of the unconscious memories of the fluidly moving spectators, a provocation of nostalgia to the many unstable private minds. The shift from the twentieth century to the twenty-first invites a memorial of everyday acts in the visual graffiti, and in tandem, a desire to explode new acts of theatrical creativity.

The 'walk' embraces the aerial view, the experiential, and the poetics of the city space, re-writing a place through the act of walking. Walking is wandering, drifting or grazing, in the natural environment of weather and sky, and as a theatrical event of undirected moving. Everything signifies, "he wonders about the moment the rain begins, the turn from forming to falling, that slight silent pause in the physics of the sky as the critical mass is reached, the hesitation before the first swollen drop hurtles fatly and effortlessly to the ground."[38]

Where are we *now* in the politic of the moment, in the politics of non-category and cross-art forms across post-feminist, interdisciplinary landscapes? Is it at the cusp of something, crossing borders, boundaries, all of which are blurred, so that there is a need to make interdisciplinary, interconnected works, which come out of and from the inter-textuality of texts, including new technologies and multimedia? Disruption prevents categorisation. The politics of power is in the re-definition of categories of production. I am not rejecting the definitions of arts boundaries in the performance space and ask only for a celebration of the blurring of boundaries, of the unfamiliar, of risk and spatial porosity. What is emerging out of a new understanding of space, in the found non-theatre spaces of the architectural performance space of the city, the environment and the cross-art form, is the creation of new performance texts. These texts discuss the notion of memory, history and autobiography, attempting to record what has gone before. We live in a blurred sonic, spatial, sensual, visual environment, filled with 'stop and go' gaps and in-between moments; moments of interruption in a discontinuous montage of fragments of reality, media, audio, the music of daily life, "the twenty-first century promises to be an aetherial landscape of images, sounds and disembodied voices, all connected by invisible networks and accessed through increasingly transparent interfaces."[39]

In-between spatial, sensual moments where nothing is noticed, and yet, it is in the listening process of the in-between moment of transition, that the spectator loses sense of time, interpreting fragments of narratives, re-constructing and re-configuring them into something new, a half-narratives' invitation for completion. It is in this mark of time, that the spectator is forced to be aware of their personal situation, their own autobiographical space, so that the concept of 'time out' enables an in-the-moment evaluation of the now, based on the events of before and after to understand the moment itself. In the gap of the space in-between is a space for scrutiny, a momentary glance, and the contradiction of different senses in the mental and bodily creativity of the spectator. The spectator conducts her own listening within the composition of both real living environment and theatrical context, 'writing the moment' of narration with sounds, sonorities, imagination, image, real experiences, memories, scenography and the possibilities of the Other. The spectator's creation of texts is the making of meanings in these in-between spaces, the making of unexpected connections between diverse ideas, discourses, rhythmical bodily patterns and structures, narratives and memories of the moment. That caesura in the theatrical landscape outside of the theatre building requires a willingness to be silent, in order to expose the passing of time. Silence. In order to linger, float or drift, "a free association in space", defined as a technique by the Lettrists in Paris in the early 1950s and evolving into a Situationist polemic in the late 1960s.[40]

The crossover of the poetics of architecture, space and performance is in the interdisciplinary composition of the landscape, shaped by the human and temporal dimensions of blurring the boundaries of the imaginative unconscious with the reality of everyday living, and how that architectural landscape offers spatial empowerment to the spectator. It is in the spectator's relationship to space, light and ambience, which affords a compositional work of multi-layered texts of non-linear narratives of sound, objects, music, bodies and words. The crossover of poetics is in these 'interrelationships', in the shifting perceptions and body of the spectator; in the complexity of their own composition of emotion, intellect and being in relation to the theatre landscape of architecture, autobiographical space and performance. The sensory is integrated and used by art and memory; art evokes and is an evocation of memory; the art is in the idea of poetic wandering and the composition of the journey. These multi-layered sonic, recorded and live, scenic, environmental, visual and ambient texts explore and experiment with perceptions of the world as poetic texts, new performance texts, inviting new definitions of wildernesses and paradisiacal places, celebrating the multi-cultural and multi-forms of the interdisciplinary landscape that lead towards new forms of theatrical spirituality and 'a willingness to be silent'. "I'm not waiting. I'm resting. I'm having a quiet conversation with my soul, whilst watching others pass by on their own journeys – reflective or not. …I'm on my own. I'm looking after myself – my self, soul, being, person, body. I'm resting 'in the moment' right now. I'm giving to my soul. The body is weary, but my heart and soul are alive."[41]

"as the rain fades away there is stillness and quiet, light flooding rapidly into the street and through windows and open doors, the last few drops falling conspicuously onto an already streaming pavement, …there is a quietness like a slow exhalation of tension that lasts only a moment …"[42]

NOTES

1. Cixous, H., *The Laugh of the Medusa*, p.ix, in Champagne, L., (ed.), *Out from Under: Texts by Women Performance Artists*, Theatre Communications Group, (1990).
2. Shapcott, J., in Allen, P., (ed.) *art, not chance*, Gulbenkian, 2001, p.44.
3. Shapcott, p.52.
4. Ibid.
5. Taylor, C., *Sources of the Self: The Making of the Modern Identity*, Cambridge University Press, 1989, p.289.
6. Derrida, J., *Memoires: for Paul de Man*, Columbia University Press, 1989, p.7.
7. Oddey, A., *Nurturing Creativity and/or What shall I do with my Inspiron 3700?*, script performed Edinburgh, 2000.
8. Beaujour, M., *Poetics of the Literary Self-Portrait*, New York and London: New York University Press, 1991, p.139.
9. Carlson, M., *Performance: A Critical Introduction*, Routledge, 1996, p.6.
10. McGregor, J., *if nobody speaks of remarkable things*, London: Bloomsbury, 2002, p.31.
11. Interview with Alison Oddey, unpublished, 1999.
12. Ibid.
13. Ibid.
14. Oddey, A., *Nurturing Creativity and/or What shall I do with my Inspiron 3700?*, script performed Edinburgh, 2000.

15. de Certeau, M., *The Practice of Everyday Life*, 1984, pp.117–118.
16. Phelan, P., *Unmarked: The Politics of Performance*, Routledge, 1993, p.147.
17. Jousse, M., *L'Anthropologie du geste*, Gallimard, 1974, in McAuley, G., *Space in Performance: making meaning in the theatre*, University of Michigan Press, Ann Arbor, (1999), p.90.
18. Oddey, A., *Devising Theatre*, Routledge London, 1994, p.1.
19. Belbin, R., *Beyond the Team*, Oxford: Butterworth-Heinemann, 2000. Belbin explores Team Behaviour and Psychology.
20. McAuley, G., *Space in Performance: making meaning in the theatre*, University of Michigan Press, Ann Arbor, pp.106–107.
21. Coates, N., in Hewison, R., *Future Tense, A New Art for the Nineties*, Methuen, 1990, p.139.
22. Elam, K., *The Semiotics of Drama and Theatre*, Methuen, 1980, p.65.
23. McAuley, *Space in Performance: making meaning in the theatre*, p.114.
24. Ibid., p.122.
25. Rugg, L., *Picturing Ourselves*, Chicago and London: The University of Chicago Press, 1997, p.19.
26. McGregor, J., *if nobody speaks of remarkable things*, London: Bloomsbury, 2002.
27. Flyer, LIFT, 2004. This work is discussed in detail in chapter 4.
28. Ibid.
29. Publicity Flyer, *Linked*.
30. Robertson, C., liveartmagazine.com, 6th January 2003.
31. Interview with Oddey, unpublished, 2000.
32. Donnell, A. & Polkey, P., (eds), *Representing Lives, women and auto/biography*, London: Macmillan Press Ltd., 2000, p. xxvii.
33. Stanley, L., 'Introduction', *Lives and Works*, 3:1–2, 1994, p. i.
34. Shumaker, W., *English Autobiography: Its Emergence, Materials and Form*, University of California Press, 1954, p. 45.
35. Viola's 'The Messenger' was commissioned by Durham Cathedral in 1996, by the Chaplaincy to the Arts & Recreation in North-East England.
36. Oddey, A., *Nurturing Creativity and/or What shall I do with my Inspiron 3700?*, script performed Edinburgh, 2000.
37. McGregor, *if nobody speaks of remarkable things*, p.3.
38. Ibid., p.209.
39. Toop, D., *Sonic Boom* Exhibition Catalogue, London: Hayward Gallery, p.107.
40. Keiller, P., 'The poetic experience of townscape and landscape and some ways of depicting it', in Danino, N., and Maziére, M., (eds.), *The Undercut Reader*, London and New York: Wallflower Press, (2003), p. 77.
41. Oddey, A., *Nurturing Creativity and/or What shall I do with my Inspiron 3700?*, script performed Edinburgh, 2000.
42. McGregor, *if nobody speaks of remarkable things*, p.213.

Collaborative Explorations
Reformulating the Boundaries of Scenographic Practice

Roma Patel

This chapter presents some reflections of a scenographer's personal and collaborative explorations of virtual reality technologies. By using the city, in the widest sense, as raw material, we combined video and selected VR (Virtual Reality) technologies to build a virtual interactive space, composed of abstractions of this material. The Living Image is an immersive, interactive real-time installation. It is based on a series of modelled environments. The imagery centres on the night-time spaces of the city of London, UK, filtered through our memories and fantasies. I use 3D digital visualisation tools for set designs and animated stage projections. I am also interested in the possibilities of real-time 3D computing, that is the technology used to make computer games and virtual environments, virtual reality, that is known as VR. Without computer programming skills it is now possible to create navigable, fully textured theatre sets whose properties one can modify and view instantly. I am compelled to think this could really replace the card model and further bridge the gap in the creation process between the idea and its visualisation. A few years ago I began researching the potential use of real-time immersive environments within performance space and as installation art. Relatively few artists seemed to be exploring the medium of real-time 3D. I questioned whether a group of artists could make something with this exciting but amorphous and ever developing group of technologies? What could be done outside of the games industry, outside of a university research structure, within the limitations of a non-commercial budget?

My opportunity presented itself in June 2002, when I responded to London International Festival of Theatres' (LIFT) call for proposals from artists interested in exploring the poetics and politics of London's urban landscape.[1]

Concept

According to philosopher Gaston Bachelard, "All great, simple images reveal a psychic state".[2] He proposes that imagination and memory transcend and augment the values of reality to create a psychic state in everyday objects and spaces. As a scenographer these ideas are quite familiar, a good stage set will reflect the poetics of a play. The idea of combining these concepts, of pursuing specifically 'artistic' aims, with VR was very exciting. To create a 'living' environment in which the artists could experiment with and modify virtual time and space formed the premise for *The Living Image*.

Working Collaboratively

In my role as project curator, finding co-artists was my first task. I was determined to find artists whose work showed a preoccupation with exploring the poetics and psychology of spaces, without necessarily placing emphasis on technology.

Trudi Entwistle is a site-specific architectural sculptor with a background in landscape architecture. Her works respond sculpturally to the external environment and displays a particular sensitivity to the essence of place, its presence and the intimate subtleties of human interaction with both natural and imposed forms. Graham Nicholls is an installation and video artist who creates immersive psychological spaces. He experiments with different forms of trance hypnosis and sensory deprivation. My own familiarity with designing narrative spaces, 3D modelling and real-time software completed the required skill set.[3]

My experiences of working in the theatre helped to facilitate my curatorial role. I divided the project time over a year. After the initial workshop we planned ten 2- and 3-day workshops between May 2003 and May 2004, and two 1-week workshops for testing the environment. This gave us the incubation period we needed to develop the artistic content and get our heads around the technology. This method of working, over an extended period with relatively short sessions, meant that we had to do a bit more juggling with our other projects and ensure that we stayed in contact. The 'official' time for the project was two months but inevitably we spent much more time on it. With hindsight I would have planned more workshops with the entire installation set up in the last month of the project.

I was aware that time and effort was required to develop the group's rapport and confidence in each other. In the initial workshops we concentrated on getting to know each other and to develop the original ideas. This was the first time I had worked in developing a piece with two other visual artists. Although we had our own specialities, which created natural divisions of labour, all of the artistic decisions on concept, location and the aesthetic had to be made jointly if the project was to be successful. I quickly realised I needed to be conscious of when to switch between the roles of curator and artist.

Some of the ideas in the original proposal became defunct quite early on. After lengthy discussions we realised that they were too ambitious and that we needed more focus. It is imperative when working within a collaborative group that each person believes they can make the project their own, to a degree, especially when another artist has initiated the concept ideas. It is within this area that the support and experience of a commissioning body like LIFT should be commended, for trusting us and putting few constraints on our process. This approach allowed us the creative flexibility to develop, make changes and take more risks, making this a truly experimental project.

TECHNOLOGY, TECHNOLOGY, TECHNOLOGY

The Living Image is an immersive, interactive real-time installation; the project had a major technical dimension to it.

- Immersive means engaging as many of the senses as completely possible.
- Interactive means giving the subject scope for decision-making, and is part of the immersive aspect of the experience.
- Real-time means the viewers can move around spaces using an input device (joy stick or mouse.) This may or may not be projected in stereo.

I was already practiced in building 3D computer models using 3D Studio Max. Such models would be the basic ingredients of the piece. I was also familiar with the real-time software that enables a person to move within these models with the aid of a navigation device. The other hardware components required for an immersive virtual environment, such as the stereo display technology, motion trackers, user interface and large-scale screen, were new to me. I embarked on an intensive research period.[4] I found that there is no established consensus on what an immersive real-time environment is; it is still very much in flux and under development. It is a range of disparate technologies, which must be mixed and matched according to one's priorities, the budget and what can actually be made to work at the technical level.

I looked at commercial and non-commercial developments in VR software and hardware. The industry is geared to commercial VR applications, such as military training and academic research, and to larger budgets than are typical for arts projects. Non- commercial hardware, available through some European universities is usually bundled up with proprietary software, which would need expertise to make compatible with components we were already using. This was an option we could ill afford. Hardware is expensive and choice is still limited, so securing exactly what we wanted within the budget whilst allowing for experimentation and artistic flexibility was going to be a tall order. We got some technology support and advice through our artist mentor Amanda Oldroyd, from the company BT Exact. During the spring and summer of 2003 we experimented with real-time software including beta software from BT Exact. We eventually opted for Quest 3D because I was familiar with it and it allowed us more artistic control. Crucially, I knew it could interface with 3D Studio Max, so long as I adopted certain modelling practices. Additionally, I had established contacts with the software house and this allowed us to request feature enhancements. It became clear how much of a demand on time the technology side of the project would make. It is important to decide these issues as early as possible.

ENVISIONING THE VIRTUAL ENVIRONMENT

We started by building simple 3D environments and playing with various effects such as transparency variation, layer texturing, sound triggering, light placement and the mapping of pre-recorded video footage onto surfaces. VR makes huge demands on hardware and was constantly forcing us to re-think and sometimes re-scale our artistic ideas.

In November 2003 we were able enlist the help of the technology consultant Flavio Zanchi from Zeta Networks. His advice and support on hardware issues was invaluable. He built the exhibition computer, which needed dual processors and extra RAM, and helped us with the development of a wireless user interface. By the end of 2003 we had decided on most of the components we wanted for the installation.

These components consisted of:

1. A large curved screen
2. Passive stereo projections using polarised glasses, as used in IMAX cinemas
3. Wireless motion tracker (a person's movements and position within the defined area are registered by a sensors tracking camera)
4. Surround sound

The project could have been presented in many different ways. For instance, we could have dispensed with the screen and used VR headsets, that is, with head-mounted display.

Or we could have simply used a computer screen, with VR glasses. We decided that the aspects of immersion that we wanted to emphasize involved scale, distance, freedom of movement and gaze.

LOCATION: LONDON

At times we all seemed to be able to agree on what we did *not* want, but what specifically was it that we wanted? This was not always clear! We spent hours thrashing out ideas, questioning concepts and playing with visual styles. How do you create a sense of presence in a virtual environment? How do you achieve an atmosphere? How stylized should the modelling be? What time of day should we simulate? What locations should we select? How were we to re-create the poetics of a place, and what strategies would keep someone engaged?

In the early months of 2004, we explored the streets of London by day and night, both familiar places and alien spaces. We wandered, looked, photographed; we recorded sounds and video together and on our own. We began to be drawn to the 'invisible' city at night, the non-places and in between, banal spaces, the areas in the city that we pass through but which are often not 'seen'. In the chapter *Dead End Street* from his book *Warped Space*, Anthony Vidler examines Walter Benjamin's idea about why cities are not seen, Vidler writes, "We seldom look at our surroundings. Streets and buildings, even those considered major monuments, are in everyday life little more than backgrounds for introverted thought, passages through which our bodies pass 'on the way to work'. In this sense cities are 'invisible' to us, felt rather than seen, moved through rather than visually taken in."[5]

Figure 8. Photographs from our night walks

We felt these spaces were a metaphor for the character of a modern city, the alienation, anxiety, loneliness and fear. But they also possess an allure and a beauty against the red night sky, a florescent-tinted landscape with towering shadows cast by the street lights. We wanted to express the subtle beauties we witnessed on our night walks. We finally decided on five locations: 1) the Westway, skating ramps, tunnel, footbridge; 2) a street in south London, row of Victorian houses; 3) an east London council estate, 1960s styled, garages and surrounding area; 4) Farringdon train station; 5) Smithfield market. The latter two locations were not used in the final installation. Three-dimensional models were built and video sequences of people and sounds were then recorded on location.

EXPERIMENTING IN REAL TIME

In constructing the environment of *The Living Image*, we identified essences of each place, pondered what drew us to them and which specific structures, colours, shapes, textures, shadows and lights appealed to us. We chose selected objects in each location to model. Some were worked into more detail than others, and we experimented with semi-surreal mergings of different models into each other's artistic spaces. The processes involved in developing a virtual environment include:

■ Taking photographs, making sketch plans & elevations
■ Modelling the locations on computer (3D Studio Max)

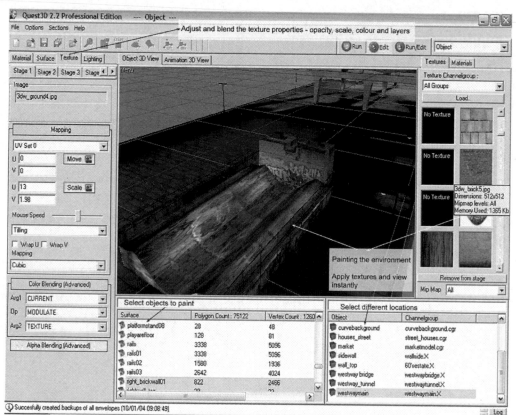

Figure 9. The real-time design environment

- Transfer of the models to real-time (Quest 3D)
- Painting/ texturing/ colouring/ light and shading virtual surfaces
- Animating objects (eg moving lights in the night)
- Composition of the virtual environment – linking the models in virtual space
- Adding environmental sounds
- Embedding video sequences
- Placing "triggers" to initiate video and/or sound at specific locations

Together with trying to convey the artistic ideas we always had to consider the technical constraints on things such as texture resolution, model complexity, embedded video size, sound compatibility and other hardware, and budget, determined limitations of the VR medium.

The real-time software we used has an intuitive interface that allowed us to work out virtual environments collaboratively. We could make changes quickly, add and test out different ideas and, as a result, changes then became less 'precious' to the individual artist. It does take some time to learn this type of software, in particular the logic of linking events to trigger interactive elements, for example, using the distance of the user to a virtual object to trigger a video sequence, but I feel it paid off in the end. However, in the last month of the project it was difficult to balance the technical with the artistic and it would have been a less stressful experience if we had someone to concentrate on the technical software issues, which inevitably arose.

MAPPING THE ENVIRONMENT

During the process of developing the aesthetics of the environment we tried to use the properties of the medium creatively, there are things in VR that can never be created in the real world and we were interested in how we could use these proprieties to enhance and challenge the participant's experience. For example, 'collision detection' on a virtual object stops a user from 'accidentally' walking through a solid object; it reacts like a real world object. But this can easily be turned off, allowing the artist to play with the definition of 'real' in Virtual Reality. Alternatively, for the triggering of videos we planted transparent or invisible walls to create boundaries that the user could not walk through. We used different levels and layers of opacity on structures and videos to further upset perception and enhance the 'off-real' properties of the experience. This period of experimenting was very invigorating because it was pure play, not knowing what to expect and welcoming the unexpected. This partly arose due to the nature of the creative software, which is so full of options, so capable of re-thinks, of quick experiments and small accidents, which send the imagination in completely new directions.

An important component in developing any virtual environment is how the user is going to interact with it. Initially we had ambitious goals. We wanted a natural user interface with a wireless motion

Figure 10. Identifying the interactive elements in each environment

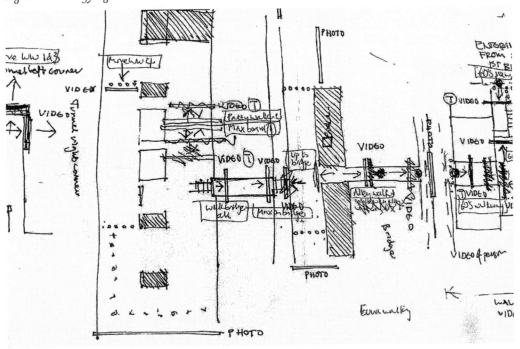

tracker, but this was too expensive so we started to experiment with a head tracker and a wireless mouse. The software company Quest 3D wrote special channels for us to use for head tracking. Having direct contact with a software company was an important technical asset. However, we should have considered and tested these options much earlier in the process. In an arts project in which technical components are so important, goals must be kept in focus and constantly re-examined, keeping in mind the unexpected possibilities that can occur while working with this medium.

THE INSTALLATION

The Living Image is a single-user experience. At the exhibition each person was allotted fifteen minutes in the darkened projection room.[6] They wore 3D glasses and used a hand-held navigation device. Navigation was calibrated to slow down the person's virtual movement to encourage observation and exploration.

Written comments and discussion with participants after the experience indicated that many of them found the allotted time too short, but most enjoyed the experience; some felt frustrated by the slow speed whilst others had a dreamlike experience. The sense of presence and validity was very high, for some a sense of foreboding and personal vulnerability was felt. Some of the participants wrote:

[I] enjoyed the knowledge that I didn't have to attack or shoot anything which seems to be the main aim of many …worlds in virtual reality and 3D games.

I enjoyed the sense of surrender…I felt very safe…

The other humans in the environment made it more real. They were quite a surprise when I encountered them. I experienced a defined sense of place as well as space.

Sense of beauty and trepidation.

The attention to detail and hazy images flashing in every now and again really added to the effect.[7]

Afterwards, we felt that what contributed most to the sense of immersion in this piece was:

- The stereoscopic projection
- The large curved screen
- Surround sound
- The single user nature of the experience
- The use of video as opposed to computer generated characters
- Setting in the night time
- Slowing down the participant's movements
- Mixing stylised and realistic environments

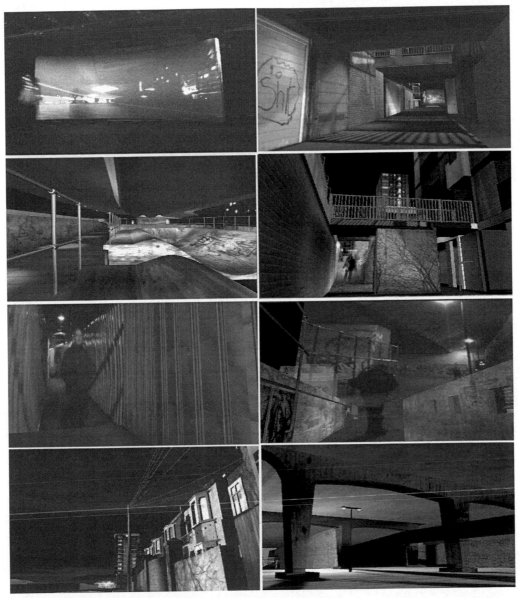

Figure 11. Screenshots from the Installation

The nature of the VR environments in *The Living Image* hopefully challenges the distinction between the artist as the sole creator and the participant as the passive observer. It aims to offer the participant degrees of freedom and removes the distance from the image, so one is relocated 'inside' the image. Oliver Grau in his book *Virtual Art* writes: "It is not the format of virtual reality that defines its genealogical relationship to illusionism; through real-time computation, interaction and evolution, the observer is attaining a power to form the image that is unparalleled in history. At the same time, the observer is subjected to the greatest ever suggestive potential of images, which are now dynamic, interactive, evolutionary and 'alive' in immersive image space."[8]

This project confirmed to me the artistic potential of this medium. A scenographer's attention to detail and experience in creating imaginative spaces are all skills perfectly relevant to VR development. In fact, I feel they can bring something unique to this field. By no means was it a perfect experience, we made compromises with the technology, time was a problem, ambitions ran high but we certainly learnt a lot. We want to continue to develop it and experiment with new user interfaces and we hope to exhibit it again soon.

NOTES

1. *The Living Image* was commissioned by the London International Festival of Theatre (LIFT).
2. Bachelard, G., *The Poetics of Space*, Boston, MA, Beacon Press, 1994, p.72.
3. *The Living Image* artists are: Trudi Entwistle (artist) www.trudientwistle.com, Graham Nicholls (artist) www.grahamnicholls.com, Roma Patel (artist and curator), www.digitalsetdesign.com.
4. Beckman, J., (ed.), *The Virtual Dimension: architecture, representation and crash culture*, 1st edition, New York, Princeton Architectural Press, 1998. Sherman, R. S. and Craig, B. A., *Understanding Virtual Reality: interface, application, and design*, USA, Morgan Kaufmann Publishers, 2003. Candy, L. and Edmonds, E., *Explorations in Art and Technology*, London, Springer-Verlag, 2002.
5. Vidler, A., 'Dead End Street', *Warped Space: art, architecture and anxiety in modern culture*, Cambridge, MA: MIT Press, 2001, p.81.
6. *The Living Image* was first exhibited at the London Science Museum's Dana Centre, London, May 2004 as part of the LIFT 04: Enquiry, www.thelivingimage.org.
7. From questionnaires completed by participants at the time of the installation.
8. Grau, O., 'Perspectives', *Virtual Art: from Illusion to Immersion*, Cambridge, MA: MIT Press, 2003, p.348.

FLATNESS AND DEPTH
REFLECTIONS

Nicholas Wood

This chapter seeks to explore the relation between the use of depth in the staging of work for the theatre and the discovery by the audience of depth in the meaning of the work shown. If a relation is found to exist, is this relation accidental, or does it suggest a correspondence in our ways of thinking/remembering, organising our thoughts and the physical arrangements of the stage? To assist in this exploration, reference will be made to the spatial images we carry of the workings of the human mind, the quest to represent depth of field, as well as examples of depth of staging pertinent in contemporary theatre.

I would like to begin this short personal reflection on depth, and the place of depth in the theatre, by saying a few words on what may be conceived as its opposite – that is, flatness, since it was an interest in flatness, which provided the main drive and principle for my earliest work in the theatre.

Emerging in the 1970s, with a typical word-based education, I first encountered the contemporary visual arts in the form of the great abstract expressionists Pollock, Newman and Rothko,[1] who held sway, especially as interpreted by the art critic Clement Greenberg,[2] whose formalist approach dominated art criticism at that time. Like many others, I immediately became intoxicated with the idea of flatness or "the all-over field."[3] The idea of an approach to painting which accepted that the surface of the canvas was flat, and celebrated this, rather than fought against it, felt to me like the arrival at a wonderful quietus, where the stresses and strains of the history of the previous five hundred years, based on hierarchical values and a pressure to *represent* the world, could fall away, and the dawn of a better world seemed possible, based on the unassailable logic and beauty of the principle of equality. Just as each part of the canvas was to be equally valued, suddenly, so was each human being. And it is important to emphasise here how integrally flatness seemed to be bound up in all this. Depth or rather the desire to explore depth seemed to me at that time a retrograde step, a kind of heresy, a step back into a dark and gloomy guilt-ridden world of superstition and ancient discredited values. And the rightness of all of this seemed to me to be neatly in accord with my recent exposure to Oxford philosophy, with its emphasis on the careful and critical examination of each and every proposition; a kind of constant and rigorous pairing down to the essentials, which looked so critically at any sort of metaphysics, or unsubstantiated speculation.[4]

In my first stage play therefore, *Country Life*, produced at the Hampstead Theatre in 1973, which was directed by Chris Parr and designed by Bernard Culshaw, I attempted to explore flatness as a notion, which might be applied to dramatic writing, and you will notice an apparent contradiction or tension at the outset. Here, the main protagonist, Richard, played by George Cole, was a character so beset by flatness that he found it difficult to stir from his chair, or undertake any normal or perhaps uneven activity. Spurred on by his frustrated wife, Diana, played by Virginia McKenna, attempting to bring some meaningful contours to his life, he finally agrees to go for a drive in his car but falls asleep, we are told, in the garage, overcome by a kind of perennial lassitude or flatness of mind.

Set "in the garden behind a house" the presence of the house behind the characters limited any physical depth in the staging, assisted, of course, by the 'narrowish' shelf, which constituted the Hampstead Theatre stage at that time. The characters were pinned to that shelf, facing to the front and towards an imaginary space, which, in a tradition of more literary theatre, they were able to describe, but not of course visit.

Having described my interest in flatness derived from a broad identification with certain basic precepts of modernism, as I interpreted them, I would now like to describe certain instances in the theatre where that notion has been challenged, for me, and the curtain has been lifted, so to speak, on depth as an area to be explored, and the expressive possibilities of the uses of depth in staging, given in my mind, due weight and prominence. I will describe a few instances of these insights as they occurred, to me chronologically, and then begin a process of seeking to draw some conclusions from these individual events.

The first instance I would like to record took place in the Bargehouse on the South Bank in London 2001. One of the first performances to take place in the attic floor of that building was Primitive Science's production of *Icarus Falling* designed by Dick Bird, directed by Marc von Henning, with dramaturg Boz Temple Morris. As I remember, the first scene of this performance took place close to the seated audience in a confined space before a projected image of Breugel's famous painting. I remember two characters interacting with some wit and 'theatrical' badinage, a sense of some kind of lecture taking place, and some humour at the expense of foreigners, Italians, I think, and their unusual ways. The audience was laughing, hugger-mugger, warm, reassured, operating according to clearly understood rules within a confined and recognisable space. Then the scene ended and the unexpected occurred. The screen bearing the projected image of the 'Fall of Icarus' was removed and suddenly we the audience were in darkness, our senses feeling the existence of a much larger space before us, extending the full length of the Bargehouse attic space. A dimly lit door opened, perhaps thirty metres away, and our senses grappled to make sense of this apparition. Where was it in relation to the floor? What size was this door? A figure appearing in the doorway appeared to be the 'wrong' size? Was it a very large door or a very small figure? From a state of comfortable knowledge and reassurance, as an audience, we had moved to a state of unknowing, poised uncertainly on the brink of an apparently endless void. Just as the performance space had been suddenly and unexpectedly extended, so the space in our minds in which we would be feeling and responding to the event was extended to a much stiller and darker place.

As a second example, I would like to cite a recent performance of a company of graduate students from the Central School of Speech and Drama called Shunt, which took place in their railway arch in Bethnal Green, and which shares a key element with the previous experience – that is surprise, or craft, in that the audience suddenly found themselves in an extended space, far larger than the one which they thought they had occupied, up until that point. In this case, for their show, *Dance Bear Dance*, Shunt had acquired the neighbouring railway arch, a fact unknown to many members of the audience. By some extraordinary sleight of hand they managed to assemble two audiences, one in each archway, each unaware of the other's existence. And at a critical moment in the piece the audience were led to a large sliding door, standing between the two archways, the door was suddenly thrown back, so that each audience found itself contemplating the other, a kind of penetrable mirror, through which each audience was eventually able to walk and enlarge their experience, to the other side.

As my final example, I would like to make reference to AKHE's award-winning production, *The White Cabin*, seen at the Edinburgh Festival in 2003, and again at the Purcell Room in London 2004. One of the clearest arcs, or journeys, of this piece is an exploration of the space in which this ritualistic event takes place. A strange and manic figure, for example, uncoils a rope, moving from side to side and gradually more deeply into the playing area, like some latter-day shaman, marking out a territory in which the play will take place. A threatening metallic geometrical device swings from the side, bearing a mirror, defining space in a more cold and scientific manner, interacting with and probing the space around the single woman performer, almost as might an instrument of torture. Three cloths, with a gentler, more theatrical, provenance descend from above, each with a square cut out from its centre, each further back from the other, through which the performers cross and re-cross, playing a game of concealment and revelation at various distances from the audience. On to these flat, ever retreating, surfaces, are projected an extraordinary array of religious and iconic images, from the front, while from behind, as I remember, moving images reminiscent of silent films are projected onto a small screen, occupying the furthest of the ever-retreating squares and frames.

This was the strangest and fullest enactment of the workings of the inner mind on the stage I had ever seen. The effect was to open up the thoughts and emotions of each member of the audience. One of my current students for example, a South Korean, spoke of reliving his childhood during the performance, of remembering events which he had not thought about for many years. There is much here which seems to chime with Alison Oddey's prophetic vision of the theatre-maker of today as the creator of "a contemplative space".[5] Mischa Twitchin, a member of Shunt, reviewed the show for *Total Theatre*[6] and there are a few key phrases, which seem to echo thoughts about the role of the theatre-maker, and also give some clues about a direction in which many contemporary theatre-makers appear to be moving:

> One of the joys of the fantastic Aurora Nova series of 'mini-festivals-within-the-main-Festival' at Edinburgh has been the appearance of the Russian company AKHE in the UK – first with 'Pooh and Prah' in 2001 and this year with 'White Cabin.' *For if one dreams of a theatre that is not prescribed by words, then here is that dream come to life, gleefully playing hide-and-seek with our expectations of the relation between stage and story.*

> Now, thanks to the London International Mime Festival, 'White Cabin' … can be seen again, together with Plug and Play, described by the company as a kind of club night *with 'live painting' alongside live sampling by their DJ.*

> Whilst based in St. Petersburg, where most of the company were born and have studied, AKHE *doesn't have a theatre of its own. Recalling Kantor's notion of a Wandering Troupe, they not only perform internationally, they also make their work where ever they are invited to…*

> … Founded in 1989 by three members of the experimental 'Yes/No Theatre Group' of Boris Ponizovsky … *the company began by exploring their own diverse range of interests, from street happenings to concerts and exhibitions, and even to making short, black and white films.* Since 1996 … AKHE has devoted itself more to theatre-based projects. *Both of them painters, Isaev and Semtchenko fashion all of the objects that appear within the shows themselves, with both sound and light also produced by the company.*

> Besides notable collaborations – which are set to continue – with, amongst others, Derevo, *each of the artists in AKHE also does work outside of the company,* ranging from projects with Slava Polunin to the designing of cafes and clubs in St Petersburg. Now with seven core collaborators, *they operate as a kind of artists' collective, based on the shared experience that their collective projects offer greater possibilities than any one of them could create on their own for developing a sense of theatrical creation.*

> *Their word for this creation is 'engineering'* – not, however, to suggest that the small miracle of theatre is simply the workings of a machine, but to point up the identity of the creative and the technical within their art …

> … AKHE emphasises that *what they share with an audience is, like a dream, visual – calling theirs an 'optical theatre'. They stage such stories as their audiences will become the authors of.* From the theatrical reinvention of the images of things, *audiences will come to tell their own stories, putting into words what the performance has to say without them.*[7]

So what would Clement Greenberg, my critic on the shoulder make of all this? My first feeling is that he would be appalled by the presence of all this stuff, this human bric-a-brac, the mess which eventually peoples the stage with references "outside the frame" to the whole history of art, religion, magic and superstition up to this point.[8] At one level, the piece appears to lift the covers on our lives, prying more and more deeply into our collective feelings and unconscious, the deepest and darkest secrets we normally keep covered with our mask of social normality. In some ways, this glimpse into the deeply human would appear to be strongly antithetical to the formalist point of view.

But now I would like to raise another point, a realisation as an artist, which perhaps you may feel I have arrived at somewhat late in the day. A performance space is not, of course, a canvas, so much as a cube or volume, its "all-over field" is usually three-dimensional, including a deep horizontal plane. It is a cube, or volume of space, moreover, allied to a tradition of deeply human origins, combined with the presence of the human audience, make it practically impossible to divorce the activities which take place within it from our day-to-day activities, as well as our deepest interests and concerns. The implications of these discoveries are far-reaching, as I try to bring the disciplines and rigour of 'flatness' to the exploration of volume, a volume, moreover, imbued with human and social associations, and in some way linked to the workings of our own inner minds.

So what is the work of the theatre-maker to be, in relation to the 'canvas' or volume, which is waiting to be filled? I consider the work of the theatre-maker, artist, teacher, today is to occupy this space, deeply, completely but also ephemerally and surprisingly; looking to purify it to a degree of worn-out or corrupted 'space-filling' conventions, and always seeking a new and better understanding or rearrangement of the spaces which seem to exist within us, as well as outside.

NOTES

1. Sandler, I., *Mark Rothko: Mark Rothko Exhibition Catalogue*, London: Tate Gallery Publications, 1987, p.9–18.
2. Greenberg, C., *Modernist Painting*, Arts Yearbook 4, 1961, p.107.
3. Sandler, 1987, p.14.
4. Ayer, A. J., *Language, Truth and Logic*, London: Victor Gollancz, 1964, p.33–36.
5. Oddey, A., 2004 Scenography & Performance International Symposium, 'a willingness to be silent', *Scenography International*, Issue 8.
6. Twitchin, M., *Total Theatre*, Volume 15.4: winter 2003–4, p.23.
7. Ibid., p.23. (Italics sic)
8. Greenberg, 1961, p.107.

PART II: PERFORMANCE POTENTIALS

Digital Dreams
Sleep Deprivation Chamber

Lesley Ferris

This chapter articulates and examines the various digital performance techniques used in a collaboration between the Advanced Computing Center for the Arts and Design (ACCAD) and the Department of Theatre at The Ohio State University. When the Director of ACCAD, Maria Palazzi, approached me in 2001 with the idea of collaborating with them in a fully produced theatre production the department declared a strong interest. We had already initiated several digital collaborations. These included the creation of the Roy Bowen Virtual Theatre which we use when we teach our Introduction to Theatre class and our virtual and digital lighting class that included students from Theatre and the Advanced Computing Center for the Arts and Design (ACCAD) team, taught by Resident Lighting Designer Mary Tarantino and Maria Palazzi. But a fully produced play? What script would we use? Mindful of the fact that technology, "has rarely enabled new forms of dramatic literature", I set my mind thinking of possible scripts that would work. While Burke and Stein's thesis on the inadequacy of technology's generative powers in the realm and dramatic texts may hold true, another view of dramatic literature is also possible. Namely, that there are writers who have written scripts that cry out for the innovative possibilities of digital technologies long before such technology was available. Of course, Artaud is perhaps one of the first to come to mind, for example, *The Jet of Blood*. I would also suggest some of the German Expressionists such as Kokoschka and Kandinsky, *Murderer, the Hope of Woman* and *The Yellow Sound*, respectively. More recently we have Heiner Müller and the playwright I will consider here, the African American writer Adrienne Kennedy.

PRODUCTION TIME LINE, PERSONNEL AND CONTEXT
The production time line was very different from time lines used by either collaborator. Discussions began in 2001 and we finalised a script choice in March 2002. The Kennedy script

was also chosen because Adrienne Kennedy had graduated from Ohio State University in 1953. The Ohio State University gave her an honorary doctorate in June 2003 and the production and a symposium celebrated the 50th anniversary of her graduation.

In April 2002 I developed a draft concept as the director of the project and began meeting with members of the production team. By June 2002 the concept was developed further and there were several summer meetings. In September 2002 a team of students from ACCAD started to meet weekly with the Art Director/Scenic Designer, Who Jeong Lee and the Director of Technology and Live Integration, Katie Whitlock. The director joined these meetings twice a month. By January 2003 much of the video and some of the animation were well underway. In February 2003 the video beating sequence was shot. The reason for the delay was we needed to cast the show and auditions took place in late January 2003.

The production staff was much larger than that required of a theatre production without digital design aspects. The Director of Technology and Computer Control was Matt Lewis, who programmed jitter sequences as well as made it possible to link and control all the live feed video and the five video projectors. Other staff included: Costume Designer, Adam M. West; Lighting Designer, Mary Tarantino; Computer Animators, Carrie Wilson, Jeff Ostergaard, Jenny Macy and Mike Altman; Sound Designer, Stacy Siak; Video Processing, Hyun Jung Chae, Carrie Wilson, Who Jeong Lee; Computer Programming, Jon Woodring, Matthew Lewis, Fran Kalal, David Tinapple; Assistant Director of Technology/Moving Light Programmer, Sean Hennessy; Dramaturg, Anthony Hill. Maria Palazzi, Director of ACCAD, was the Computer Animation Producer. Mark Shanda was the Theatre Producer and the Technical Director.

The video projectors were tested several times in the theatre space with animation sequences in March. The testing was to see what throw was necessary and to see what kind of screen surface was best for the projections. Several kinds of material were used before a final choice was made.

The production opened on 7 May and ran through 23 May 2003 in the Roy Bowen Theatre on The Ohio State University campus in Columbus, Ohio.

Established by Professor Emeritus Charles Csuri in the 1970's, The Advanced Computing Center for the Arts and Design (ACCAD) is a multi-disciplinary center, located in the College of the Arts, which supports research that fosters innovative ties between the arts and sciences. ACCAD and its associated faculty have a long and proud pioneering history in computer graphics and of teaching OSU graduate students from across the University. Graduates who have studied at ACCAD make a huge impact on the American film industry in special effects and computer graphics. Our former students have had a hand in movies like *Star Wars: Episode I, The Phantom Menace, Toy Story II, Titanic, A Bug's Life,* and *Ice Age.* They work at major studios like Disney, Industrial Light and Magic, Blue Sky Studios and Dreamworks.[2]

Since the beginning of ACCAD's history the staff of the Department of Theatre at Ohio State have formed creative teams that are multidisciplinary since that is the only way we can successfully explore and invent. For this production of *Sleep Deprivation Chamber*, Theatre and ACCAD formed a partnership in part because our students were sharing and discovering connections between live and digital theatre and it seemed like the perfect time to collaborate on a performance. This collaboration features new research for us in live performance including computer-generated graphics, real-time interactive triggering devices, post-processed video sequences, and live video signals.

Our process with Theatre started in the summer of 2002 as the team read the script with the director and her crew and started to imagine how technology could be used to enhance action, meaning and interpretation of the live events. Our team was made up of artists, programmers, designers and animators. For the graphics, we start by conceptualizing on paper, then creating still digital images, then building three-dimensional models and making them move. The computer scientists on the team were inventing and programming to enable us to run the visuals for the show through interactive computer interfaces, creating real-time visual effects, and integrating triggering devices into the live performance.

As a result the ACCAD team is producing animation and video treatments and programmed triggering sequences that support and explore the live actors' interpretation of the Kennedys' written word. Examples of these graphics, video, and programming include particle systems controlling the movement of swarming moths, actor-controlled video manipulation, a three-dimensional metamorphosis of an African mask to a human skull in the metaphorical reference to March, and real-time writing that transforms into blood.

Carver and Bearden's edited work, *New Visions in Performance: The Impact of Digital Technologies*, summarizes the various authors' common concerns, which include:

> the virtuality and fluidity of space and time, and the potential for alternative realities, spaces and narratives; interactivity and the active audience/participant; the role of the body (and its double) in technologically enhanced or mediated performance and the ensuing questions around identity and presence; the ability of performance to extend itself beyond the circumscribed moment and place of its enunciation; and the 'problem' of liveness in multimedia work....[3]

Every one of these 'common concerns' of digital performance can be found in the majority of Kennedy's scripts, work she has been producing since 1964. Indeed, let us look at the critical response of several scholars to Kennedy's work. Alisa Solomon, in her introduction to Kennedy's *The Alexander Plays*, talks about how Kennedy's, "poetic theater of images" frightens many traditional producers and directors. But for Solomon it is "their looping, lilting language and their fuguelike, fragmented form" that makes them so exciting. Solomon continues: "Dialogue takes place not through the conversational exchange of characters addressing each other, but through the fluid interplay of visual and verbal imagery."[4] Linda Kintz explains: "Their mesmerizing complexity, horror, and grotesque beauty works like Möbius strips that keep turning inside out to show what goes on in the ambiguous, troubled process called acculturation."[5] It is exactly this mesmerizing complexity, this fluid interplay of visual imagery, the turning Möbius strip, and the looping, fragmented form of Kennedy's work that I felt would lend itself to our experiment with live performance and technology.

THE AUTOBIOGRAPHICAL DOUBLE

Adrienne Kennedy is known for finding dramatic inspiration in autobiography. Her early scripts, such as *Funnyhouse of a Negro* in 1964 that established her career, employ a fractured dream imagery grounded in her personal memories and experiences. While her self-reflexive quality becomes a signature of her work, it was not until much later that she created a character that becomes her autobiographical double. The dramatic cycle she wrote in 1992, entitled *The Alexander Plays* aligns itself to autobiographical models. The four plays in the cycle, *She Talks to Beethoven*, *The Ohio State Murders*, *The Film Club*, and *The Dramatic Circle*, include geographical locations that are the 'real' settings of Kennedy's life: Cleveland, Ohio State, Ghana, London and New York. And the central character, named Suzanne Alexander, has lived a life much like Adrienne Kennedy. Suzanne Alexander is what critic Werner Sollors calls an "authorial projection" or what I call a shadow-self of Kennedy.[6] Suzanne, like Adrienne, is a writer who interweaves personal narrative with fantasy, ritualistic repetition, fragmentation and violence. In *The Ohio State Murders* Kennedy charts her student life at Ohio State University in the early 1950s. In the script the character of Suzanne Alexander is doubled appearing both as a young student between 1949 and 1952 and in the present tense, as Suzanne Alexander, an established writer who has been invited to Ohio State to lecture on her work. So Suzanne Alexander is Kennedy's double, and the play itself has two Suzannes, as if to demonstrate this fact. The Kennedy doubling has a resonance within African American theory, touching on, "what W. E. B. Du Bois called the double consciousness of African-American life, a life that must reconcile the yoked forces of European and African experience, while refusing synthesis."[7]

I now turn to *Sleep Deprivation Chamber*, which was first produced by the Signature Theatre Company in 1996 and became the script chosen for our digital theatre collaboration. Here, Kennedy deals with a major difference from her previous plays: instead of using autobiography as a landscape of memory from her distant past, she is faced with using a very present personal, traumatic moment.

In 1991 while Adrienne Kennedy was working on *The Ohio State Murders*, which premiered at the Great Lakes Theatre Festival in Cleveland in 1992, Adam Kennedy, her son, was beaten and arrested by a white police officer. The crime? DWB, Driving While Black, is a term coined by African Americans who are frequently stopped by police and harassed. Driving his own car, on his own street, with a broken tail light, Adam Kennedy was stopped by a policeman, who could not believe that Adam lived in the middle-class neighbourhood. The policeman's aggressive questioning led to a violent beating of Adam in the driveway of his father's house. This act of brutal racial profiling is the source of *Sleep Deprivation Chamber* and the play becomes Adrienne's first co-authored work as she wrote it with her son Adam Kennedy. The play utilises the trial transcript as well as a variety of testimonies from the people involved in this incident. It also includes a variety of dream sequences, memories, and disjointed visual images. Locations change suddenly and abruptly and some scenes occur simultaneously. For example, the play starts at Antioch College in Ohio, where Teddy is a student. 'Teddy' is the character name for Adam Kennedy. He is directing a production of fellow students in *Hamlet* and snippets of the rehearsal, including "the murder of the sleeping king" and Yorick's grave and skull are woven throughout the play.[8]

Here is an example of an early dream scene from the script: "Teddy's body is drawn in sunder and dismembered, his carcass cast into a fire."[9] The challenge of staging such a scripted direction faced the design and production team time and again, as we considered ways to represent the multifarious visual aspects of this work. In this particular instance, the actor playing the role of Teddy stood on stage while computer-generated images of fire and flames created by jitter were projected on screens. Referring back to Carver and Bearden's 'common concerns', Kennedy's script easily provided, "the potential for alternative realities, spaces and narratives" and it experimented with "fluidity of space and time".

WRITING AND RIGHTING

As the director, and after much thought and consideration, I decided I wanted to locate the meaning of the piece in Kennedy's act of writing. I realised that with this play 'writing' is about 'righting' the grievous wrongs to Adrienne Kennedy's son and family. I focused much of my research on women's autobiography as a way of coming to terms with this challenging play. I used Sidonie Smith and Julia Watson's important work *Reading Autobiography* in which the authors have created a theoretical template for considering and interpreting this literary genre. As the co-authors state: "To theorize the autobiographical we need an adequate critical vocabulary for describing how the components of subjectivity are implicated in self-presentational acts…[W]e have defined five constitutive processes of autobiographical subjectivity: memory, experience, identity, embodiment, and agency."[10] For Smith and Watson these terms are the foundational groundings that make it possible to come to terms with, "women's acts of self-representation in twentieth century narratives." While all five 'constitutive processes of autobiographical subjectivity' are actively present in the play, I was particularly interested in pursuing the concept of 'agency' and its relation to Adrienne Kennedy's life as a writer.

Kennedy's first reaction to the brutal beating of her son was to write. The work, a prose essay entitled "Letter to My Students on My Sixty-first Birthday by Suzanne Alexander", was originally written in 1992, and predates the play by several years. The letter is a narrative telling of the trauma and foreshadows in detail and styles, much of the script. In it Teddy Alexander screams the words, "What did I do? What did I do?" And Suzanne Alexander/Adrienne Kennedy follows this with, "And that's what I'd wondered ever since. What did we do? What did our family ever do except try to be excellent citizens? What kind of country was this where a policeman could beat you and then you had to defend yourself with letters of character?"[11]

Sleep Deprivation Chamber is filled with a sense of tension and apprehension that comes primarily from Suzanne Alexander. The concern she feels for the well-being of her son is made manifest through her disjointed dreams and her obsession with writing. Writing, the foremost method, one could argue, for controlling self-representation and for positioning, articulating and negotiating subjectivity, is a central concern of the play. Alexander/Kennedy identifies herself as a writer. The first stage direction in the play is: "Suzanne sits at a dressing table *writing*."[12]

One of the scenes in *Sleep Deprivation Chamber* is Suzanne attending a rehearsal of her play *The Ohio State Murders* in Cleveland, Ohio. Suzanne listens to an actress rehearse the role of Suzanne in her earlier play and the lines are a monologue taken verbatim from *The Ohio State Murders* script. The monologue situates Suzanne as a celebrated writer who is invited to speak about her work. The Suzanne, of the present, in *The Ohio State Murders* script says:

> I was asked to talk about the violent imagery in my work; bloodied heads, severed limbs, dead fathers, dead Nazis, dying Jesus. The chairman said, we do want to hear about your brief years here at Ohio State but we also want you to talk about violent imagery in your stories and plays. When I visited Ohio State last year it struck me as a series of desperate dark landscapes just as it had in 1949, the autumn of my freshman year. I used to *write* down locations in order to learn the campus: the oval, behind the green, the golf hut, behind Zoology....[13]

For Smith and Watson agency is the idea that people are agents in their own lives, rather than passive spectators or "unconscious transmitters" of knowledge or knowing.[14] Thus, Alexander/ Kennedy's early years at Ohio State include writing as a key to knowing, to learning the layout of the large sprawling campus. Her writing defines her in multiple ways; it has served as a method for articulating her self while simultaneously making her who she is. With writing she is clearly an active agent in her own life. In *Sleep Deprivation Chamber*, however, the act of writing becomes troublesome and potentially threatening. One of Suzanne's main activities in the play is to write letters. An example from the script: "Dear Governor Wilder: My name is Suzanne Alexander. I am a black writer...I have written you before – I am writing you again."[15] The letters are written by Suzanne to various people, in addition to the governor, there are letters to the prosecuting attorney, her son's lawyer, a state senator, and the county manager. The letters are Suzanne's attempts to try and explain why her son, Teddy, should not be arrested and tried for assault. Teddy's lawyer advises Suzanne to stop writing letters. Instead of helping, it may in fact damage his case.

It is painful for Suzanne to realise that her writing could cause harm to her son. In a letter to Attorney Edelstein, her son's lawyer, Suzanne says, "You say I must see Teddy's case realistically. Few people win cases against the police; the judge tends to side with them. And you are doing everything possible that I must understand it is your profession to prosecute the police and you hope I won't write too many letters."[16]

In addition to the numerous character texts, such as those quoted above from Suzanne's letters, the script also contains numerous stage directions that reinforce Suzanne's major dramatic purpose, writing. Examples include: "She walks, writes."[17] "Light on Teddy. He remembers as Suzanne writes."[18] "Again, as she writes...."[19] "Again Suzanne is writing letters...."[20] "Suzanne continues letter to Governor Wilder."[21] "Writing."[22] "In the Ohio Theatre Suzanne writes".[23]

In addition to the realisation that the act of writing is crucial to understanding the play, I also noted that hands, the physical body's instrument for writing, played a significant role throughout, both for Suzanne as well as other characters. Below is an excerpt from my Director's Concept:

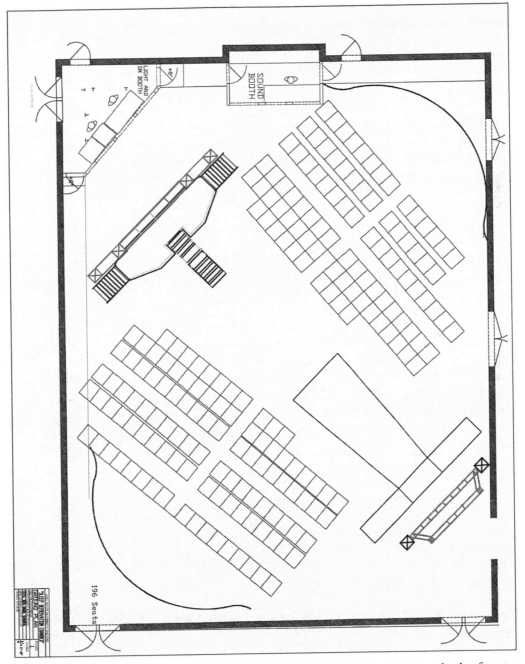

Figure 12. Ground plan *for* Sleep Deprivation Chamber, *showing trestle staging, two banks of seating facing each other, and the screens for projections: behind each seating bank the screens were curved and layered, while the screens were flat at the ends of the 'road'. The computer operators sat behind the audience in front of the curved screens in view of the audience.*

Hands: Hands writing (Suzanne,), hands-cuffed (Teddy), hands violated (finger tips lost in accident: David), Finger-prints/Palm prints (Teddy, being finger-printed when arrested); hands writing to represent March, Teddy's uncle (a Stanford professor). Hands are the source of doing, of writing, of changing things; for that very reason, they are also the target of aggression and entrapment. And they are also the agent of Suzanne's life as a writer....[24]

My concept paper was provided to the design and animation team and it helped us all to focus on certain elements that we could realise on stage. Before considering the digital design work we did on writing and hands, it is necessary to understand the stage layout or floor plan. A crucial decision made early on was not to stage the play in the traditional presentational, proscenium arch way. When working with projected images this is the most obvious choice and often necessary because of the theatre space one is allocated. I was lucky to have our 250-seat thrust stage for this production. We broke down the seating and totally transformed the space to represent a road with audience seating on both sides of the road's berm. So the visual presentation of the performance space was environmental rather than presentational, against the traditional use of multi-media in a filmic way. The surfaces for projections, there were five of them, surrounded the audience and included a projection on the floor.

Another excerpt from my Director's Concept on the stage space:

The image of the road: a journey, a pathway, going from one place to another, travel, right of way, intersection, junction, artery, interchange. Implies movement, motion, activity, speed, velocity, restlessness, mobility. The road as Möbius strip: a constant return on and into itself. The road as landscape for freedom and movement contrasted to the road as the site for terror and racial violence. The notion of the 'road' as a particularly American image...It is on the road, the street in front of Teddy's father's house that the violence occurs.

Other notes that I gave the design team about realising this space arrangement helped to articulate a rationale for the audience seating arrangement.

Audience facing each other in a trestle-like seating arrangement. This is reminiscent of the effect of Maya Lin's radical sculpture for the Vietnam Veterans: shiny black marble in which viewers see their own faces overlaid the engraved names of the dead. In the newly reconfigured Roy Bowen Theater audience members watch the action in front of them but behind the actors are other spectators, watching. Thus the audience must confront itself throughout the performance.

The use of the road as the 'stage', the performance space, was reinforced by other scenic elements. One end of the road rose up on a ramp that diminished in size as if moving toward a vanishing point. The projection screen at the end of the ramp often had moving 'street' footage projected on it. Miniatures of the Alexander family house, the family church, and a police car were props situated along the road's berm. The actors occasionally used these when they referred to them in their text.

WRITING DIGITALLY REALISED
The first aspect of 'writing' that the production team developed was the use of real-time handwriting executed by the actress playing the role of Suzanne. A small desk with wheels, so that

Figure 13. The Alexander family, David Alexander, the father (L), Suzanne Alexander (centre), and the children, David Jr., Patrice, and Teddy. Projected on the screen are the signatures of all the family members that are on a letter Suzanne has written.

it could be easily moved to change position on the stage floor, was designed that had a hidden Wacom writing tablet embedded in the desktop. As Suzanne wrote her letters, her writing would simultaneously appear on the screens surrounding the audience. In a few instances, the writing was recorded ahead of time, such as the letter, which Suzanne writes to Governor Wilder. After Suzanne writes the letter, the entire family signs their names to it, and each name was pre-recorded and projected on the screen while each actor playing the family roles stepped forward.

Also in this same letter, Suzanne talks about Emmett Till, the fourteen-year-old African American boy who was murdered in Mississippi in 1955 for allegedly saying "Bye Baby" to a white female store clerk. Till's murder was the spark that set the civil rights movement in motion. As Suzanne started to talk about Emmett Till, his photograph came on the screens, and she wrote his name and it appeared across the screen.

The computer programmers also developed methods for turning the real-time writing into different visual effects. For example, the first letter Suzanne writes to the County Manager occurs right after the fire effect mentioned above. "Dear County Manager" appeared on the screen in real time, turned to ash and slowly blew away. Another effect turned the real-time writing to blood red, which slowly dripped down and fell off the screen.

Suzanne's desk was ever-present and moments were staged to give a sense that her writing is a constant presence in her life. For example, when a lawyer is cross-examining her husband in a

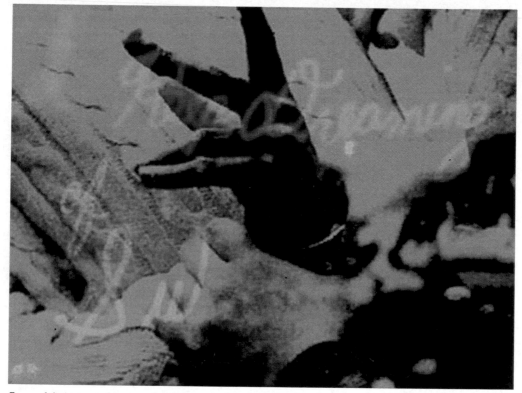

Figure 14. A screened image of still from the beating video shows Teddy's hands cuffed and the policeman's hand holding him. Suzanne's line "I am dreaming of suffocation...' is partially written on the image.

disturbing, aggressive way, she sits at her desk between them, in her own world, writing. Such simultaneous staging confirms the double consciousness of Kennedy's writing, and suggests a dream-like, conflicting surreal moment.

As I quoted from my Director's Concept above, 'hands' became a central image that we used throughout the performance. "Hands are the source of doing, of writing, of changing things; for that very reason, they are also the target of aggression and entrapment." Suzanne's hands write, they act, they create. Suzanne is plagued with nightmares and fears of loss. She has a recurring dream that all the letters she wrote to help Teddy have been intercepted by the police. Figure 15.

Teddy's hands become the focal point of the police aggression. His hands appear projected in two key ways. First, as palm prints, in an animation that had numerous open hands slowly coming into focus, overlapping, and fading from view. We wanted a quality of pressing the hand on a pane of glass, to suggest a fingerprinting operation. Figure 16. Teddy crouches to avoid an imagined blow from the police. The palm print, which is used throughout the performance at key moments, is projected behind him mirroring his own outstretched hand.

Figure 15. One of the nightmares that Suzanne has centres on her letters being intercepted by the police. Here all the members of the chorus, who play the roles of the students in the production of Hamlet Teddy *is directing, are studying their rehearsal scripts while at the same time offering letters to the police.*

The second time Teddy's hands were featured was when the police handcuffed him. The handcuffing was part of a video written into the script. Teddy's brother took a home video of the beating and this video appeared several times in the script. The first stage direction referring to the video reads: "The brief film is very dark with violent sounds of Teddy's scream."[25] The video was played several times on all the screens as the script required. The camera focused on the policeman handcuffing Teddy's hands. At the end of the play the beating is literally staged as Suzanne, his father, and other characters observe. Part of the enactment included Teddy's brother videoing the violence. For our staging, the brother's camera was rigged with a live video feed and the beating was projected on the screens. The embodied 'live' beating performed by the actors is doubled with the live video projection. The script's insistence that the beating, which was projected previously as video, makes the audience confront the theatrical 'reality' of this violent act of police brutality. The spectators sat facing each other, the staged beating taking place in front of them, while surrounded by screens with the real-time video. There is no escape.[26]

While the imagery of the hands was a crucial visual statement that we developed throughout the creative process, Kennedy's innovative writing would never allow for a single image, no matter how refracted or variously played.[27] In the following are some of the effects we achieved

Figure 16. Teddy crouches to avoid an imagined blow from the police. The palm print, which is used throughout the performance at key moments, is projected behind him mirroring his own outstretched hand.

using other images in the text including 'suffocation' and 'drowning', both physical states that Suzanne identifies in the script. For example, at the end of Scene I, she says: "I keep dreaming of suffocation"[28] Later in the script both Suzanne and Teddy refer to a creek in their Cleveland neighbourhood that is submerged, flooding.[29] We used these ideas for three visual concepts that reinforced aspects of the script, and added to its non-linear, fragmented quality. What we called the 'suffocation sequence' occurred between Scenes I and II, following Suzanne's line quoted above. Drifting smoke appeared from the bottom of the screen, which turned into two hands. These smoke hands dissolved, and the handprints appeared, slowly fading in and out. Suddenly, a close-up of the handprint zeros in on the veins in the hand, which turns bright red. There follows a second close-up of the red veins, which slowly turn black, and clouds appear blowing past. The veins are now tree branches in the night sky. The sky is slowly blotted out by grains of earth that are being tossed and the picture turns black, covered by earth. An animated swarm of moths flew around the audience from

Figure 17. The Conference Room in the Advanced Computing Center for Art and Design during the year-long creative process. The strip of numbers is the page numbers in the script.

screen to screen. The moths finally swarmed and landed all over Teddy's body as he lay on the floor at the moment in the script that he said: "Mom, I may have to go to jail."[30] And the third sequence, which we called the 'drowning' interval, occurred between Scenes II and III. Suzanne reads a letter from her daughter telling her that Teddy was a victim of a previous instance of police brutality, which he never told Suzanne about. The letter is projected on the floor of the stage, and a pool of water appears overlaid, on top of the letter. As Suzanne approaches the pool of water, the letter sinks and dissolves. Suzanne reaches down and touches the water, causing the water to ripple. This affect was accomplished by using a laser sensor aimed across the correct spot on the floor. When Suzanne's hand crossed the laser beam, the movement immediately triggered the water to ripple.

It is important to remember when using a theatre script combined with a high level of computer animation and projections that the visual imagery does not obscure or swamp the text. We worked hard to keep a balance between the spoken text and the visual design to maintain the integrity of the written word. In order for us to visualise and keep track of the many distinctions, one member of the team created a spreadsheet, which divided the work into the five projection screens, the two live videos, and the writing desk, so that we would know page by page of the script what was happening. This kind of planning was crucial because of the nature of the non-linear script, the simultaneous staging, and the many other effects we were using. From the beginning the technology design team was sensitive to these issues. As Maria Palazzi, Director of ACCAD, states: "We read the script with the director and her crew and started to imagine how technology could be used to enhance action, meaning, and interpretation of live events." The ACCAD team met weekly in a special room used as the think tank space for the production. As the director, I joined the discussions on alternate weeks. The room was in constant transformation as new visual imagery was posted on the walls to consider.

We also read and discussed various scholars and critics, who continued to remind us of the uniqueness of Kennedy's work. As Linda Kintz says, "there are few North American playwrights who have brought together a study of the symbolic construction of racism and sexism so powerfully."[31]

CONCLUDING THOUGHTS

Frantz Fanon, whose work *Black Skin, White Masks*, 1952, had a major influence on civil rights, anti-colonial, and black consciousness movements around the world, has been compared to Kennedy in the following way, Fanon, "draws on a painful re-membering, a pulling together of a dismembered art to make sense of the trauma of the present."[32] So for Fanon and Kennedy the only way to approach a retelling of the racialised past is through carnivalesque heterogeneity where we are unhinged in time and space, hierarchies are collapsed, categories are mixed, there is an inversion of ranks and memory is dismembered.

As audience/reader of *Sleep Deprivation Chamber* we witness the aftermath of this trauma, this re-membering, this putting back together, which leads to a fragmented, sleep deprived state for the central characters, a state that is transmitted as well through the staging of Kennedy's hypertext narrative, a narrative that is non-linear, non-sequential and uses multiple storytelling modes. By staging the writer writing in ways that I have discussed above, *Sleep Deprivation Chamber* demonstrates how the autobiographical subject is implicated in her own self-presentational act.

Through the spoken text of the letters and the literal embodiment of the act of writing, Kennedy/Alexander exposes writing's dilemma, is it efficacious? Does it produce change? Can it affect the course of events? Suzanne Alexander cannot stop writing; she writes too many letters, she writes plays, memoirs. This time at least it has no affect. Her ability to articulate the world around her through her prose and playwriting; her talent for expressing feelings and telling stories, the very thing that has made her what she is, her talents and ability to write, has no impact on protecting and saving her son. In some elemental way her writing defeats and fails her. At the same time, however, her writing does record a sense of loss, a loss of innocence. And, of course, it gives us this play, the one we are watching or reading about right now.

NOTES

1. Burke, J., and Stein, J., 'Theatre of Context: Digital's Absurd Role in Dramatic Literature', in Carver, G. and Bearden, C., (eds.), *New Visions in Performance: The Impact of Digital Technologies*, Lisse, Netherlands, Swets & Zeitlinger Publishers, 2004, p.93.
2. *ACCAD and Theatre: a collaboration* – Programme Note by Maria Palazzi, Director of ACCAD, May, 2003.
3. Carver, G. and Bearden, C., (eds.), *New Visions in Performance: The Impact of Digital Technologies*, Lisse, Netherlands, Swets & Zeitlinger Publishers, 2004, p.2.
4. Solomon, Alisa, 'Foreword' in Kennedy, A., *The Alexander Plays*, Minneapolis, The University of Minnesota Press, 1992, p.xiv.
5. Kintz, Linda, *The Subject's Tragedy*, Ann Arbor, University of Michigan Press, 1992, p.142.
6. Sollors, Werner, (ed.), *The Adrienne Kennedy Reader*, Minneapolis, The University of Minnesota Press, 2001, p.xiv.
7. Solomon, p.xiii.
8. Kennedy, Adam P. and Adrienne, *Sleep Deprivation Chamber*, New York, Theatre Communications Group, 1996, p.6.
9. Ibid. p.6.
10. Smith, S., and Watson, J., *Reading Autobiography: A Guide for Interpreting Life Narratives* Minneapolis, The University of Minnesota Press, 2001, p.9.
11. Kennedy, A., 'Letter to My Students on My Sixty-first Birthday by Suzanne Alexander' in Sollors, W., (ed.), *The Adrienne Kennedy Reader*, p. 199.
12. Kennedy, Adam P. and Adrienne, *Sleep Deprivation Chamber*, New York, Theatre Communications Group, 1996, p.5, (author's italics).
13. Ibid. p.22, (author's italics).
14. Smith and Watson, p.42.
15. Kennedy, Adam P. and Adrienne, p.7.
16. Ibid.p.25.
17. Ibid.p.6.
18. Ibid.p.7.
19. Ibid.p.15.
20. Ibid.p.21.
21. Ibid.p.22.
22. Ibid.
23. Ibid.p.26.
24. Ferris, L., "Director's Concept for *Sleep Deprivation Chamber*", unpublished manuscript, May 2002.
25. Kennedy, Adam P. and Adrienne, p.20.

26. For an interesting discussion of 'the digital double' see Steve Dixon's essay of the same name in the Carver and Bearden collection sited above, pp. 13–30.
27. Due to space limitations it is impossible to discuss all the imagery, animations, and mediated video that was created for this production. In order to see a full account of the visual material please visit the ACCAD website at http://accad.osu.edu/research/interactive_performance_htmls/SleepDep.htm.
28. Kennedy, Adam P. and Adrienne, p. 20.
29. Ibid. p. 31–32.
30. Ibid. p. 32–34.
31. Kintz, p. 142.
32. Ibid., p. 144.

Re-Designing the Human

Motion capture and performance potentials

Katie Whitlock

This chapter begins to address the questions created by the use of motion capture in relation to theatrical performance. Seizing human motion as data, motion capture provides a record of individual movement characteristics that can then be manipulated, embodied, and projected into a live performance. Live performance can potentially be re-fleshed and transformed in the moment. Although motion capture is a standard in the film industry and often considered as beyond the reach of theatrical exploration, the ramifications of this technology must be explored as part of the digital media age, which has become integral to the theatre of the twenty-first century. In a new age of mediated bodies and avatars, the potentials of motion capture in performance suggest a new method of character creation as well as new possibilities for recording and re-using human motion.

Using two practical examples developed through collaboration between the Department of Theatre and the Advanced Computing Center for the Arts and Design (ACCAD) at The Ohio State University, this chapter examines the manipulation of the human movement data for prospective theatrical use. The first used a human subject to drive a character animation utilising puppet architecture to reinvent human motion. The second explores the manipulation of a single performer's motions translated to multiple avatars in a blocking interface designed to explain the rudiments of performance. Both projects and practices have further possibility to become integrated into live performance. As motion capture technology continues to evolve, so must the dialogue, which surrounds the critical implications of digitized performance. With motion capture the human body becomes data and this transformation expands the very idea of the physical body to new limits.

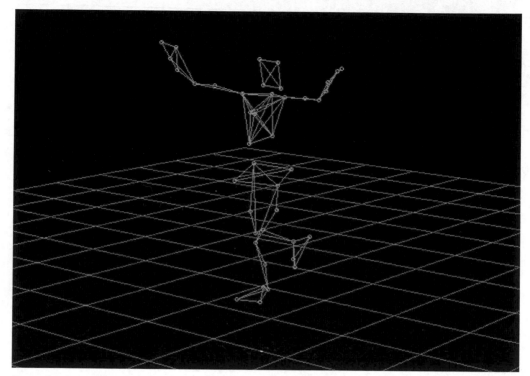

Figure 18. A screenshot from the hOuse Of mOves DIVA™ software package in which the skeletal structure is viewed as a series of interconnected points.

Motion capture, now a standard practice in film, animation, and gaming, allows motion of any sort to be transformed into numerical data. Once in the computer, software 'sees' the data as a cloud of points that exist in virtual space. The user reconnects the points to create a linear skeletal structure.

Once captured, motion can be connected as the user desires, manipulated, re-fleshed, or transformed to fit the performance. Human actors or other objects are covered with several markers, which are small reflective balls, at key joint locations to generate the numerical data then used in a three-dimensional environment. Once data is captured, the possibilities for manipulation and repetitive use make the expensive technology a worthwhile investment. Films such as *Final Fantasy: The Spirits Within* and *The Lord of the Rings* trilogy have proved that characters created by human motion are accepted as substitutes for living actors; for example, in the creation of Golem for *The Lord of the Rings*. When applied to theatrical performance, the questions that naturally arise include the following:

- ■ What does this offer to performance?
- ■ What does this offer to historical inquiry?
- ■ With the 'flesh' removed, can the 'expression' of movement create the illusion of physical presence?

Theatre has yet to make extensive use of this technology. The prohibitive costs which can be borne by large film studios and the accessibility of such systems make the widespread use of motion capture improbable. However, slowly some theatre artists are gaining access to capture facilities, often in conjunction with universities, and units are also beginning to come down in price. Most notably, in 2000 at the University of Georgia, David Saltz presented a version of William Shakespeare's *The Tempest*, which used motion capture in live performance.[1] In Saltz's production, the character of Ariel was present both as a live actress and as animated character driven by the motions of the actress. In this production, the use of motion capture is balanced by the live presence, rather than relying solely on the character generated by the technology. Although the performers did not acknowledge the actress onstage, the physical presence of the performer, strapped into multiple pieces of gear, made the audience aware of the actress and the technology.

The two projects I have focused on used motion capture in a different fashion than Saltz. Both occurred at The Ohio State University, using the resources of the Department of Theatre and the Advanced Computing Center for the Arts and Design (ACCAD).[2] Each revolves around using human motion to drive animated characters with different results. Charlotte Belland developed the first project *Mo-Cap Game Reserve* in 2001 / 2002. Belland was a faculty member at ACCAD at the time this project was developed and has since joined the faculty at the Columbus College of Art and Design, specializing in three-dimensional animation. Her original interest in theatre developed from an interest in developing a character that could be driven by an actor without requiring any animation knowledge. Motion capture allows for the performer to embrace his/her skills while allowing the computer artist to then interpret or reinvent the data generated in the session. This new form of collaboration draws from the best use of interdisciplinary work, allowing artists to combine their strengths while creating new, inventive pieces.

This particular experiment used human motion in relation to a puppet armature to explore the possibilities of imbuing a three-dimensional character with human emotions and pathos for possible use in live performance. Human motion is applied to a non-human form in an attempt to craft an anthropomorphic character. A team of several programmers, designers, and developers at ACCAD developed the second project, the Roy Bowen Virtual Theatre. I, as a member of the team, served as content designer and coordinated much of the initial data capture and cleaning. As part of a larger online project, we sought to develop a repertoire of online characters that could be used in teaching simulations to explain aspects of theatrical directing and design to introductory level students. In the process we used motion capture to drive our three-dimensional characters. What became evident in this project were the possibilities of exploring a single motion as 're-fleshed' in varying body types, ethnicities, and genders disregarding the original creator of the motion. Although neither project has been fully completed, both present questions in relation to the development of motion capture as a live performance tool.

The initial spark behind the *Mo-Cap Game Reserve* was a desire to create a reactive character that could potentially be used in live performance. Potentially, this type of creature could become the ultimate über-marionette, creating a character that could be driven by a movement and a performer who could interact in real-time via projections with live performers.

The preliminary investigations into creating the first member of the game reserve generated an awareness of the following factors. First, the puppet armature needed to be durable as well as rapidly adjustable and adaptable to allow for performance conditions. Second, the motion capture system available to the creator was an optical system requiring the use of markers but allowing for a 360-degree capture setting. This creates a 'rotoscoping' effect, sometimes causing difficulty in capture but allows for a more fluid sense of motion for the performer. Third, the difficulties inherent in real-time rendering called for a simple texture map, allowing for the puppet to move, be reconfigured in the computer, and then given colour and texture in the rendering phase in a timely fashion. Fourth, the questions concerning the actual projection and space limitations required for such intensive work. Finally, the question of how to establish a reactive environment conducive to allowing for communication from live performers and the puppeteer was addressed with the hope of creating a reactive character. The last two concerns were never truly addressed as the project only reached partial completion, but the creature created has 'lived' beyond the initial creation phase as an example of the possibilities of using puppet armatures in real-time capture settings.

The choice to attempt to use motion capture to even begin such a project was a lively debate between the pros and cons of the technology. On the advantage side, motion capture is reactive technology. It records anything that can be 'seen' by the range of the cameras, allowing performers a large footprint in which to perform. Also, once the marker set has been mapped in the computer, the possibility of capturing multiple characters is open to the artists, suggesting that if one character was proved viable, dramatic interaction could occur in live performance, in virtual space, and in any combination needed. On the challenge side, the pipeline to create the characters is lengthy and requires qualified staff. The process of creating characters, placing the markers correctly on the various armatures, and then gaining a successful capture is time-consuming. Also, the space needed for capture in an optical system necessitates low light conditions and an open playing space which would need to be located near the actual performance space to allow for resources and reactive environments. However, in this case, the problems were of interest to the participants as much as the end results.

With the initial concerns in mind, the attempts to find an appropriate character began. Initially, the puppet resembled an ape, using crutches to extend human forearms. The head position was extended using a ball cap and a rigid pole, but that was soon discarded as lacking fluidity. The overall motion of this creature was slow and stiff, prohibiting a more reactive, fluid use of data. As character was the primary interest for Belland, the armature was redesigned. Using the human pelvis as the starting point for creating a basic marker set, the addition of flexible legs, neck and tail created the second character, which now resembled a bird rather than an ape.

The bird creature had no wings, instead moving like an ostrich, focusing on leg and head movements to convey emotion and character details. In developing this character, a variety of materials were explored and discarded, ending with a children's toy as the primary means of creating the armature. 'Pool Noodles' (thin floats of polystyrene) provided a durable, flexible surface that allowed for marker application while also being low-cost and lightweight. The final armature placed the actor

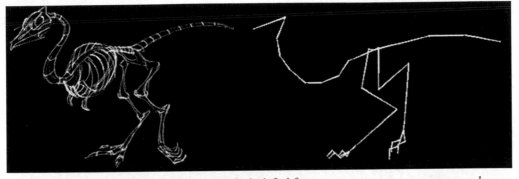

Figure 19. The sketches for the second version which shifted from a more primate armature to a truly non-human form as done by Charlotte Belland

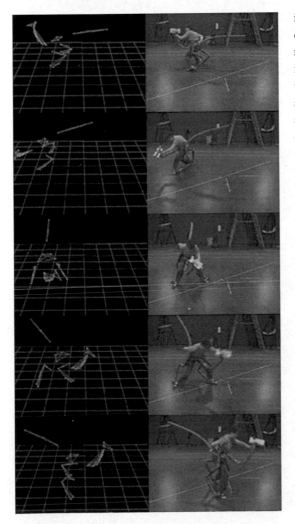

inside a loose skeletal structure that had a controllable head, tail joint and legs. The nature of the material created a natural sway in the neck and tail, which contributed to the sense of the character. The capture session was focused on developing a short series of movements, which could suggest character while allowing for a practical test of the pipeline process.

The raw data was captured and cleaned using the VICON™ workstation and the skeleton was created in hOuse Of mOves DIVA™ resulting in a prehistoric bird skeleton. The final creature was rendered using the Pool Noodle textures as a possible choice for later incorporation into a real-time capture performance. To provide character in its final state, the use of sound added some sense of dramatic involvement in a scene that showed the creature in motion.

This preliminary exploration presents the possibilities of reading human motion on a

Figure 20. This series of shots places the computer skeleton opposite the actual capture session in which Charlotte served as puppeteer to explore the creature's range of motion and potential emotional expressions.

non-human form. The bird, driven by a puppeteer, is capable of responding in real time, suggesting that our pipeline could support integration in live performance. In relation to the questions posed earlier in this chapter, the use of such a character could provide a new outlet for considering performance. For movement specialists, this type of work provides a testing ground for exploring how motions are read differently when seen on a human form as opposed to an animal or alien body. With such explorations, the understanding of how motion conveys emotion expands, allowing performers to refine the live aesthetic while adapting to the limitless possibilities of virtual creations. To then use such study in performance opens the realm of performance to a new dimension of imagination while maintaining the live reactive state of theatre. This type of character is not a progression towards the filmic but instead an expansion of the theatrical, allowing for a character that can be something other than human existing and reacting in the live experience.

In direct contrast to the capture of human data applied to non-human forms, the Virtual Theatre Project embraced human characters and human motion in a World Wide Web environment. Originally, this project was developed as an interactive teaching tool for introductory-level students. The project which spent two years, 2001–2003, in development sought to create an online space which was capable of allowing students to explore the theatrical process with variables that addressed theatrical design and direction. As part of that goal, the project developed

Figure 21. This shows the interior of the Virtual Theatre Project with two of the three-dimensional avatars standing on a set designed for Shakespeare's Hamlet.

a blocking interface to allow students to place three-dimensional avatars in a virtual theatre and to select and see motion clips, simulating a directorial experience.

The first year of the project allowed the team to develop a basic interface and some simple digital environments. In those environments, students could position a variety of prop pieces and two-dimensional costumed figures while adjusting simple lighting controls to gain some understanding of theatrical design. In the second year, the blocking interface was developed and some three-dimensional avatars were incorporated. This necessitated a discussion of what movements were 'theatrical' and would fill a wide variety of directorial needs. In addition, a group of avatars were built attempting to address issues of race, gender and weight. The avatars were built using costume renderings in an attempt to build characters rather than simple human forms. This conscious choice was also performed in the hope of inciting student interest in the casting process, recognizing that physical appearance plays a significant part in the selection of performers for a production. With the avatars built and the motions determined, an early capture session was held with a single performer to gain a stable of motions to test in the virtual environment.

The optical capture system was once again used for this project. The actor had a free range of motion in a square that measures approximately twenty-by-twenty feet square. The actor was markered in a more traditional fashion than the *Game Reserve* project, providing references on the major joint locations from pelvis to shoulders to wrist to ankle. The assembled points of data are recognisable human motions, once the data points are connected in skeletal armature in the computer. The basic motions included in that capture session were walks ranging from drunken to idle, turns ranging from quick to slow, head to full body. In addition, 'fun' movements were included to gain student interest such as a variety of death sequences, some fighting moves, and several bowing motions. Once again, the primary capture session was data provided by a single actor. This actor was a white male in his late twenties who is trained in various movement styles. He was consciously attempting to remove all his personal quirks from the motion cycles unless requested to add them, continually working in a neutral body state. Once the data was cleaned and attached to the figures, it became apparent that this raised some interesting questions concerning how we 'read' motion in relation to the physical shape that is performing the action.

When applying the same sequence of motions to three different avatars, the motions appear to take on slightly different characteristics. As the various walks and death cycles are placed on characters, the viewer consciously begins to assign different qualities to the exact same motion dependent on how they assume the avatar should walk or behave. Rather than seeing the same motion, the viewer sees character distinctions due to the 'flesh' that covers the data. This raises questions of how performers could benefit from this reaction to capture driven characters while at the same time suggesting that one actor could potentially serve as the basis for multiple characters. Rather than focusing on the puppet characters of the *Mo-Cap Game Reserve*, the *Virtual Theatre Project* allows a new understanding of motion in relation to the actor's motion serving as an animator for the mask of the avatar. Much like the phenomenon of mask work in which the mask is said to take on a life of its own, the avatars appear to take on subtle characteristics which appear as variations to the viewer.

As part of this train of thought, the question must be raised about the use of data in relation to historical inquiry. As part of the funding to obtain the motion capture studio at Ohio State, the university captured data from the world-renowned mime artist Marcel Marceau. With such a record of physical performance, the question of how to study such data must be posed, for if such data is then placed on a 'fleshed' form it may cloud the interpretation of the performance. Yet at the same time, such a record provides an intimate study of the nuances of such physical performance. Motion capture allows for the 'expression' inherent in movement, being receptive to the slightest changes in joints or other markered areas, providing numerical referents for alterations undetectable in traditional blocking or notation. Once captured, the data exists in a state of potential in which the addition of a body becomes a key factor in maintaining or shifting the original interpretation of the primary motion.

In both the *Mo-Cap Game Reserve* and the *Virtual Theatre Project*, the potential of motion capture is evident. Yet the use of technology remains challenging from both practical and theoretical perspectives. In using motion to drive either human or non-human characters, we must be aware of the visual manner in which we interpret action and interweave it with emotional meaning. The human tendency to imbue disjointed actions and/or characters with emotion and meaning works both for and against the use of motion capture. We automatically connect motion to character with mixed results. However, the importance of media in our profession demands that we at least begin to ask these questions even if we do not yet have answers. Theatrical performance can benefit from motion capture as it opens new ways for imagination to take flight in a reactive real-time state. It also provides performers with a new place of exploration for movement and how audiences interpret actions from emotional and narrative perspectives. Finally, the advent of motion capture provides a new means of recording performance, vitally aware of the body as a means of storytelling separate from text.

NOTES

1. Saltz, D.Z., 'Live Media: Interactive Technology and Theatre', *Theatre Topics*, 11.2, fall 2001, 120. Saltz refers to his production as being the first to use motion capture in a dramatic production, hence my recognition of it in this paper. Other explorations have occurred in dance but virtually nothing in live, dramatic performance to date.
2. On both of these projects I served as a consultant and project member so the information concerning the capture sessions and creation process is first-hand knowledge.

SMART LABORATORIES
NEW MEDIA

Christine A. White

This chapter explores the possibilities of new technologies and the most recent developments of research in the area of technologies, which are not yet fully available to artists. The chapter explores the development of Scenography as a practice which influences performance through the use of new technologies, projection and the mix of live and virtual media. The author suggests a need for the provision of technologies within the rehearsal spaces as a prerequisite for making performance in the twenty-first century.

The development of technologies from analogue to digital is not merely a technical response to a practical interpretation of new technologies, but rather it is brought about by a change which is also intellectually a change of wavelength. As human beings we relate to one another and speak of being, hopefully, 'on the same wavelength', especially when we are within a creative and poetic world of making performance, where inferences and symbols can be understood. These inferences and symbols are also a part of digital thinking as they are mutable and are often a spontaneous response to stimuli. In the most direct sense 'digital' defines the changes of single aspects, bites or bytes of information and these segments require us to deconstruct components of the visual and the performed and rehearsed event, in order that the singular components can be altered to evoke and provoke new ideas, feelings and associations. Experimentation with digital technologies and software actually rely on us to work through associative mechanisms in order to develop the use of the media within new contexts, often very different from the original software or hardware design envisaged by the programmer or engineer. The modernist philosophy as extolled by Adolphe Appia and Edward G. Craig to express the poetic, the mutable and the spontaneous in performance is further enabled with digital technologies. They can be used for the creation of harmonious effects, but also the creation of environments where the individual is provoked to forget themselves, where the unusual is possible, where logic and chronology are unnecessary. In this sense the free flow of the imagination is unleashed through the potentials of new media and new technologies, which allow for the mediation of the singular aspects of performance. This dawn of digital performance creation needs research into the rehearsal spaces, which provides what we might term 'smart laboratories for performance'. The laboratories need to be able to enable through new media inter-actions the possibilities and potentials, and the space to experiment in. These spaces are 'smart' in the sense of needing to be quick in reply and suggestion, intelligent and responsive to the exploration of performance-making that might be possible in the twenty-first century.

The associative nature of understanding and human experience was expressed by the modernist author James Joyce, who became increasingly convinced of the inadequacy of literature and traditional novels to capture reality. In November 1926, he wrote to his close friend Harriet Shaw Weaver, "a great part of every human experience is passed in a state which cannot be rendered sensible by the use of wideawake language, cutanddry grammar and goahead plot."[1] Traditional forms of making performance have become more complex in western culture and this increasingly relies on, and we are fascinated by, computer technology and the Internet. The Web has facilitated an incredible, often overwhelming amount of information that is multi-dimensional and multi-contextual, and it offers artistic global connections. A new dialectic, however, is emerging as artists approach their work from the positions of both manual creators and digital selves. How these new contexts are enveloping performance practice and the making of performance involves researching ideas on the Web, integrating digital processes with perhaps those of more traditional practice and recognising the seduction of digital manipulation programs the capabilities of computer technologies and the potentials of rehearsal spaces.

Digital Media allows for the mixing of media. It allows for manipulations and transformations. This approach to performance work has recently been manifest in ways which exclude the digital media but permit digital thinking, which is where the definitions of performance might provoke the question: "Are these actors dancing or are they dancers acting?" as in relation to Matthew Bourne's choreography for *Play Without Words*[2] where the dancers clearly 'acted' their parts as well as dancing them, or in Shobana Jeyasingh's *TranStep*, where the dancers are also producing work on the cusp of description as this is performance/acting/choreography.[3] In relation to the digital technology, the roles are blurred as exampled in Oli Metcalfe's work, who is arguably a scenographer, video designer or a light jock, in his work for performance contexts.[4] This is the beginning of cyberspace theory as explained in McLuhan,[5] where the phrases 'global village' and 'the medium is the message' were first coined. McLuhan's insights, some twenty years before the personal computer and thirty years before the Internet, suggested the end of humanity as it was known due to the development of these technologies. However, the new technologies are embraced by artists to review humanity, not to destroy it. Digital technologies are the tools and materials of our age, where the message can be developed, and where scenic art/scenography might be presented as installation.

As a consequence, in the post-industrial society that I live in, I am able to sit on the floor of the Turbine Hall of Tate Modern and see the theatricality that stirs the spectators of a spectacle set design, *The Weather Project*. There is a semi-circle of light produced by yellow light, indicating the sun, which is reflected in the ceiling of the whole space covered with mirror scrim sheets, seen through a haze produced by a device seen on many theatre stages over many years, a smoke machine. The visitors to this space can walk behind the free-floating sun to see the sub-structure and electrical wiring, as well as the machines distributing the fine mist. This, Olafur Eliasson explains, allows them to "understand the experience itself as a construction..."[6]

What has this visual artist created? A set design, an experience, a sculpture and environment, a place to worship the visual, a space to contemplate atmosphere? A place to worship the sun? The half sun is reflected in the mirror ceiling, which covers the ceiling of the Turbine Hall, and this reflects the semi-circle of light presenting the spectator with the illusion of a sphere. This illusion and this trickery are attractive, as most deception is. The whole of the space is turned monochrome because of the reflected yellow light and it is as if all the spectators are actors in a black and white movie, busy ants moving through this black and white space. The smoke machines operate intermittently. On stage they would be thought obtrusive, in spluttering out the smoke puffs. However, what real phenomenon are they trying to mimic? Realism is not here in this space. Verisimilitude is not required in this venue. The staging is symbolic. Excessively, symbolic. Conceptual. If you look up, you see your friends in the audience, in the picture. Some lying out on the floor, like angels in the snow. But on concrete. They look like patterns of chromosomes. Most are in twos. There are no words for this performance. The parts of *The Weather Project*, the components are worthless until the spectators are there involved.

For Adolphe Appia the plastic elements of the stage involved the third dimension, which is real. Ultimately, Appia identified four plastic elements; perpendicular painted scenery, the horizontal floor, the moving actor and the lighted space. The aesthetic problem as he saw it was the unity of these elements. Thus, he identified that painted scenery was at odds with the lighting and the actor. The consistent response in answer to this problem was related to the actor as the unifying feature and, therefore, the levels on the stage floor on which the actor walked. The theory of this as a scenic practice is most relevant in the designing of stage space in virtual worlds when these programs call the creative space 'the stage' and through this space a composition in three dimensions occurs. Appia's stage space in real dimensions was to be modelled as sculpture, and the unification of this world was achieved by lighting. In this respect, Appia was ahead of his time. Appia distinguished, "light that is empty, diffuse radiance, a medium in which things become visible, as fish do in a bowl of water, and concentrated light striking an object in a way that defines its essential form."[7] He recognised the emotional power of light; the anodyne nature of diffuse light that requires no emotional engagement of the spectator; the light that had been played with by painters for three centuries became an expressive dramatic medium. It was light then, which created the unifying form for the plastic elements of the stage.

In the model box spaces of the computer and the stage platforms of creativity in software packages, it is light that illuminates the stage space and the visual elements. These software packages use opacity, translucence and values, which for the lighting designer without the digital space has endeavoured to create with units of light from candle to incandescent and now, low voltage forms, with dichroic filters and moving mirrors, or moving heads. The nineteenth century was the century of electricity and was important in practice for the theatre, which recognised the power of this new source of energy that could be sophisticatedly controlled. In the twentieth century the digital worlds that have become possible have illuminated processes of creativity for people of different skills, the scenographer, the visual artist, the light jock, the lighting designer, the web page designer, the video designer, the automated moving light programmer.

The digital domains that we can now explore in the twenty-first century are expressive forms that enable a continually fluctuating appearance of a phenomenal world. To have recognised this phenomenon, and therefore, established a theory of the importance of phenomenology, shows Appia was already thinking about the future possibilities of emotional engagement if you involve the stage, light, sculpture and movement within a digital space. There is depth in the work of Appia and atmosphere. The light of Appia's drawings created a new reality. The movement of space and time and the play with form and dimension would have been enabled for him had he had a personal computer and some software! The toy that is the computer and the play element of most design and software packages in computers would clearly have suited Appia's need and desire to experiment. The technology dissolves boundaries, enabling the modernist theory of perception, novelty, experiment and innovation, subjective vision and freedom for the audience.

The research, which I have recently been involved in, has developed from these investigations and ideas for new equipment and possible laboratory spaces, which enable the use of computers and other digital technologies in performance and rehearsal contexts. The principles of which come from the kinds of investigations that Appia was interested in, as it is my contention that Adolphe Appia and his contemporary Edward Gordon Craig would have used computer technology if they could have, as they considered the components of performance in abstract terms: light as tone, intensity and colour, stage space as volume, direction, mass and texture. All of these form the language of digital space.

The eloquent images, which both practitioners developed in card, model and finally on stage can easily be reproduced in a virtual environment. These are performance principles of virtual reality, whether such designs are later to be used as a realised and material form, or whether they are to be used within the virtual space of the computer, or projected and brought to a real-time performance as conventional presences, automated features or digital avatars of environments and their potentials. These initial experiments have been the bedrock for the development of smart laboratories, such as the Scenography & Performance Laboratory at Loughborough University.

Theatre design exists in time; whether apparently static or changing, the Scenography is seen over time, facilitating action over time and movement, reflecting time in response to the text or themes of the piece. The designer must consider time as much as space. If we look at Edward Gordon Craig's monolithic screens, which are designed to be fluid and flexible and to offset the plastic body in motion, they move, and set off movement,[8] "...the scene was furnished with great moveable screens which could be placed on the stage in a large variety of positions. These screens were Craig's notorious invention designed to offer 'a thousand scenes in one.'"[9] His studies for movement and illustrations of steps in *The Steps*, 1905, all express motion through a combination of line, human form and architecture, even when rendered as still images. Craig described them as:

> Four designs for a drama I created called 'The Steps'. I call it a drama because acts are performed upon these steps – not because something is 'said' upon them. Let a person relate in the most perfect words how someone walked up steps, and no drama is either created or performed. The distinction between literature and drama is as simple as it is profound.[10]

Since the Renaissance the ability to change scenery and create spectacle for the audience has been a central feature of theatre. It celebrates the ability of humanity and art to control its world, signifying the importance of transformation both politically and culturally. The delight of witnessing clever or spectacular transformations has always been a crowd pleaser, whether for the audiences of the nineteenth-century pantomimes and melodramas or twenty-first-century high-tech musicals. The ability of scenery and space to change has been one of the cornerstones of Scenography. However, often the process of producing theatre forces the designer to consider the design as a static space, or at best one that changes only sporadically at key and necessary moments in performance. Ironically, of course a director may be working in a rehearsal room dealing very specifically with time and performers in time, but not necessarily with space.

In working on a project the following may be of concern to the designer:

- The changing setting, either in detail or in whole;
- The changing atmosphere and lighting environment;
- The changing look of characters;
- The rhythm and pace of movement and change;
- The development of theme/metaphor over time;
- The balance between motion and stillness;
- Different groupings and dynamics, developing a scenography of the actor in space;
- The fact that nothing changes;
- The compression or expansion of time.

There are two ways in which a designer can explore the design in time during the design process, the storyboard and the animation. Both are in some ways related to each other. I have used the term 'animation' here to refer to any moving element or elements in the design presentation, not simply animation in a movie sense; a storyboard can bring life to a design as much as a moving sequence might. Storyboards and animations have two useful, and related, purposes. Firstly and most importantly, they are tools with which the designer can visualise time/change, and having the means to visualise it the designer may then experiment with it, in essence they can design it. Secondly, of course these are communication and presentation tools, devices by which the designer can illustrate to the director and production team what it is that their intentions are. As with all aspects of design it is important to know why you are using a particular tool or approach.

The storyboard is a simplified animation; it illustrates key moments or frames from the complete drama. In a few images it sums up the Scenography of two hours' passage upon the stage. It illustrates key moments in the production, traditionally as still images, often selecting one or two moments from each act or scene. Movement will generally be illustrated by showing the beginning and end states that bracket change. In traditional approaches a storyboard may be a set of paper, like a cartoon strip, thus sketching the production over time in a method that is easy to see. Examples of this technique can be seen in Craig's *The Steps*, and more contemporary work of Laurie Anderson[11] *Songs and Stories from Moby Dick*, and the most recent British film animation *Valiant*,[12] which, although an animated film in 3D, was constructed with pencil and paper cartoon strips. All of these ideas are developed and expressed from the notion of a storyboard image, which communicates the moment.

At its most impressionistic, at the very early stages of a design and performance-making experience, these may well be scraps of found material, research images, abstract washes of colour, written metaphors, a suggestion of music. These can be quite rudimentary in presentation but the idea is to plot through the developing Scenography as it changes and develops. A small series of sketches may help the designer visualise the whole project prior to embarking on detailed designs of each scene. In these early versions the designer may not illustrate the whole stage but may sketch important details, derived as much from an emotional or dramatic response as a spatial one.

An animation, of course, shows the movement and transformation itself, as movement. It is quite possible to construct models that do what is required of them. For his 1963 production of *Romeo & Juliet*, for example, Joseph Svoboda built a complex model[13] where every piece moved as it was intended to in the production, thus he could plan the changing environment as part of the Scenography, rather than leave it as a technical necessity. Only by experimenting with scenic choreography in real time can it be perfected. The kind of resources required for this are beyond those available to most designers, but even the act of lowering an object on a piece of fishing wire into a model gives insight into movement. Similarly, light can be one of the most fluid elements of Scenography and it is perfectly possible, though again a little expensive, to equip a design studio with a miniature lighting rig, and explore the effects of lighting changes in real time. Naturally, failing this, a couple of torches and a gel swatch-book, which offers a range of colours, often create the effects.

Through the use of animation tools within computer modelling programs the theatre designer can take the production team on a walk through the set; they can set up a series of shots or frames which can then be played as a sequence to show the movement of scenic units such as flats or a revolve. The theatre designer can illustrate dynamic scenic features to be viewed by the production team in real time on a virtual stage. The team can then discuss the mechanics by which this movement might occur. Thus, in the pre-production period animating the flying pieces of a set design can enable a sense of time for the movement of these features and allows the designers, director and production team to fully understand the type of look and movement of complex flying sequences.

For the purposes of the theatre designer, one is rarely looking for a faultless animation technique but rather an indication of the way in which objects or light move in the three-dimensional space. Furthermore, animation is time-consuming and generally very processor intensive, so one must account for it in planning a project and identify elements that will really benefit from animation rather than a storyboard treatment; animation can sometimes be used more as window dressing than a useful design process towards the final performance aims. Two apparently conflicting attitudes need to be addressed throughout the design process and kept firmly in the mind of the designer. In his excellent overview of digital modelling Peter Weishar, 1998, in *Digital Space: designing virtual environments*,[14] observes that in creating virtual worlds for many purposes, product design, games creation and so on, a digital designer must think like a set designer. The creator of imaginary realms is not making them to be lived in for real but rather to offer the appearance or illusion of reality.[15] The effects of these imaginings and simulations does not as Baudrillard posits create a 'hyperreality', as this is our cultural reality, it is very clearly a part of our social and cultural predicament.[16] We must consider what is and is not seen, what needs to be three-dimensional and what can be falsified. A cut-out pillar with a texture applied, for example, rather than a fully rounded object will still look like a three-dimensional pillar in the image. This is useful for the set designer as the approach required by virtual worlds for the computer is equivalent to the approach needed in creating worlds for the stage, which are, of course, equally unreal. However, it is possible for the designer using the computer, as it is for the card model maker, to become involved in their creation to the extent that they may forget that its purpose is to illustrate something that is to serve a different purpose.

So the theatre designer needs to consider the experience of working with the digital tools versus the pressure to complete the project. Most modelling programs, even the simplest, take some time to learn and certainly require practice to use with any sophistication and ease. Inexperience may not only restrict and frustrate creative development but at worst it may create errors that are not easy to recover from. The designer is in dialogue with the computer, but if the conversation is stilted, it is unlikely that poetry will be made. Therefore, the first few projects need to be free from pressure, and potentially will require an extended development period working with collaborators, perhaps working alongside a card model and using the computer as a digital sibling. Again, collaborators must be able to read the computer screen or else you lead people to false expectations. Similarly, lighting designers and directors must understand the modelling process as a sketch and understand the opportunities and limitations of the medium in order to avoid misconceptions, both positive and negative. Ultimately, there is likely to be some crossover between methods, and a design studio needs to be established that allows for portability between physical and digital domains.

There is no doubt that computer images can be beguiling and engaging. They allow for animated walk-throughs of the environment, the display of lighting effects and even smoke, and they provide a high-quality final image. They indicate high-tech sophistication and high-tech production values. The look and the nature of this work can send certain messages to the producer or client, and, in the more commercial sector, this might be an important signifier, winning confidence and contracts if used well.

Certain designs lend themselves far more to digital approaches than do others. Projects that are likely to utilise modern materials and forms, for example, geometric shapes, projection and kinetics, are more sensibly approached in the digital model, where the modelling and rendering process are likely to produce a more convincing result than traditional techniques. Designs that are likely to draw on chaotic and run down or organic forms may be better served using card, fimo, balsa and fabric. However, with the development of more sketch software and sophisticated textures, the use of scanning devices and digital cameras, the applications are becoming more varied, more evocative and more flexible.

It is obvious that the personal computer has changed working practices in many working environments. How useful the computer is, as a tool for exploration, research and design will depend to a certain extent on the level of engagement the user has with the programs. The use of computer software requires continual research but more recently it also requires practice, as it is only by practice with the tools that the success of certain programs versus others can be ascertained and then disseminated. Again, as theatre concepts change so will the working practices for digital tools. It is obvious that practitioners will make developments with an inquisitive nature, investigating, exploring, playing, thinking and dreaming. Digital images have been experimented with as part of live performance, in immersive and interactive performance. The digital modernist thoughts of Adolphe Appia and Edward Gordon Craig were translated yet again into kinetic film interactions in the work of Svoboda and demonstrated the need for opportunities to explore these fields in practical experiments. Therefore, this technology opens doors on new design processes, collaborative working relationships and experimental performance outcomes.

There has been an explosion of ideas in art and design, multimedia and performance studies in the area of digital interfaces and whilst these interfaces have generally accepted the nature of the computer interface as reflected in Barbara Laurel's work,[17] that is the instruments of the alpha-numeric keyboard and the mouse, there have been initiatives, and experiments, such as those at Loughborough University, "the development of highly configurable wireless networked wearable/mobile computing environments,"[18] with interfaces for artists which involve a more tactile approach using digital gloves for the manipulation of the digital image. In performance, however, what has not been addressed is the nature of the performance contexts, which is where a polymath approach to experimentation is necessary. In performance, people learn different skills, roles and techniques, as they need to find the means of expression, dependent on the urgency of creation. However, what is needed is the establishment of an environment where that expression works within a digital studio, which is not simply a student laboratory with a range of PCs or Macs networked in a relationship to software and where seating and chair positions restricts the activity and engagement with a process of making performance. To this end I have been working with companies who produce and develop hardware for lighting and light projection. Again, quite a new area of this element of performance has developed and the crossover of light as a source for illumination, projection of atmosphere and then projection of Scenography for performance has become enhanced by technologies such as the DL1 and DL2 from High End Systems.[19] These units enable multiple media, that is, light, projections and video images to be played back and developed in the performance space. The notion of experimentation is, therefore, developing even more and again with light technologies, it is being led by the concert and music industries. All these advances have developed from automated moving light technologies, otherwise known as intelligent lighting. Whilst this type of work has most typically been developed recently within a West End (UK) context, for example in *The Woman in White*, the use of these technologies and the ability to learn and explore their potentials needs to be given a primary place within the rehearsal studio in order that new techniques of performance practice can be experimented with and integrated into new media and new performance making contexts. For example, in *The Woman in White*,[20] the video projection has been supplied by XL Video and the projection designers were Sven Ortel and Dick Straker of Mesmer, and both these companies and individuals were needed to realise the ambitious technical requirements of the designer Bill Dudley's ideas. According to Michael Billington in *The Guardian*, the projection opened up, "new possibilities in the marriage of theatre and cinema".[21] The notion of a marriage is where I believe there is difficulty, as is usual in marriage, as it suggests that one art form or another is dominant, whereas we are really talking here about performance, and this should perhaps be pointed out to Billington, as the live and the projected are played in real time; they are not edited but are prone to the vagaries of live performance and the immediate perceptions of the performers interacting with this projected reality. All the show's settings, locations and backdrops are projected onto a thirty-metre-wide-by-five-metre-high cylindrical projection surface, which at certain points in the performance moves and the screen tracks all the way around the stage to form a surface across the front of the stage. For more intimate scenes a section of the track splits off and tracks into the central stage revolve, complete with its own set of video projections. What has been developed here is a stage, which has been treated as a three-dimensional environment, where there is a mapping capability to move shapes and images across the stage in real time, which is also keeping pace with the screen movements. Members of the company were also filmed in order for them to be included in the animations later to be projected with and alongside the live performers. This is a landmark production for its use of, and near total reliance on, video visuals for setting the scenes, moods, and for special visual effects. This show has, therefore, developed a new piece of hardware, the Mesmerist media server,[22] so named after Mesmer, the company of the projection designers.

All of these developments suggest the need for the development of a new studio for interactive creation, where performance can develop alongside ideas for visual expression, where artists can learn new techniques for performance, and skills to engage with digital creativity. There is no need to lament the marginalisation of theatre, as Johannes Birringer does[23] believing that the nature of theatre and that theatricalisation cannot embrace and subvert cutting edge technologies, using them to repossess the theatre and explore the contradictions of contemporary culture.

I have been involved in an investigation of voice-operated technologies, which has developed from my research and practice with automated moving lights and communicative interfaces for performance. The impetus for this is to create a user-friendly interface system, which develops from voice-operated software, such as word processing programs but also from more complex forms of medical voice-operated equipment designed by companies such as Stryker,[24] for operating theatres in hospitals.

The project is developing a software interface, which enables theatre makers to use and manipulate, light, projection and sound easily within a new laboratory space for developing art forms within the creative industries. This means a development of technologies, which are interactive in the real-time space of the studio and or performance venue. The user interface may then be applied to a number of operational technologies for theatre production that will enable a command position for the artist's creation of atmospheres, projections and sounds by voice command. The ultimate objective is a performance studio, which enables play and creation using a vast array of multimedia facilities and Information Communication Technologies, which have so far not been developed as integrated mechanisms. The development of the integrated system will inevitably enable new works to be developed and the use of new media for platforms such as Web broadcast and broadband applications. The added value of the development of these technologies will be the accessibility of these creative technologies to people from a variety of differently abled backgrounds. This research will also enable individual artists to share information and digital ideas. It is the gesamkunstwerk which Wagner wrote about in, "The Artwork of the Future".[25] It is that which has developed into Total Theatre, and it was termed the meta-medium by Alan Kay, a researcher in the 1960s, who developed the object we now use as a laptop. Digital experiments in performance, which dissolve borders and heighten our awareness of subjective experiences, through the use of multimedia technologies for performance enable the modernist vision of Total Theatre.

To be transported to another realm is a primal desire. To lose oneself in the veracity of the drama is an immersive experience. In this room the computer can control the existence of matter. Such an environment will involve a participatory, interactive electronic theatre. William Golding wrote the science fiction version of this in his novel "Neuromancer" in 1984.[26] The cyberspace created has a structure, which is programmable, where environments are fluid. Designing in this space allows the artist to transcend the laws of the physical world; the provocations and interactions. Helping us to understand the world in a rehearsal for expressing and behaving, "as we may think", coined by Vannevar Bush in 1945.[27] The flexibility of this laboratory brings together devising practice, which is also based on associative theories of play and creativity, digital devising with the tools of the new media and artworks located in the laboratory outlined above.

Theatre has always developed from the position of "as we may think", as have computers. It is a rehearsal of issues and ideas that are part of our lives, some themes of which are timeless and, like children, who must always learn by their own experience, and, therefore, we must revisit these themes again and again. The ever-developing form for these rehearsals, however, is made by a replication of the tools for living at the moment in our contemporary culture.

Artists of the twenty-first century are required to make immediate use of developing technologies; to understand the way we think and the way we are now. A smart laboratory must include the most relevant expressions and means of thinking for making performance. For what is smart about the laboratory? It needs to exude vigorous activity and provide an intelligent space for creativity and perhaps in its other meaning, a lively pain, but most importantly a place where digital media is prepared for use.

Notes

1. Costello, P., *James Joyce: the years of growth 1882–1915*, London: Random House, 1993.
2. 21/02/04, *Play Without Words*, Royal National Theatre, directed/created by Matthew Bourne.
3. Shobana Jeyasingh Dance Company, *TranStep*, spring 2004.
4. Oli Metcalfe, new video media designer, working in rock concerts and events entertainment.
5. McLuhan, M., *Understanding Media*, Routledge, 2001.
6. Eliasson, O., *The Weather Project*, programme notes, exhibition October 2003 – March 2004, Turbine Hall, Tate Modern.
7. Simonson, L., 'On the Ideas of Adolph Appia', from *The Stage is Set*, Brace & Co., 1932, re-print Theatre Art Books, New York, 1963, cited in *Effective Theatre: a study with documentation*, John Russell Brown, Heinemann, London, 1969.
8. Craig's screens developed both as a prototype for scenic movement and for use in *Hamlet* at Moscow Art Theatre 1924, directed by Constantin Stanislavski.
9. Styan, J.L., *Modern Drama in Theory and Practice 2, Symbolism, Surrealism and the Absurd*, Cambridge University Press, 1981, p.20.
10. Catalogue of an Exhibition of Drawings and Models for *Hamlet*, *Macbeth*, *The Vikings and other plays*, by Edward Gordon Craig, City of Manchester Art Gallery, November 1912, no.162.
11. *Songs and Stories from Moby Dick*, visual design, music and lyrics by Laurie Anderson, May 2000, Barbican Centre; her work is renowned for the use of electronic music, striking visual imagery and her own stage presence.
12. *Valiant*, released 2005, Vanguard Animation, a small UK animation company.
13. *Romeo & Juliet*, designed by Josef Svoboda, for Czech National Theatre, Prague.
14. Weishar, P., *Digital Space: designing virtual environments*, New York: McGraw Hill, 1998.
15. White, C., Carver, G., *Computer Visualizations: 3D modelling for theatre designers*, Focal Press, 2003, p.186.
16. Baudrillard, J., *The Mirror of Production*, St. Louis, Telos, 1975.
17. Laurel, B., *Computers as Theatre*, Reading MA: Addison-Wesley, 1991.
18. Roy Kalaswky, Advanced VR (Virtual Reality) Centre, its mission is to develop multi-sensory interactive human-computer interfaces.
19. High End Systems, Lighting Technologies group, these systems enable designers to mix light and video projection.
20. *The Woman in White*, West End, The Really Useful Group, designer Bill Dudley, director Trevor Nunn, 2004–
21. Billington, M., *The Guardian*, 2004.
22. The Mesmerist, a customized playback by a tripartite of XL Video, Mesmer and Digital Antics.
23. Birringer, J., *Theatre, Theory, Postmodernism*, Bloomington, Indiana University Press, 1991.
24. Stryker, medical equipment specialists of voice-operated instruments for surgeons.
25. Wagner, R., *The Artwork of the Future*, 1849, translation Ellis, W.A., 1895, Kegan Paul, Trenchy, Trubner & co., Ltd.
26. Golding, W., Neuromancer, 1984.
27. Bush, V., 'As we may think', The Atlantic Monthly, vol. 176, no.1, July 1945, pp.101-8.

A Place to Play

Experimentation and Interactions Between Technology and Performance

Scott Palmer

This chapter explores issues associated with the use of technology in performance. Why is the use of technology seen by many as a threat to the liveness of the performance event? Does the use of technology necessarily distract the audience and detract from the art? Can there be a seamless integration within the performance event? What are the implications for designing for performance in and for, an increasingly technologically oriented world?

Drawing on the work of key practitioners including Robert Wilson, Josef Svoboda, and Robert Lepage, I aim to investigate the links between the use of technology and the creation of scenographic statements on stage. Whilst concentrating primarily on the convergence of digital and projection technologies, this chapter will advocate new ways of working if such technology is to be integrated successfully into performance work. An account of an exploratory project involving dance, digital media and projection is provided as part of an argument that attempts to counter suggestions that performance and technology, art and science are fundamentally incompatible.

Peter Hall's assertion that: "Advances in technology have allowed for greater scope, potential and excitement but has also created potential problems in the cohesiveness of making theatre",[1] which has been echoed by other practitioners within theatre and dance, and suggests that the use of technology is somehow at odds with the nature of making performance work. The implications are that despite the possibilities that new technologies provide, their impact on performance is not entirely positive and their incorporation has profoundly affected the way in which performance is made. If there ever was cohesion in creating theatre, then technology seems to make the process even more difficult. It is as if technology is seen by some as anti-artistic, and alien to the creative process and those who use it are criticized for being more concerned with the mechanics of operation than the creative impact of the technology on stage. As a lighting designer, who has to use technology to practice his art, I have experienced this perception first hand, and have argued elsewhere for ways in which this particular situation and relationship should be addressed.[2] Hall does, however, acknowledge that technology offers new possibilities, and it would be odd to suggest otherwise when at the end of a century where we have seen artists who have consciously sought to embrace and absorb new technologies in their work. So why is technology regarded with so much antipathy in the theatre?

Partially, this mistrust is borne out of a basic misunderstanding. Technology frustrates, it baffles and it is often surrounded by mystery and its own jargon, which alienates those who do not speak the language. Directors and performers may feel disoriented, threatened or feel that they are losing overall control which exacerbates the problem. The technology is therefore seen as detracting from the very 'liveness' of the performance event, an unnecessary adjunct, and diversion from the primacy of the performer, the text and the spoken word.

Newer technologies tend to be more complex and by their very nature 'foreign'. The technologies can be time-consuming to set up and may be more prone to failure than longer established or conventional techniques. When these technologies are located in the digital domain, they are also subject to the vagaries of software instability and hard drive crashes. The integration of such technology is often compromised by flawed production practices, which do not seek to embrace the technology through the devising and rehearsal process, but rather apply it as a 'bolt-on' accessory relatively late in the production process. Attempting to integrate such elements under the considerable pressures of the production period is a recipe for frustration and this may explain Hall's statement. This suggests that there is a need for new ways of creating theatre if potential new discoveries are to be made at the same time as preserving a 'cohesive' approach to making performance.

Is the opportunity to use new technology worth the effort and physical investment or does it risk damaging the creative process? In the commercial theatre, apparent technological innovations are heralded as 'must see' events and the resulting visual effects are frequently used to define the show itself; for example, the helicopter in *Miss Saigon*, the hologram in *Time*, the 'flying' car in *Chitty Chitty Bang Bang*. Sometimes performances in the recent past seem to have been staged precisely because of the possibilities that new technologies provide; for example, computerized flying techniques in *The Witches of Eastwick*. Despite the undoubted spectacle that these moments can provide, such high-profile examples of the use of technology have had a reductive effect on the overall performance event. Christine White argues that, "new technologies have enabled West End musical spectaculars to become personality proof products", which are, "transferable and mutable from nation to nation through the technology that has been created." White alludes to this regurgitation as "technological colonialism", a theatre transformed and "Disneyfied into a theme park of spectacle."[3]

Artists and theatre practitioners have, of course, always used technology and it is interesting that in the field of music the use of new technologies to create and innovate has never appeared to be an issue in quite the same way, as it seems to be in the theatre. Perhaps one reason is that in this medium, the technology is invisible; we hear the resulting sounds but are not distracted by the immediate visual presence of the technology itself. When performance technology is placed within the stage environment, however, the audience is more conscious of its presence. The equipment itself may be visible, and therefore perceived as a principal aspect of the performance. Even when the technology itself is hidden, the audience is often complicit in their suspension of disbelief. We may not be conscious of exactly how effects are achieved, but we do know that the transformation of the stage has taken place with the aid of lighting changes, a fly tower and traps in the stage floor for example. Such moments may contribute to the view of theatre as a place of magic, but their appearance of sophistication often belies the relatively simple technology that is being employed. Since these are traditional techniques, one can argue that their effect on the contemporary audience is a tribute to the skill and creative endeavour of the designers and technical operators rather than any innovative use of new technology. A performance of *Waiting for Godot* staged in the mid-1980s offers a good example;[4] "The light suddenly fails. In a moment it is night. The moon rises at back, mounts in the sky, stands still, shedding a pale light on the scene."[5] A simple scenographic solution to Beckett's stage direction was provided by a domestic light bulb in a spherical paper lantern, which had been laid flat on the stage floor. It was slowly lifted up into the flies at the same time as the light faded up. This elegant solution of course required the use of technology, twentieth-century developments in thyristor dimming, lighting control systems and the vacuum light bulb. The paper lantern itself uses Chinese technology from over 2000 years ago and the vertical movement into the flies could be argued to have arisen from Renaissance staging practices. The point is that the technology is not important, it is a means to an end, to creating a theatrical moment, which stays in the mind long after all else relating to this production has been forgotten.

TECHNOLOGY AS A VEHICLE FOR DEVISING WORK

New technologies, however, can make a significant impact on production practices. In the Eurodans project,[6] the technology of the World Wide Web and custom-made software allowed for a devising process to be undertaken simultaneously, in seven different countries. The technology in this case was used as a sophisticated communication tool that facilitated dialogue through the rehearsal process. The Eurodans collaboration instigated by the University of Leeds, Ultralab and ELIA, used the technology of the Internet, harnessed through *Snugfit* software to allow fourteen groups of dancers from Higher Education Institutions from all over Europe to collaborate online to create a dance performance. Movement sequences were rehearsed, recorded on video and posted on web pages for sharing and development with other groups. The choreography was refined online with feedback from all other collaborators, the lead choreographers and the project coordinator. Other student groups were then able to learn the material and develop it further. Scenography students were also able to share design ideas relating to the costume and lighting of the space through posting their ideas in a similar way. Virtual renderings of lighting ideas, using Cast Lighting's WYSIWYG™ software, and scanned images of a range of costume ideas triggered a debate that helped to shape the final performance, and showed the value of using digital techniques to share visual ideas in the collaborative production environment. The range of digital material posted on the website, became a comprehensive record of the devising and rehearsal process and allowed the development of the movement to be tracked and re-traced. Earlier ideas, which had been discarded, could be tried afresh and existing movement phrases used as a reference for further development. Over a period of five months the Web had become a place to experiment with ideas prior to the culmination of the project in performance. The online aspect of this project was followed by a rehearsal period in Dublin and performances at the Project Arts Centre with live performers from most of the online choreography groups and projected sequences from the few unable to travel. Without the Web-based technology, this performance could not have happened. It was interesting to note therefore, that this aspect of the project worked seamlessly, in direct contrast to the failure of the engineering technology of the theatre space itself, which restricted what was able to be realised and necessitated original lighting design ideas to be modified substantially.

TECHNOLOGY, ART AND EXPERIMENTATION

Technological failure has always been an accepted risk in making performance. Occasionally, these failures are serious enough to cause the cancellation of a show, such as *Marisa Carnesky's Ghost Train*[7] in Coventry and Manchester in 2004. This fascinating project, proclaimed as a feat of twenty-first-century engineering, attracted NESTA (National Endowment for Sport Theatre and the Arts) innovations funding and involved the collaboration of numerous artists, engineers, designers and an illusionist. A dilapidated ghost train was created as an installation within which the audience were transported on a theatrical ride in which a combination of live and projected performers unravelled a moving narrative. Digital technologies were employed to recreate contemporary versions of nineteenth-century visual illusions such as 'Pepper's Ghost' and 'the floating lady'. However, the ambitious nature of the work caused severe technical difficulties and a number of performances had to be cancelled due to safety concerns.

Robert Lepage's *Elsinore* is a well-documented example of technological failure.[8] This solo re-staging of *Hamlet,* used a kinetic stage structure as an acting machine, which became an integral performer in the drama, but its complex series of movements caused the production to be plagued by a spate of technical problems. These difficulties occurred so regularly that the company kept records charting their progress and during the lifetime of the production run there was a record of 24 consecutive performances when no technical problems were encountered, which contrasted with difficulties in over 100 performances during the entire run.[9] These technical failures often caused the performance to be halted for some time and in the case of the run of performances at the Edinburgh International Festival, to be cancelled altogether. However, the technological ambition of this venture in itself generated considerable interest and the performance when realised on stage, did not disappoint. The element of danger actually contributed to the intensity of the performance with both performers and audience not knowing if things were going to break down. This sense of risk, an essential ingredient in all live performance, seemed particularly apt in this version of Shakespeare's text. Whilst the ambitious combination of kinetic stage, live video and projected image created a wealth of stage spaces for Lepage to inhabit, it also reinforced the sense of play which was central to this stunning tour de force. However, Lepage does not view *Elsinore* as particularly sophisticated from a technological perspective: "Elsinore is extremely low-tech. It looks extremely high-tech, ...but I've replaced traditional shadow play by simple live video work...it's actually very simple, the way it functions and there are a lot of people backstage like the good old days, pushing the set and turning things with their hands."[10]

In retrospect, although the technology was very much in the foreground in this production, it is not the technology that one remembers but individual moments of creative brilliance. At one point Lepage's Hamlet transmutes into Ophelia, with the stage-machine descending around his solitary figure and dressing him from above in a white lace shroud. As we are drawn into this image, we forget about the technology that enables this to happen and are fascinated by an apparently simple, pure moment of theatricality. It is a captivating transformation, a vision of body, light, and fabric, which transcends the mechanics of the technology that we know, has enabled the moment to be created. Lepage's use of technology has been regarded as a tonic for a complacent theatre. New media allows practitioners to create new forms of communication and creative expression. Lepage sees these dialogues as vital to communicate with today's audience. He is therefore critical of the majority of current practice: "People in theatre are still working to the old code of the early twentieth century, the old conventions."[11]

Many of the most interesting contemporary theatre artists seek to find ways to incorporate technology as an essential response to what is happening around them. New technologies offer creative possibilities, which extend the boundaries of the art form whilst also providing the potential to fascinate modern audiences with a new kind of theatrical spectacle that brings together the worlds of art and science in the entertainment arena as they have developed in the domestic environment. The Czech scenographer, Josef Svoboda, refused to acknowledge any distinction between art and technology and his work demonstrates how such boundaries have been extended. Svoboda argued that it was essential for the scenographer to embrace all of the existing tools at their disposal: "Of course every new technical element represents only a fragment of the technical foundation needed by all scenographers. People, presumably in the interest of theatre, take up arms against its industrialisation, to which experiment allegedly leads...it is impossible for theatre to remain totally behind in technical advancements without becoming a museum."[12] Svoboda's work was characterised by a ceaseless exploration of scenographic solutions to staging problems and his work demonstrates a willingness to employ whatever materials and means were necessary to fulfil his artistic vision. These solutions frequently involved collaborations beyond the theatre world in order to employ any available technology, which would assist in realising his scenographic vision on stage.

Svoboda's unique combination of technical expertise and a scenographer's sensibilities resulted in a number of landmark technical innovations and a legacy of stunning performance imagery, which was often created through a direct rejection of standard theatre equipment. Tools and techniques were invented specifically to meet the particular requirements of each production. Collaborations with technical and materials specialists, engineers and other partners in industry created new technologies to fulfil precise artistic needs. Svoboda argued that, "This union of art and science is

Figure 22. Josef Svoboda's hollow cylinder of light for the 1967 production of Tristan and Isolde, *Wiesbaden, Germany (Printed with kind permission of Sarka Hejnova).*

essential and vitally necessary for our time. It provides art with a rational basis and helps us to carry our investigations further."[13]

Famously, low-voltage lighting battens were developed to produce the intense high-angled backlighting or 'contralight' effect, which characterised many of Svoboda's productions in the 1960s. This distinctive effect has become a commonly adopted way of lighting the stage space, but the technology also allowed stunning images to be created with light in space.

In the 1967 production of *Tristan and Isolde*, Svoboda also used a collection of low-voltage lanterns to create the famous hollow cylinder of light. However, the effect that was so easily created when first employed in the dusty stage environment in Prague was found to be impossible when the production toured into the much cleaner German theatres. A technological solution was again found through collaboration with local engineers to spray tiny fog droplets into the air, which were loaded with an electrostatic charge. This device, the forerunner of the haze machine, enabled the vapour to be uniformly spread throughout the space and the scenographic image to be recreated as it was originally intended.

Svoboda argued for real experimentation as an integral part of theatre-making: "Production space should be a kind of piano, on which it is possible to improvise, to test out any idea whatever, or to experiment with the relationship among various components. Only so, by means of concrete experimentation, is it possible for everyone's words and creative ideas to share the same objective reality."[14] The use of the projected image and interplay with live actors was central to Svoboda's work. Discoveries were made through experimentation with equipment and techniques to create installations and performance work in the Czechoslovakian pavilion at the 1958 Expo in Brussels. The time, and more importantly, the resources that were provided by the State enabled true experimentation to occur. Discoveries made during the making of the *Polyekran* and *Laterna Magika* presentations, were subsequently developed in mainstream theatre performance work in Prague and led directly to the establishment of the *Laterna Magika* experimental theatre space, dedicated to artistic creation through the interaction of technology. Additional state funding also allowed new techniques to be developed for future international presentations at Expos, and the results of this research were crucial to both Svoboda's own scenography at the Czech National Theatre in Prague and, through international collaborations, to developments in twentieth-century dramaturgy. "Everything I've ever done has, in fact been borrowed from exhibitions, prolonging the exhibition's short-term investments into theatrical life."[15] Technological developments and experiments to integrate the live performer and the projected image were developed further in work at Laterna Magika. Productions such as *Magical Circus*, 1977, and *Odysseus*, 1987, still play in repertoire alongside newer explorations of scenic space like *Graffiti*, 2001, Svoboda's final production, which uses the emerging technologies of projected VR (Virtual Reality) scenic environments, and investigated ways of projecting into the stage space without a physical screen.[16]

The creative freedom and new possibilities inherent when live performance and projected images are juxtaposed has been increasingly recognised by contemporary practitioners. Emerging developments in digital technology are having a profound affect upon performance work since they allow for the creation of a new imagery, even though in many cases the 'grammar' of these techniques is not in itself new; projected film has been with us for over 100 years and filmic techniques such as montage have been widely embraced by theatre directors, scenographers and choreographers alike. However, the advent of the digital age has enabled practitioners to embrace the possibilities of the virtual stage space and of projection far more readily.

Recently, William Christie and José Montalvo's production of *Les Paladins*, 2004, has been hailed as ushering in a new era of theatricality.[17] Critics have argued that the use of live video interaction and digital effects makes projected scenery look distinctly old-fashioned. "Singers morph into serpents, dancers into butterflies, before your very eyes. An elephant lumbering across the stage turns into a tiger mid-stride...and is one of the most striking theatrical events that you will ever see."[18]

Robert Wilson chose to use three-dimensional projected holograms in *Monsters of Grace: A Digital Opera in Three Dimensions*, 1998, although the quality of the images of virtual worlds sat uncomfortably alongside the live aspects of the performance.[19] The production seemed to be an interesting experiment with the technology rather than an integrated, scenographic solution with the computerised aesthetic of the digital world, sitting uncomfortably alongside beautifully staged theatrical moments on the physical stage. This contrast, coupled with the need for the audience to put on, and take off 3D glasses to see the projected images, also had a profound effect in lessening the overall engagement in the event. It is clear, however, that computer-based animation offers new possibilities in scenographic expression and we should consider such techniques, "not as a replacement for the stage, but as an extension of its formal possibilities and an addition to its repertoire of expressive devices."[20]

In the past, criticism that technology has been used for its own sake with little regard to the overall artistic concept has often been fully justified. Emergent digital and projection technologies have sometimes been employed simply because they can. We must avoid the temptation to use technology for its own sake. There are parallels in the field of entertainment lighting with the advent of, 'intelligent' light units in the late 1980s, which allowed sources to be controlled remotely. Led by the needs of the rock and roll world to create spectacular images in light, their use in theatre often seemed gratuitous at first. Moving lights were used because they could be. Where their use was appropriate, designers tended to overuse them, seemingly in an effort to justify the significant financial outlay of the equipment. Recently, however, there has been a more sensitive use of this technology where the designer's approach doesn't necessarily draw attention to the techniques being employed. Perhaps such subtlety can only emanate from maturity, at a time after the initial wonderment of what is possible with the new technology has worn away.

A Place to Play

Performance work in the twenty-first century cannot ignore the tools that are available but it seems that it is essential to create an environment that allows practitioners to explore, test and create. World Expositions have provided funding and space for many to experiment in the past with results later cascading into the performance domain. In contrast, other groups have sought to align science and art through specific collaborations. The pioneering E.A.T. project (Experiments in Art and Technology) led and inspired by the visionary engineer Billy Klüver in New York in the 1960s provides an inspirational model. However, such collaborations can also occur on a smaller, local scale. In the UK the need for 'a place to play' in which technologists and theatre-makers can experiment side by side, can be met through the performance laboratory model. Blast Theory worked with computer engineers at Nottingham University on *Desert Rain* 1999 to create a performance installation of astounding resonance.[21] The actual experiences and mediatised versions of the 1990 Gulf War were explored through the integration of the virtual worlds and the 'real' in performance. The link between emerging gaming technologies, and the public's experience of the war via news broadcasts was well made through the technologies employed in the performance. The sophistication of battle-zone technology, 'smart bombs' and pilot's head-up displays, was translated directly into the audience's experience of the event, which transposed the technology of the computer game into the performance domain.

The Interactive Performance Telematics Project

Open-ended projects, without the requirement or pressures of a performative outcome can also be valuable in exploring the potential of technology. The Interactive Performance Telematics (IPT) Project brought together software and graphics programmers from KMA Interactive Media and staff and students in dance and performance design at the University of Leeds. KMA are involved in a diverse range of creative work within the digital domain, which has included the design and manipulation of vibrant, morphing scenic projections for large-scale popular music events. Another key activity has been the design of interactive abstract digital forms for use on websites. Through initial discussions, between University academics and the company, it emerged that there might be some interesting possibilities in combining these two products with a live performance setting. The IPT Project's (Interactive Performance Telematics) objective was to investigate the performance potential inherent in the combination of digital media and human dancers and the collaboration was realised because of a common desire to explore synergies in the work that both parties were already undertaking. KMA were keen to explore the further potential of their work without the constraints associated with the realisation of specific briefs for televised music events and it was significant that the company expressed the need and the value of working in a more exploratory way without the limits of a commercial deadline. The project was, therefore viewed by all participants, as a research and development opportunity, which would allow space and time to play with the technology and to investigate the interactivity between the digital space and the performance space without a fixed end product in mind.

A team of individuals was assembled with skills that seemed to be appropriate to the artistic and technological aspects of the project. It was important that the project provided space for open-ended creative interaction and it was refreshing to observe that all members of the team were able to commit to working in such a divergent way. The main processes that we discussed were based on improvisation and devised dance performance. Kit Monkman, company director of KMA, admitted afterwards that he had had a few reservations, and he was initially concerned, "that it might be embarrassing. That we might waste each other's time, that our working practices might prove to be fundamentally incompatible."[22] The performance academics too were apprehensive that the collaboration might prove to become technology driven with little room for aesthetic exploration, despite the initial clarity about the need to achieve synthesis between the two. The technology would be clearly visible in the performance space, and the technicalities and practicalities of setting up and getting it to function could potentially take primacy. However, such fears proved unfounded, as there was much commonality in methods of working. Monkman describes KMA's usual working techniques as, "experimentation and serendipitous discovery",[23] a process remarkably akin to devising and creating performance work.

The University of Leeds provided a studio space as a performance laboratory for the project. This had a perfect blackout, and was equipped with a full lighting grid, sound and projection facilities and a range of additional theatrical equipment was available for exploration throughout the duration of the project. An important feature of the studio, which contributed directly to the quality of research, was that it was flexible and allowed for the rapid testing of ideas. Experimentation with the technology could therefore take place without the typical lengthy delays of re-rigging equipment that is usually associated with technical production work in similar environments.

The first day of the residency was reserved for KMA to set up their digital equipment and for the performance designers to prepare the space theatrically. A scenic gauze was rigged across the space

Figure 23. Dance students from University of Leeds interacting with yellow and blue sprites projected on the gauze in front of them. (Note: Some of the vibrancy in the images is lost in the transition to greyscale.)

to provide a semi-transparent wall, as a surface for projection. Whilst this plane bisected the stage space, dancers were still visible behind it. Theatrical lighting was prepared to allow for a variety of options in lighting both the space and the performers. The computers, which were to generate the projections were set up and linked to a data projector, which was then focused on the gauze. Initial software programming was then undertaken in preparation for the arrival of the dancers. This preparation of the space was important to ensure that the technical aspects of theatrical production work did not interfere with the momentum of creative discoveries. Ideas could be tried out quickly and then either discarded, recorded for future exploration, or developed further. Ultimately, this potential for rapid experimentation contributed significantly to the range of discoveries that were made during the two further days of intensive work.

The KMA programmer created a series of simple animated images as starting points for the exploration. Most of these digital creations or 'sprites' were based on basic geometric shapes such as lines. They were then given a variety of parameters that created flowing abstract images when moved across the screen, allowing each position of the sprite to be registered for a short time before allowing it to decay. These left echoes of the sprite's movement as a trail, which was visible temporarily across the monitor screen and duplicated in the performance space through its projection onto the gauze on the stage. The form and behaviour patterns of the sprites could be governed by a variety of input devices. Primarily an operator with a mouse achieved control, but other inputs could also be employed to modify the way in which the sprite behaved. A sound reactive variant, for example, provided a more organic image when music was introduced because it was never static. A further experiment introduced a live microphone to the space to investigate the impact of the sound of the dancer's feet and voices in affecting the movement patterns of the sprite. Other parameters such as the colour, speed and delay times influenced both how the sprite appeared and the way in which it moved, and these could be altered through swift re-programming between experiments. One of the sprites dubbed 'ribbon' became the chosen version for further discoveries and created an image reminiscent of the visual impact achieved in rhythmic gymnastics, where trailing fabric in the air provides a fleeting echo of the movement. Later in the project a second 'ribbon' sprite was added, allowing for more complex interactions to take place.

The individual sprites were each controlled by an operator working initially with a computer mouse. The operator used the mouse to draw the path of the sprite, leading it around the screen and therefore the gauze. The dancers could see the images on the gauze in front of them, and they were able to respond to the sprites, improvising movement with them in the performance space. Key discoveries were made through allowing the dancers and operators to experiment freely within both the digital domain and the physical stage space, exploring how they could relate to each other through the performance medium. The experiments began with simple improvised movement from the dancer, which the operator of the sprite attempted to follow on stage. This tracking process provided an almost instant mediatised echo of the movement content, which was manifested in the space with the dancer via the gauze. At first, the dancers found the inter-relationship with the sprite a strange but exciting one, with one dancer commenting: "I'm not used to dancing with a light."[24] The tendency at first to think of the sprite as being merely a scenographic element was gradually overcome to reveal a richer relationship between dancer and sprite as the operator became more familiar with the dancers' movement. It soon became clear that the operator could also lead the movement of the dancer, who would respond to the speed, direction and qualities of the projected image's movement. The dancers reported that they felt increasingly as if they were dancing with another person, rather than a computerised image. The way that the sprite reacted to them and improvised with them was more akin to a human partner than a computerised interaction, as it had potential for the unexpected, the humorous, and the quirky. This realisation coincided with the decision to remove the computer monitors altogether, thereby allowing the operators to work entirely by watching the sprites on the gauze in the performance space.

At this point in the project, the operator moved from being the 'technologist' to being, a performer, albeit by a proxy arrangement. This transition represented a major discovery and challenged pre-conceived expectations about the efficacy of the relationship between performer and remote technical operator. It is common industry practice for technical operation to occur away from the place of performance, removed physically from the stage space itself and distanced by glass, screens and layers of technology. This tendency has been criticised,[25] since the operator often experiences little engagement with the creative act of performance and may simply be following instructions and pushing buttons. In the IPT project, however, the operators were engaging in dynamic creative expression, with a direct relationship between their embodied movements of mouse control through the sprites' movements. The dancers also explained that their awareness of the dancing partner slipped between the image and the technologist, so that sometimes they felt that they were dancing with the sprite and sometimes with the operator. Consideration of how the movement could be simulated by a computer program suddenly appeared redundant, and was replaced with a new focus on the relationship between performer-dancer and performer-operator.

This shift in emphasis led to the suggestion to replace the mouse-driven input device with graphic tablet and pen. The new equipment allowed for more expressive movement as the pen was more intuitive and precise to use than the mouse, engaging the operator in free-flowing action based on drawing or sketching, and the sprite immediately became more infused with the operator's own movement style.

The operators of the technology reacted strongly to the experience of 'dancing' via their sprites with the performers on stage. Afterwards, they described the fluid interface that the pen provided which allowed them to experience their movement embodied in the sprite. The operators were still sitting amongst the technical paraphernalia, but their experiences transcended that situation and they felt 'drawn in' to the image of the sprite on the stage. They were aware of the technicalities of what they were doing in one sense, but the differentiation between the performance and the technology had been erased in the moment. The operators' contribution had become inseparable from the dance to such an extent that they considered themselves to be performers in the piece. The intensity of the creative experience and the accompanying adrenaline surge that they felt was described as being akin to stage performance. The choreography created from this point in the project included both dancers and operators as choreographed performers.

The excitement at these discoveries was articulated at regular meetings to evaluate progress, throughout the two days of experimentation. The team attempted to quantify what had been achieved and to identify likely avenues for further exploration. All participants, in a spirit of open collaboration, suggested alterations to the parameters of the sprite. Changes were undertaken through speedy programming and ideas were tested and modified further. Audience members, from outside the research team, were invited into the space to share examples of the work and to comment and this helped the team to identify a host of possibilities for further investigation and exploration.

The initial results of the IPT Project are the product of careful preparation that established methods of working at the outset. This influenced the nature of the creative collaboration in which, despite the variety of experience and backgrounds, each individual's contribution was acknowledged on an equal basis within a supportive environment. There was a major reduction in the sometimes, intrusive distinction between the art and the technology, between the performers and the programmers. The focus remained on using the technology as an expressive tool to explore a performative outcome. At the end of the three days of intensive work, a quartet performance had been created in which two performer-dancers danced with two sprites controlled by two performer-operators. It was unclear whether the quartet was between the dancers and the sprites, or the dancers and the operator-performers, and it seems likely that these relationships were in flux for much of the performance. Monkman described the outcome as being twofold, "we ended the project with a very real, and strong performance idea AND a strong working relationship. Both of which we'd like to pursue."[26]

CONCLUSIONS
This method of experimentation has demonstrated that the performance laboratory is an essential way of working if the impact of technology is to be evaluated properly in a live context. Despite

the difficulties and necessary uncertainties in working in this way, the range and quality of the discoveries suggests that it has greater validity than a more prescriptive approach. The shift in the focus of the IPT work to address the performer-operator relationship became a fundamental basis of the research which had arisen directly as a result of the open exploration described by Monkman as, "an extraordinary valuable way of collaborating on projects."[27]

However, the collaborative approach is not necessarily straightforward or easy to achieve within the rehearsal room, and much depends on the nature of the individuals involved. This is not a model of research and development that is necessarily comfortable for its participants. Performance making can be a difficult, messy process in which its participants may feel exposed and vulnerable but the most interesting creative discoveries are often made by taking risks and seizing the opportunities that these moments can provide. A level of honesty and trust is required between team members to enable truly exploratory work to develop and this openness of approach is difficult to attain, especially amongst individuals who are not familiar with the languages of each area of specialty or of this experiential method of working. A longer timescale than was possible on the IPT project is also usually required for members of a team to build up a relationship, which acknowledges each individual's skills and ways of working. Importantly, for the outcome of this particular project, the technologists from KMA were both happy and, more fundamentally, able to work in this collaborative way. "Sadly, the creative freedom that we all had [...] to play (with so much resource and support) without expectation is rarely possible in the commercial world."[28] New connections between specialists in different disciplines should not be restricted to performance work. The designer and sculptor Thomas Heatherwick believes that "Art and science and engineering should get together more often, with a view to marriage."[29] Like Klüver's work, this statement acknowledges that there are mutual benefits to this collaboration, which can create both better engineering and inspirational art.

It is clear that the potential of new media to provide new ways of creative expression will ensure that technology will continue to remain as a vital aspect of contemporary performance practice. However, there are clear implications for the way in which these technologies are incorporated into the performance domain. Working practices need to adapt to acknowledge the creative contribution of all members of the production team, and to provide both time and space to allow experimentation to take place. If such collaboration between performance makers and scientists, and technologists can be accommodated, then the theatre space itself has the potential to genuinely become a place in which to play.[30]

NOTES

1. Hall, P., Keynote speech, *Theatre in Britain and Europe — A Visual Dialogue? Conference*, Royal Haymarket Theatre, London, UK, 8th May, 1998.
2. Palmer, Scott 'Technology and Scenography — Teaching Lighting for Performance' in *Lighting 2000*, CIBSE edited, The Chameleon Press Ltd, 2000, pp. 222–228.
   'Virtual Light — Using Digital Technologies in the Process of Lighting Design' in *Tradition and Innovation in Theatre Design* Jagiellonian University, Cracow, 2002, pp. 81–86.
   'Making Light Work — Lighting Design in Contemporary British Theatre' in *Theatre; Espace Sonore, Espace Visuel* edited by Hamon-Sirejols, C. and Surgers, A., Presses Universitaires de Lyon, Lyon, 2003, pp. 267–276.

3. White, C., 'Scenography and the fourth dimension – the use of computer rendering to replicate the 'time' dimension of theatricality', in *'4D Dynamics Conference on Design & Research Methodologies for Dynamic Form'*, Robertson, A., (ed.), Proceedings 4D Dynamics, De Montfort University, Leicester. UK Revised Edition Cyberbridge 4D Design, 1996. http://www.dmu.ac.uk/In/4dd/synd2b.html.

4. Not the National Theatre's UK touring production, 1986, designer Russell Harvey.

5. Beckett, S., *Waiting for Godot*, 2nd edition, Faber & Faber Ltd, 1965, p.52.

6. Eurodans Project, October, 2000, Popat, S, Butterworth, J. & Palmer, S., http://www.eurodans.net Also see Popat, S and Butterworth, J 'The Eurodans Project: A European Collaboration through Choreography and Technology' *European Journal of Higher Arts Education*, 2004, http://www.elia-artschools.org/ejhae.htm/.

7. Marisa Carnesky's Ghost Train, UK touring installation, summer 2004, http://www.carneskysghosttrain.net/.

8. *Elsinore*, Robert Lepage in collaboration with Ex Machina, English version first performed April 1996, Toronto, Canada. see also Ex Machina, http://www.exmachina.qc.ca/intro.htm.

9. Robert Lepage in conversation with Richard Eyre, *NT Platform Papers*, 10th January, 1997, Lyttelton Theatre, London, UK, 1997, http://www.nt-online.org/?lid=2627&cc=1.

10. Ibid.

11. Lepage, R., in Kustow, M., *Theatre@risk*, Methuen, London, 2000, p.207.

12. Svoboda, J., 'A Few Notes on Scenography' in *Josef Svoboda Scenographer*, Giorgio Ursini Ursic, (ed.), Union des Théâtres d'Europe, Paris, 1998, p.64.

13. Svoboda, J., *The Secret of Theatrical Space*, translated and edited by Burian, J. M., Applause Theatre Books, New York, 1993, p.17.

14. Ibid., p.20.

15. Svoboda, in Ursic, p.62.

16. See Laterna Magika, http://www.laterna.cz.

17. Les Paladins, Rameau (first staged at Theatre du Chatelet, Paris, France May 2004) Design by Jose Montalvo for more information see http://www.operabase.com/fr/critiques/20040516-Chatelet-Paladins.htm/.

18. Holden, A., 'Is This the Future of Musical Theatre ?' *The Observer* Newspaper, London, UK, 6th June, 2004.

19. *Monsters of Grace :A Digital Opera in Three Dimensions* by Philip Glass and Robert Wilson, first staged UCLA, Los Angeles, California, USA 15th April 1998, staged at Barbican Theatre [BITE:98 Festival], London, UK 19th –23rd May 1998.

20. Packer, R., 'Monsters of Immersion', http://www.cyberstage.org/archive/newstuff/monsters.html, May 1998.

21. *Desert Rain*, Blast Theory first performed in Nottingham, UK 1999, http://www.blasttheory.co.uk/bt/work.desertrain.html/.

22. Monkman, K., Director of KMA, taken from email correspondence with the author on 15th September, 2004. More information about KMA can be found at their website http://www.kma.co.uk.

23. Ibid.

24. Dancer, Clark, in post-project questionnaire response.

25. Hunt, N., 'A Play of Light', *Showlight 2001:International Colloquium on Entertainment Lighting*, Edinburgh Festival Theatre, Edinburgh, Scotland, 21st –23rd, May 2001. White, C., 'The Changing Scenographic Aesthetic', *Scenography International Issue 1 New Departures*, October, 1999, p.10, http://www.lboro.ac.uk/research/scenography/, White, C., 'New Technologies of Theatre Lighting design and their influence on Practice' in *Space and the Postmodern Stage*, Eynat-Confino, I and Sormova, E, (eds.) Prague, Czech Theatre Institute, 2000, p.106–114.

26. Monkman, K, see n.23.

27. Ibid.

28. Ibid.

29. Thomas Heatherwick in interview with Tamsin Blanchard, *Observer Magazine*, London, UK, 26th September 2004.

30. The author gratefully acknowledges the work of the following people on the projects referenced in this chapter: Dr Sita Popat and colleagues in the School of Performance & Cultural Industries at the University of Leeds; Nicola Greenan-Tammaro (Arts-Stra Management) for her help in setting up the project with KMA; Paul Clark, Elizabeth Collier, Lydia Sewell (students from BA (Hons) Dance at University of Leeds); Paul Halgarth, Lisette Wright, Carley Marsh, Alistair West and Helena Rose (students from BA (Hons) Performance Design and Production at University of Leeds); Kit Monkman, Tom Wexler and the team from KMA Interactive Media.

PART III: Aesthetic Visions

Scenographic Avant-Gardes
Artistic Partnerships in Canada

Natalie Rewa

Recent examples of scenography challenge the concepts of perspective by their engagement with the spectator. Essentially, this inquiry by designers revolves around the creative experience of performance for the spectators, which has a lot to do with the conceptualisation of the act of seeing as a dynamic negotiation between the stage and the auditorium. While the visual experience of perspective in the theatre has often linked the proscenium arch with active framing as in film or painting, and the manipulation of sight lines has been associated with camera angles, such an approach is being augmented by the attention to the way in which specific details can break out of a sense of two-dimensionality. One of the major characteristics of recent scenography is an apparent emphasis on focal distance and spatial arrangement of objects on the stage, at the same time as breaking with concepts of a pictorial representation of place. These new scenographic experiments effectively drive the mise-en-scène by encouraging in the audience an engagement and analysis of the animation of the stage space as it contributes to a complex and multivalent performance. It does so by challenging perspective as static. This silent and often unacknowledged process of analysis engages spectators in a strong visual narration and begins to make the links with linear perspective and cinema more tenuous. In effect, what I am noting is scenography as a performance practice.

Michael Levine[1] and Ken MacDonald are two Canada-based designers who actively employ perspective, and intensify the spectator's experience of space by a scenography that flows between the two-dimensional pictorial and the three-dimensional experiential, as it embodies an integral metaphor or enacts a narrative role within the mise-en-scène. Their designs contest the co-ordinates of the stage as primarily those of 'place' in favour of characterizing it as 'interactive space', where the aesthetic vocabularies make the spectators actively see the elements of the design. The distinct relationships that the designers engender between the elements and performers encourage active viewing that breaks through the concept of the stage as a screen, and thus pictorial. The original use of the term scenography and recent revisiting of it is helpful to consider more fully.

Vitruvius used the term 'scenography' in his *Ten Books of Architecture* (c. second century B.C.), making a fundamental distinction between architectural drawings, which specifically acknowledge the position of the viewer and those that offer a ground plan or section elevation. This orientation of architectural drawing takes into account an adjustment for the angle of vision and focal distance from the building by scaling the image so as to represent the front and sides of it. It is a geometric transcription of vision. Co-opted into painting and theatre design, scenography is often characterized as linear perspective, represented as the view through a window, therefore, pictorial and graphically depicted as a cone emanating from the eye of the spectator, which arrests the object on an imaginary screen, interposed between the viewer and the object. This screen allows identification and conceptualisation of an object in relation to a vanishing point. Geometry serves to translate the process by which the horizontal landscape can be represented in the vertical plane. Contemporary scenography, however, might best be served by the insights gained from the questioning representation of contemporary architectural theory in which perspective has been reworded to inquire into how buildings represent themselves within the streetscape and therefore, experientially. The nature of programmability, which identifies the function and scale of a building, while it is analogous to painterly pictorialism has been supplemented by attention to a more interactive role, greater than the shell of the building. Architect and theorist Bernard Tschumi has investigated concepts of architectural space in *The Manhattan Transcripts*, 1981. He likened his method of inquiry into architecture and its narratizing role, to a stage script or Sergei Eisenstein's storyboards. Tschumi's sequences denote encounters with architecture as 'events' and in his manifesto he lays out sequences that employ different means of showing an event. Initially, the sequences consist of ways of considering the space, for example a photograph of a real location is placed alongside a map, and a notation of a route through this space. Tschumi invites the viewer/reader to engage with the "internal logic"[2] of each form or language of notation, be it photo illustration, line drawing, map akin to a bird's-eye view and finally the pattern traced by the human route through space without the presence of a physical context. He points out that "looking at them also means constructing them."[3] This process begins to search out what is dynamic about space as it is differentiated between "type" of place and its "program," so that he concentrates on finding the moments when "a disjunction among use, form, and social values" occurs.[4] Tschumi's mises-en-scène point to an intensification of details, as themselves; the practice of such investigations is evident in his design of Parc la Vilette in Paris, an urban park full of architectural and spatial encounters drawn from distinct architectural vocabularies. His argument that, "the definition of architecture may lie at the intersection of logic and pain, rationality and anguish, concept and pleasure" accents the experience of space, and this aspect is what is germane to this discussion of contemporary scenography.[5] Events such as those described by Tschumi are evident in the design by Michael Levine and Ken MacDonald. Their efforts invite the spectator to map the floor and to abstract the geometry of the configurations, in effect, to create their own overhead views, ground plans and movement diagrams akin to Tschumi's *Transcripts*, simultaneously with the performance. The material of the stage becomes dynamic as it turns to 'becoming' and the narration operates synaesthetically. The selected examples illustrate how Levine and MacDonald's scenography invites the spectator to engage in such a process of creation.

Michael Levine's design for *Rigoletto*, Amsterdam, 1996, enacted a closed world where entrances were clearly not evident. Jean Kalman's lighting plunged the stage into a total and unmarked darkness and only lines drawn by light beams provided a sense of physical structures. An enormous banquet table that accommodated the whole of the large chorus around its perimeter would dominate the stage in one act and in another the same area was characterized as a large red-rimmed box which contained the chorus, but never was there a clue as to how the smooth rhythm of the scenes of the chorus, followed by appearance of the principle singers, could be maintained without prolonged blackouts. How and where did the 45 members of the chorus disappear instantaneously to, if the wings were not used for entrances and exits? Levine's design was fundamental to the building of tensions that these effects created. His solution was a hydraulic platform relative to stage level, the table when slightly raised and the box when lowered below stage level aided the solution to the apparent 'decorporealisation' of the chorus and was a carefully worked out choreography that provided each member of the chorus with an individualised exit under the platform. Kalman's lighting had the effect of detaching the action from gravity and floating the table or box in space. In the final scenes the emotional poignancy was evident when the platform was tilted towards upstage with only an edge visible high up above the stage floor and when it was picked out by a stark white light the sense of a horizontal depth was lost. This closed world did not conceive of Rigoletto and Gilda appearing in the same plane, Monique Wagemakers' direction capitalised on this play of light and so Rigoletto is isolated on the thin white line and truly alone in the final act, and Gilda's body is discovered lying in the vastness of the platform while Rigoletto can only look on helplessly from the stage floor. Here the clash of the vertical with the horizontal perspectives removed the emotional import of the opera from the trappings of the court succinctly.

By contrast Levine's scenography for *Eugene Onegin* at the Metropolitan Opera in New York, 1997, played on the monumentality of that stage, as here too he eschewed any nostalgic reference to period reconstruction. Levine created a large box defining the height and width of the stage and introduced a blizzard of leaves in amber light that emphasized the stage space as a large solid cube which then absorbed the solitary figure of Onegin reading Tatiana's letter. Scene changes were effected simply by a cadre of attendants who swept the leaves into various configurations, while the stage was reset by Jean Kalman's lighting design of colour fields on the walls. Often the stage walls would be of a very different colour and hue than the lighting for the stage area and this dynamic made one aware of the whole of the Metropolitan Opera's stage, as much as it paradoxically reduced it to a small intimate area. The historically detailed costumes, which particularised the human presence in time, were in strong contrast to the monumentality of the set. The effect of the scenography was to bring time and memory together almost like looking at a very rich piece of amber.

Levine often returns to work with specific directors. His most frequent collaborations, over a dozen, have been with Canadian-born opera director Robert Carsen, beginning with *Mephistofele* in 1988 in Geneva until their most recent *Capriccio* at the Garnier Opera in Paris, June 2004. He has also collaborated with Canadian theatre artist Robert Lepage on the internationally acclaimed production of *Bluebeard's Castle* and *Erwartung*. In addition he has worked on opera with film directors Atom Egoyan, *Dr. Ox's Experiment* for ENO, 1998, and *Die Walküre* with the Canadian Opera Company, 2004, and with François Girard on the production of *Symphony of Psalms and Oedipus Rex* again for the Canadian Opera Company, 1997.

A brief examination of Levine's collaborations with Egoyan and Girard are helpful to an appreciation of Levine's scenography collaborating with cinematic imaginations. For the premiere of *Dr. Ox's Experiment*, Levine's scenography conceived of the stage in layers, a shallow forestage, limited by a scrim was for Dr Ox and his assistant Ygène, with their sphere of activity flattened onto the surface of the scrim and oriented vertically. They arrive in their hot air balloon along the upper rim of the stage high above the street of miniature houses of the Quiquidone that were ranged along the stage floor. Ygène's descent into the village is presented to the spectators as a rope the height of the proscenium opening, which bisected the vast flatness of the scrim and disappeared into a trap in the forestage. Ygène arrives in the village by climbing up onto the stage to join the village of Quiquidone.

Dr Ox's world is set in bright light, where a black scrim isolates Quiquidone, as the next layer of the stage. Levine devotes the mid-stage area, behind the scrim, for Quiquidone and the slow-moving somnolent citizens who are revealed as human installations resembling peaks of whipped cream in the costumes by Sandy Powell. This motionless, "crystalline beauty of clear ice blue light" that Levine created contrasts with Dr Ox's scientific bustle with his instruments, paraphernalia that allows him and Ygène to measure the atmosphere and observe the citizenry. Quiquidone is suspended in time. The saturated blue lighting is broken up when a candle-bearing chorus, which fans out on the stage as if new constellations of light that gently transform the darkness into a distinguishable place. The upstage layer to the stage Levine apportions to the technology of the citizens, the oversize churns for the cream represent urban architecture and tall ladders reaching into the flies serve as perches for citizens during a council meeting. Small lights on the handles of the slow-moving churns are initially the only signs of activity in the darkness. The shift from place to space is apparent when Dr Ox injects the city with gas, a white scrim rises giving the audience a measure of the volume of the stage, thereby seemingly filling out the vastness that the spectator could contemplate only moments before. Ten booms holding 400 lights descend from the flies to create a smaller and more defined stage space as they meet up with pipes of light brought in from the wings in the lighting design by Rick Fisher. Egoyan and Levine further define the new pace of life in Quiquidone when the electrical lines of the churns snap under strain of this new order of productivity. The precariousness of the new liveliness is made immediate as the audience becomes conscious that the ice that they saw at the beginning has melted into a puddle that covers the stage floor and is dangerously close to these 400 lights. This holding off of potential disaster is as much actual as metaphorical as the audience takes in this new Quiquidone. Ripples are a record of every disturbance on the surface of the pool and the lights glinting off the water create a 'live gobo', reminiscent of the clouds projected onto the scrim when Dr Ox arrived. The repetition of this visual image short-circuits concepts of nostalgia. A question of Dr Ox's ethics arises as Levine and Egoyan bring this structure of performance to the forefront; the large light box contributes to the metaphorical shudder for the spectator.

In his collaboration with François Girard on the double bill *Symphony of Psalms* and *Oedipus Rex* in 1997 at the Canadian Opera Company in the Hummingbird Centre, the scenography made a powerful gloss on the ease with which statistics eliminate individuality. *Symphony of Psalms* opened with a male chorus, dressed in plain black suits, distributed throughout the auditorium. Individually, they read aloud lists of names of those who have died of AIDS from thick notebooks, as they slowly make their way to the stage. Once on the stage, each of the two dozen readers lies down and transcribes these names onto a raked forestage using white chalk. And now all the spectators recognize that they were not all hearing the same list, since any one reader cannot have read all the names. Simultaneously with the names being written down they are transcribed and projected onto an upstage screen that takes up two-thirds of the upstage wall, the final third given over to a 'frieze' of the singers lit by green-shaded suspended lamps. The invisible hands that inscribe the names on the large screen take on a ceremonial function bringing together two perspectives, the individual horizontal as if a blank sheet of paper and the vertical, and highly public one, of a memorial plaque. The physical horizon is replaced by a temporal one of memory.

For *Oedipus Rex*, Levine's scenography extended the concept of those whose lives become part of the great list of names by using real bodies and mannequins to be the foundation for Oedipus's throne. The mound was not static as the 'not-yet-dead', could be seen, albeit imperceptibly, climbing over the mannequins to get to the throne, and once there, created another heap, and perhaps a more terrifying one, as it obscures the throne. All that remained at times amid the sea of bodies was a red line, a red cloth reminiscent of Oedipus's costume descending through the bodies as if blood were flowing from the throne. Upstage, a scrolling Cocteau-esque line drawing narrates Oedipus's fall. Levine and Girard ask the viewer to consider the mound of corpses and the dying as distinct from an architectural transcription of a palace by its horrific combination of the inert dead and struggling survivors. However, if illumination is meant to allow the audience to see, Levine's concept of lighting for the stage provides a fine insight into colour taking precedence. Alain Lortie's lighting design concentrated on strong colours of reds and yellows instilling an expressionist, if not also a Cocteau-esque surrealist tone to the stage. His lighting contrasts the narrative positions with Jocasta in yellow and Tiresias in blues, often dividing up the stage space, not in terms of civic immutability, but as a remaking of the environment of the stage as, "a chromatic irradiation of colours arising out of the theatrical action – colours standing in for leitmotivs – as taking on the emotional power of the seen scene".[7] The almost electric luminous intensity of the lighting sharpens the mise-en-scène yet further when in the final scene the male chorus, costumed as they were in military uniforms, trains large, harsh white lights onto the auditorium. As Oedipus crosses a narrow red bridge to a forestage this human wall turns its back on the monumental mound of bodies now re-animated in the spectator's view by the scrolling line drawing, which has changed in colour from white to red.

Figure 24. Walkure A — Die Walküre *by Richard Wagner, production scenography by Michael Levine, lighting by David Finn. From left to right, Paul Hunka as Hunding, Clifton Forbis as Siegmund, Adrianne Pieczonka as Sieglinde.*

Currently Levine is the production designer for the Ring Cycle being mounted in individual installments from 2004 until 2006 when the Canadian Opera Company will move into its new home. In April 2004 *Die Walküre* was mounted with Egoyan as director.[8] Levine's scenography for *Die Walküre* does not insinuate Wagnerian location rather this scenography juxtaposes significant developments of the twentieth century, both technological as well as socio-cultural. The structure of the design remains the same throughout the performance, taking as its point of departure an organisational composition, using seven borders distributed asymmetrically towards the upstage area. Levine has designed towers, which resemble remnants from the construction failure of a bridge, which by the shadows that they cast the image offers an ever-complicating, view of the stage. This expression of a modernist mythology of steel and girder construction becomes multiplied into an urban industrial forest. Lighting is grafted directly onto the stage set with these girders given two sorts of lights, the strong 1000 candle light power of night-time area lighting on pipe extensions, which now defy their intended directionality. The yellow-hued light bulbs spaced over the expanses of the girders define the structure as they trace the geometry of the once intact bridge in a night sky. But where usually borders serve to focus the view to a vanishing point, here the upstage area is an abrupt stop in a non-descript wall, blocking any seeming perspective of distance. In the first act these girders create a natural urban canopy and the lights turned to a low intensity suggest urban constellations, altogether displacing any domestic architecture suggested by Wagner. Downstage centre and stage left offer a site where the rhythms of the stage are distinct; the paving stones are broken and create a pit with a large tree that has been felled dividing the stage in yet another manner. Woodchips covering the stage floor in this area provide a richness of texture, more so as they extend onto the tiles, frustrating the demarcation of clear boundaries. Here, in contradistinction to the electrical lighting, the glow of a small fire draws the spectator's eye to the dwelling of the apparently homeless urban dwellers Sieglinde and Hunding.

In this scenography Levine has provided a stimulating unprogrammable world. An architecture that cannot be attended to, but which speaks to the investigation of materials, twentieth-century achievements, bridges taming the topography, or modernist steel and glass constructions of buildings shooting into the sky, and shadows become abstracted as a strange foreboding forest. David Finn's lighting design in the first act stays close to a monochromatic palette of grey and white, with the exception of a deep red block created upstage to bring to life Sieglinde's retelling of her misfortune to Siegmund. This scene is presented silently on an imaginary battlefield, out of reach of the glow of the fire where Sieglinde stands. Significantly, it is only in this vision of the past that distinctly military uniforms are brought onto the stage, showing how *The Ring* conceives of itself in a post-military world, where the power of national armies taint all that they come in contact with. By contrast to the red of memory, Hunding's entrance from stage right cuts a swath through the shadows of the detritus of the 'underbrush of industry' with a harsh white light. So Levine and Egoyan manage the entrances and intrusions into the stage orienting them perpendicularly to the flow of perspective and the lighting by David Finn creates the effect of

Figure 25. Walkure B — Act 3 in Valhalla — the Valkyries

shutter inserts. Without any scenery changes Levine enacts the move to Valhalla in Act 3 in a bold revelation of the stage by the elimination of shadows. By superimposing the Valkyries onto the same set as that inhabited by Siegmund and Sieglinde, Levine invites the spectator to look again. In this new light the black girders and drooping electrical lines contrast the neatly bagged bodies that the Valkyries stack into organised piles, which further increase the starkness of the stage. The objects that seemed to be big stones on the set in Act 1 are now re-evaluated by the spectators and identified as bodies that the Valkyries had already stored, so that the audience is seemingly attending to two places simultaneously. In Valhalla, the overhead catwalk that looked menacingly unstable earlier, now becomes a crossover for a Valkyrie, and several of the precariously poised girders readily bear the weight of the busy Valkyries. Here, Wagner's mythology and our own belief in technological prowess are melded on the human actors when lighting from the grid becomes a prop for Fricka, and one or two of the Valkyries. The historical elements of our twentieth-century accomplishments are wrested from the scenography and made to perform; urban lighting becomes a flashlight when in the hands of a god.

The costumes for the Valkyries differ from the weathered and worn attire of the humans and Wotan by their elegance; the Valkyries wear the structure of their garments with flair. Levine's costumes for some of the Valkyries reveal a femininity that is between historical periods. While Fricka and Brünnhilde are fully corsetted and enclosed in their nineteenth-century fashions, the Valkyries stack the bodies in elegant taffeta gowns with thin shoulder straps and tracings in gold on the bodices. They are nowhere near any approximation of military dress. Levine and Egoyan characterize these Valkyries as ceremonial, as occasional. Their link to human life is made evident in the red cord wound around a hand and wrist, which they uncoil with some ceremony as they deal with the corpses of the fallen warriors. The use of the cord shows up well in the stark white light and becomes all the more significant against the backdrop of the pristinely shrouded corpses as its presence effectively rhymes with the disconnected wires that seem to hang as urban vines. These Valkyries move precariously through the same environment as the humans, of broken tiles and decaying natural matter, but they do not all manage it as well and one of them is choreographed to slip and fall in her high heels, to the great mirth of her sisters.

Finally, Levine blends the environments by the volatility of live fire torches brought on by the Valkyries to create the cave around Brünnhilde. Just as the bulbs on the girders were reconfigured in their use for Valhalla, so too is fire on the stage. The Valkyries create a circle of fire around the sleeping Brünnhilde as they stand their torches in the 'soft earth' and their departure then traces a path on the stage through the stacked bodies to the cave's opening. This final image brings the action back down to the downstage area where the small hearth fire first illuminated the stage.

Contrasting these opera productions by Michael Levine is the work of Ken MacDonald whose training as a painter comes to terms with the four-dimensionality of the stage by emphasizing perspective and then disturbing the spectator's security in it. Ken MacDonald, an actor, director and Governor-General, and award-winning playwright Morris Panych work in Vancouver and Toronto. Their collaborative venture *The Overcoat* was featured in the 2004 Mime Festival at the Barbican and is now enjoying an extensive international tour. In the early 1980s they wrote and performed political cabarets that toured Canada and for the last twenty years they have worked on music videos, operas and plays both in tiny theatres and in very well-equipped performing arts centres. MacDonald has designed the premieres of all of Panych's plays, and his scenography is integral to the mise-en-scène, both of the script and performance. Their work is significant for the way in which they compose productions scenographically.

For *Seven Stories* that premiered in the tiny Arts Club, Seymour Street Theatre in Vancouver in 1989, MacDonald created a stage that was eighteen inches wide, a ledge. This set was akin to a line drawn in space within the vastness of the sky and MacDonald completely disoriented the spectators by resorting to an elaborate Magritte-like scenographic 'canvas' to contain the action. This design took its inspiration from architecture of the late twentieth century; for example, the mirrored building, where the building reflects the sky or buildings around it. This effect can be surreal when the building seemingly disappears from the streetscape but in this case the surrealism is physical. MacDonald's conception was a brilliant solution for a performance space with no depth, and not much height, but also for Panych's script, which sets adrift a character from society. As the man prepares to jump, he encounters groups of characters behind each of the windows. At all times the spectators remain on the ledge with the man, but we see as if through a rear-view mirror the encounters with the other figures, through the windows, and this punctures holes in what we begin to settle on, as actual.

Figure 26. Earshot, *by Morris Panych, set design by Ken Macdonald, lighting by John Thompson, Tarragon, Extra Space Toronto, Ontario 2001*

On the other side of the country in the 'Extraspace' of the Tarragon Theatre, with seating for 100, MacDonald designed *Earshot* in 2001, Panych's play about a man with overly sensitive hearing. In this case, the thematic was realised as the physical, so if the sound design exaggerated the aural, the set playfully employed a forced perspective which realised the distortions of the protagonist as it was crammed into a footprint of about 12' x 10'. With skilful trompe l'œil painting, right down to the floorboards and clever choreography, MacDonald and Panych managed to create a fishbowl view of what the audience knew logically was implausible. As long as the man keeps to the first three feet downstage all proportions are maintained, but as the man begins to roam around the room when the sounds increasingly intrude from the neighbouring apartments and become unbearable, the perspective was made to perform its existence. As he prepares to leave the seemingly cavernous apartment his 'take' on reality is sorely challenged when he picks up a proportionally correct, but impossibly small pair of jeans, or becomes giant-like barely fitting in between the floor and the ceiling. For the audience the effect is hilarious and also greatly unsettling because what they know to be logically plausible is unseated by what they actually witness.

MacDonald's work for large stages exploits the relationships that the added focal distance in a large house can accommodate, and this is where MacDonald's delight in linear perspective is clearly evident. The large theatre at the Arts Club on Granville Island is a proscenium arch theatre built as part of a national programme of the mid-twentieth century of municipal theatres, part of

Figure 27. Pens & Figure

Figure 28. Cogs both from: The Overcoat *conceived and directed by Morris Panych and Wendy Gorling, set design Ken MacDonald, lighting Ala Brodie, Vancouver Playhouse, Vancouver, British Columbia, 1997*

a network of theatres to allow touring, to rationalize the performing arts in a vast country such as Canada. MacDonald revels in the proscenium arch, and no where more spectacularly than in his scenography for *The Imaginary Invalid* in 1996, for which the forced perspective of the home was the sole 'location,' its use, however, afforded a captivating simultaneity. The set itself comprised of nine doorways and the elaborate cornice and door frames along with Raoul Dufy-esque intense wallpaper suggest an idiosyncratic set of residents. Downstage the doorways were oversized and informed the audience of an especially large room but the tiny chair in the apex of the room corroborated the sense of distance from the upstage door. The geometry of this set made this a very large room. Moreover, since MacDonald furnished Orgon with all manner of medical equipment to gauge all his bodily functions, all slightly out of proportion with the intimacy of the function they were to perform, and which appeared with increasing frequency throughout the performance, the sense of the space being proportional to him became part of the visual story. Panych's mise-en-scène augmented the physical environment by specifically drawing attention to it. Orgon's privacy and pomposity are theatrically undercut as the servants all become a chorus of observers as they peer over the walls from upstage and thus playfully confirmed that the upstage chair really was tiny, only a foot high, and that MacDonald's scenography was poised egocentrically.[9] For the spectators, trying to assess which of the frames that they were seeing would stop the stage from reflecting itself into itself, this mise en abîme and dialogue between designer and audience was delightful.

Part of MacDonald's fascination with the framing of the stage is the way in which he has made not only forced perspective integral to his work, but other kinds of manipulation of perspective as in Panych's *Vigil* in Tarragon, 1996, mounted in a new production by the Canadian Stage Company Bluma Appel, 2004, and produced at Wyndhams as *Auntie and Me* in 2003. Here, MacDonald's scenography for this dingy apartment slips off reality into a doubling of its real self. The perspective may be forced, but the scenography is a refusal to stay aligned to a vertical-horizontal grid. Throughout the performance one was conscious that the clash in geometries created a series of frames that did not ultimately make sense. The details of the dressmaker's mannequin, the empty birdcage and the vista onto the street consisting of papered-over windows allowed the audience to attend to what was not there. These kinds of questions of space and organizations came to the forefront in their production of *Arsenic and Old Lace*, 2003, in Vancouver. Here the building appears to have been set adrift from architecture by the evident sliding down of the upstage wall from the ceiling line to reveal a blue sky, and the staircase to the second storey simply, and insistently, ascends into the flies without remark.

The Overcoat at Vancouver Playhouse, 1997, is perhaps one of their most exciting productions that have maintained the interest in cinema-like perspective and framing and has also emphasized a cinematic fluidity. It is not surprising that the Canadian Broadcasting Corporation commissioned MacDonald and Panych to adapt the stage version for their flagship performance series four years later. Composed as a wordless drama by Panych and Wendy Gorling to Shostakovich's music, the story is derived from Gogol's novella of the same name. The process consisted of Panych and Gorling devising the choreography to the music with several professional performers and the students of the conservatory Studio 58 at Langara College in Vancouver. MacDonald was present at all the rehearsals and his scenography reflects the integration of design in the conceptualisation of the performance.

Instead of quick changes of scene all the furniture is set on casters and arrives elegantly and silently. The drawing tables in the architect's office are drawn into the conspiracy of creating chaos in the office when they are taken up as the dance partners. Proportions, emotional as well as physical, are present in MacDonald's design, as for example when the 22-foot nibbed ink pens descend from the flies seemingly dwarfing the architectural office, or when large cogs that come down on either side of the stage to orchestrate the machine age of the tailor's sweatshop. The infernos of Gogol's characters become menacingly present as themselves in a profound scenographic hybrid between the nuances of silent film, choreography of the factory and modern dance. The pens come into dialogue with the floor, as if with a sheet of paper, as MacDonald characterized the floor as an architectural drawing with lines in red. Panych exploited the 1930s factory-like quality of the upstage wall to great advantage, opening the windows to create a series of frames for 'stills' intermittently pausing in the action, to emphasize a moment, and to contrast the whirlwind of the lower level. Alan Brodie's lighting gives the hues of industrial lighting and the clarity of outdoors, and a single light bulb in the rooming house. However, he never suggests that we become more interested in action beyond our frame, so remaining tied to the very immediate present.

These experiments in scenography rise to the challenge of creating dynamic space akin to what Bernard Tschumi characterises as an architecture that invites new engagement. The design by Levine and MacDonald insists on the conception of space that includes shifting proportions and potentialities of negative space as aesthetically significant. Spectators enter into a dialogue with what they are seeing and this complex interaction between actors, object and lighting creates its own event. In such scenography the concept of place gives way to the 'practiced space'[10] that becomes interactive with the imagination of the spectator as the spectator engages in an experiential ordering of the elements and choreography, beyond mere identification. Such scenography does not seek to be understood as a two-dimensional landscape captured in the frame, rather such scenography performs itself.

NOTES

1. Michael Levine, has been designing professionally since the early 1980s after graduating from the Central Saint Martin's School of Design. He has worked in Glasgow, London, New York, Paris, Niagara-on-the-Lake, Toronto, Vienna, Antwerp, Chicago and Denver.
2. Tschumi, B., *The Manhattan Transcripts*, 1st edition, New York, 1981, p.8.
3. Ibid., p.9.
4. Ibid., p.7.
5. Ibid., p.9.
6. Michael Levine, Interview 27th July, 1998.
7. Prampolini, E., 'Futurist Scenography', 1915 in Kirby, M., (ed.), *Futurist Performance: with manifestos and playscripts*, translated by Victoria Nes Kirby, New York: Performing Arts Journal Publications, 1971, p.205.
8. The second and third installments take place in 2005, 2006: *Siegfried* directed by François Girard and *Gotterdammerung* by Tim Albery 2006. When *The Ring* is fully mounted as three four-day extravaganzas in the fall of 2006, the operas will be presented in sequence with the production of *Das Rheingold* unveiling the last of Levine's designs for the tetralogy and marking his directorial debut. The excitement of this Toronto *Ring* is that the designer will become his own ultimate collaborator and the scenography and mise-en-scène will be seamless.
9. Reid, G., 'Perspectives on recent set design by Ken MacDonald' *Canadian Theatre Review*, 91, spring 1997, p.68.
10. de Certeau, M., The Practice of Everyday Life, Translated, Rendall, S., Berkeley, University of California Press, 1984, p.117.

CODES AND OVERLOADS
THE SCENOGRAPHY OF RICHARD FOREMAN

Neal Swettenham

During the last thirty-six years, New York–based writer, director and designer Richard Foreman has developed a distinctive style of work. From the very start of his career, he has involved himself in every aspect of the theatre-making process, including the detailed design of the performance space. Throughout the entire fifteen-week rehearsal period, actors work in a fully dressed set which, nevertheless, changes and evolves constantly, along with the other performance elements. His sets are never mere backdrops to action: rather they are an integral part of the performance discourse. Specifically, Foreman works by assaulting the audience with an overload of codes and signs, creating an effect that is both disruptive and exhilarating. His productions bombard the spectator with an excess of semiotic information, but the ultimate aim is not to create confusion: it is to disrupt over-familiar ways of seeing and enable new ones.

"I realise it has sort of relationships to schizophrenic art. I mean, it's cluttered, there's not a free inch that's not decorated, much like schizophrenic artists, and perhaps that means I'm schizophrenic".[1]

"One might say that the force of its significations, felt all at once, overloads the artistic circuit, as in the filaments of those early light bulbs that glowed intensely with the first surge of power..."[2]

Something is definitely wrong. Sitting in the cramped auditorium, waiting for the performance to begin, one's gaze moves restlessly around the over-crowded stage, looking for a focal point, on which to settle, or some kind of key, with which to unlock its meaning. But the attempt is futile: the disordered picture retains its secrets — and its fascination.

The stage set for Richard Foreman's play, *King Cowboy Rufus Rules the Universe*, 2004, echoes and reconfigures the clutter and confusion of all his most recent productions. Foreman does not tend to do things by halves, or even seven-eighths: instead, he crams the entire performance area with a wealth of contradictory visual information, incorporating strangely awkward angles, half-familiar objects and defiantly jarring patterns.

Combining and switching between the roles of writer, designer and director, Foreman has been producing plays at a steady rate of approximately one a year since 1968, when he first established his New York–based Ontological-Hysteric Theater Company. Although his scenographic practice has matured and developed over that period, his essential aim has remained constant: to produce work that unbalances and disorients its audience:

> I like to think of my plays as an hour and a half in which you see the world through a special pair of eyeglasses. These glasses may not block out all narrative coherence, but they magnify so many other aspects of experience that you simply lose interest in trying to hold on to narrative coherence, and instead, allow yourself to become absorbed in the moment-by-moment representation of psychic freedom.[3]

For anyone unfamiliar with this work, it should be emphasised that whilst the plays do indeed lack narrative coherence, consistent characterisation, and any recognisable sense of location, they are by no means without form, intention or, I would suggest, a singular and expressive beauty.

Foreman's sets have always been strongly influenced by the spaces, for which they were created. One early venue, an unusually shaped loft space, presented an extremely deep and very narrow performance area, the visual depth of which Foreman would re-configure constantly during shows by the use of sliding screens. By way of contrast, *Penguin Touquet*, produced in 1980, was designed for the much larger, and more conventionally shaped, stage of the Joseph Papp Public Theatre. The venue that Foreman has been using since 1991 is a compact and potentially more restrictive black box studio space that he manages, nevertheless, to manipulate and re-invent with considerable resourcefulness for each new production.

I propose to investigate Foreman's scenographic practice, by looking at the visual elements of *King Cowboy Rufus*, particularly in the light of Bert O. States' suggestion that semiotics and phenomenology, taken together, form the 'binocular vision' of all theatrical reception.

STAGE LEFT...

The setting for *King Cowboy Rufus*, as for virtually all of Foreman's other works, is an interior space. Foreman rarely ventures into the outside world in his plays, preferring instead to keep his audiences enclosed within a carefully regulated, private territory, bounded by artificial, yet seemingly impermeable barriers. This echoes the tone of the writing, which suggests constantly that we are witnessing an internal dialogue made public: a mental landscape that favours containment, rather than the unrestricted opportunity to range far and wide.

But this is not a single space: the stage is divided into two distinct areas, stage left and right, suggested not simply by the alternative décor of each, but formally separated by a strip of red carpet that creates both a barrier between each half of the space, and also a link between stage and audience, as it extends forward and up onto the central steps of the auditorium's raked seating. To either side of the strip of red carpet, as it ascends these steps, is a curiously high, metal handrail.

The cramped space on the stage left area of the set suggests a manically over-decorated chamber in some faded stately home-cum-hotel. Four large paintings, done in the Renaissance style, dominated the walls, which are themselves covered in busy vertical stripes of black, brown, fawn, white and red. The floor introduces a further, sharply discordant, note of busy-ness: a noisy grid of terracotta squares, enclosed in thick white stripes. A wooden table and four old-fashioned high-backed chairs, with red upholstery, are pushed up against the one wall, the chairs almost, but not quite, matching. On the table are napkins and two identical white vases side by side, each containing a yellow flower or two.

There are smaller pictures also: above each of the large paintings, and dotted around the walls at other strategic points, can be seen medallion-like gold trays, each holding a black-and-white portrait of some past American president. Several of them are further decorated with tiny national flags, never the American 'stars and stripes', though, but the colours and symbols of other nations, apparently chosen at random. Over one of the paintings hangs a noose.

There are other, semi-recognisable, objects that seem curiously detached from the real world, perhaps the most immediately striking of which are the red and black checkerboards, suspended by their points around the walls – at least nineteen of them at a quick count. Echoing the ludic theme, there is also a large number wheel, laid out in patterns that remind one of a dartboard or target. Then there are the 'candles': tall, thin, and constructed out of rolled-up newspaper, with silver foil 'flames', which line the walls at ground level and are complemented by little balls of scrunched up paper.

More fragments of newspaper, cut into boomerang-like shapes, decorate the walls; and there are other objects too, less easily definable, but reminiscent of bomb casings or pressurised gas cylinders, and decorated in gold and bronze stripes. Three other items are prominent in the space: an elaborately dressed china doll propped up against the table, a large empty bowl on a wrought-iron stand, and a very solid-looking, painted iron bollard, placed awkwardly in the centre of the room.

Very few of these objects come to play any direct part in the action, however. That is not their primary function in Foreman's theatre. Rather than having any direct narrative connections with the action or dialogue, they act both as obstacles to be negotiated by actors and, more importantly, perhaps, as resistant resonators within the visual echo chamber of the set.

Foreman describes this process in an early essay entitled *How to write a play*:

The way to confront the object is to allow it its own life – let it grow its own shoots in directions that do **not** re-inforce it's [sic] being-in-life for use as a tool, but that suggests a compositional scheme not centered on useful human expectations. So, let the chair that is for sitting have string run from it to an orange, because if chair was just 'chair for sitting' we would not confront, [...] its meaning is too much OUR meaning; but now chair-connected-to-orange is an 'alien' chair that we must CONFRONT.

> (To reveal an object or act, gesture, emotion, idea, sound.
> To make it seizable
> To speak its name you must
> make it part of a system not
> its own. Involve it compositionally with
> Another realm [...])[4]

The suggestion that objects should be re-encountered, in unfamiliar, often 'difficult', settings, is not a new one. It goes back at least as far as Marcel Duchamp and his 'ready-mades', and was defined by Victor Shklovsky as the need to, "make objects 'unfamiliar,' to make forms difficult, to increase the difficulty and length of perception".[5] Magritte and Dali carried such ideas into their surrealist paintings, in which can be detected both beauty and a terrible fear.

For Foreman, however, these stage objects are no mere visual puzzles, or curiosities: they are intended to create 'interference' with the thoughts and ideas expressed through the verbal text of the plays, acting not as echoes of the words spoken, but as objects that will 'bounce back' the text and constantly resist assimilation into coherence and meaning. Foreman stated:

> ... I was writing, and still am writing, dialogue or language without a thinker, and without an object towards which it is aimed. And in the staging of the play [...] I am trying to select objects, to begin with, that might be objects that the word could interestingly collide with. And the various visual techniques, as I'm doing the play and when we rehearse, I redo it and redo it and redo it, as if somebody were editing a film for week after week, because I'm not getting enough collision, I'm not getting enough spark gap – spark jumping the gap – between the said and what is there for it to be said in terms of. And that is what I keep adjusting: to make a kind of ultimate tension between the 'said' and the 'seen'. But the seen comes after, the seen is a comment on the said.[6]

STAGE RIGHT...

The area to stage right is both linked and distinct, its most prominent feature being a series of three archways hung with red drapes and bearing above it the legend, "La Maison Rouge". The whole effect is vaguely reminiscent of a Parisian brothel. Another bowl on a stand, more of the bomb-like cylinders on the walls and newspaper candles, and some smaller, more mysterious-looking paintings, echo the stage left scene. The floor is similarly busy, though the pattern is a different one. Distinctive elements in this part of the set include some large tarot cards over the archways, and not one, but four Damoclean swords suspended menacingly above the space.

Figure 29. and Figure 30. Foreman's scenography for King Cowboy Rufus Rules the Universe, *2004*

Even with the proviso that not every single detail needs enumeration, there is still more to be said about the visual impact of the set. Across the front of the stage, and dotted at various points amongst the audience, are several tall, black-and-white striped poles, each surmounted by clusters of light bulbs and decorated around the top with bullets, medals and military insignia. Suspended from the ceiling are lamps that are not quite lamps: where the bulbs should be, these contain gold tassels. There are a couple of chandeliers that are, also, 'not' chandeliers: the loops of crystal have been replaced by strings of pearls, and in the centre of each, is suspended a tiny mirrorball. Just above the eyeline, and closer to the audience, are large gold letters suspended on wires. In some earlier productions, letters like these have been displayed as isolated symbols, individual signs, detached from each other and from any kind of sense, but here they spell out a phrase: "President of the United States".

And then, of course, there's the string. A trademark feature of Foreman's work, from the very beginning, has been his recurrent use of both plain white and, more often, black-and-white dotted-line string, stretched at various angles across the performance area. What is its purpose? Foreman admits, rather ruefully, that he has had to answer this question "millions of times".[7] And, like so much in Foreman's theatre, there is not just one reason for the string, but many, since "everything is over-determined".[8] First of all, says Foreman, they represent lines of energy, analogous to the perspective lines that you might see in an artist's preliminary sketches, which define the space, direct the eye, and connect objects within the frame of the picture. He also describes them – in terms that are reminiscent of Oskar Schlemmer's directions for creating a "spatial-linear web" by means of "taut wires", as being like lines on a graph, creating a grid, against which you can chart the movement of the action.[9] More interestingly still, he relates them also to images taken from his adolescent dream life: a nightmare vision of his father with swollen head and crossed eyes, staring down at him from the staircase in his house; dreams of an aeroplane high up in the sky above, but with people in the plane also staring down at him, and between their eyes and his, these dotted lines of energy and hostility. Above all, he says, they are, "lines of force that suggest other ways to read things", alternative perspectives onto a world of familiar, and unfamiliar, objects.[10]

This, then, is the 'reverberation machine', in which the verbal and physical texts will be amplified and distorted. Simply to name the process, however, does not account for its effect. What is actually happening, and what is distinctive, in Foreman's scenography?

BINOCULAR VISION

Bert O. States provides a useful key in his account of what he calls the 'binocular vision' of theatrical reception: on the one hand, semiotics, "everything is something else", and, on the other, phenomenology, "everything is nothing but itself".[11] He highlights the distinctive qualities that enable some objects, in particular, to resist immediate assimilation into a semiotic reading. Looking at such on-stage elements as working clocks incorporated into a set, operational fountains, real fire, child actors and, finally, performing animals, he demonstrates how each of these is likely to be seen by an audience initially as the 'object-in-itself', an intrusion of the real world into the stage fiction, rather than as the narrative signs that they are intended to be. To use Foreman's terminology, these objects 'confront', by resisting their planned roles within a compositional scheme "centered on useful human expectations".[12]

And for States these are simply the most obvious examples of a dynamic that runs throughout all theatre: the ongoing interplay between object-as-sign and object-as-itself. Of course, as he goes on to point out, we quickly recover from the phenomenological shock of noticing that, for example, Launce's dog Crab, in *Two Gentlemen of Verona*, is a real animal in a live theatrical space, and begin to 'read' it as another character in the world of the play, interpreting its real doggy behaviour as narrative signs, indicating boredom with what Launce is saying, perhaps, or genuine excitement at another character's actions. The functional 'reality' of the story world re-asserts itself and the strangeness of the initial encounter is dissipated.

Foreman's theatre, by contrast, attempts to prolong and extend this strangeness to an indefinite degree: not, however, by putting live animals on stage, but by crowding the space with contradictory elements and introducing a profusion of objects that are suggestive of possibilities, rather than exhaustive of them. By their refusal to take their place within a coherent narrative world, the objects on Foreman's stage remain disordered and unfamiliar, retain their awkwardness, and yet compel us to maintain our efforts to try and recognise, categorise and explain them. The very fact that there are discernible patterns and repetitions encourages the belief that, ultimately, there is some sense to be made of it.

To the static backdrop of images already described, the basic stage setting, the performance adds much more. The costumes also are overloaded with meaning, contradictory, irreducible to a single semiotic reading. For example, the first character we encounter is dressed in a suit, suggestive of formality, a certain position: he could be a government official, or a businessman, perhaps? Around his neck, however, he wears a blackboard, with rows of medals attached, as well as letters and numbers scribbled on it. Instead of just one tie, he wears six, all of which are frayed or cut off after a few inches, and pushed back at various wild angles over his shoulders. On his head sits a strange cap, vaguely oriental, with a beaded handkerchief resting on top. The final touch is a pair of fluffy pink slippers on his feet. He introduces himself as the Baron Herman de Voto. Impossible to locate within a single context, he emerges as possibly a kind of secretary of state to King Cowboy Rufus, or maybe just a mobster with a penchant for abstract philosophy.

This multiplication and overlapping of semantic possibilities is carried into other costumes also, as the stage is successively occupied by match-girls, concubines, half-comical, half-nightmarish anthropomorphic bears, and sinister heavies, sporting, for no reason that is obvious, Highland tartan and bowler hats. The visual picture changes constantly and dizzyingly throughout, as more and more bizarre props are brought on to the stage, and sliding panels, displaying esoteric religious symbols, suddenly and unexpectedly reshape the space. This overloading of codes and signs, without hierarchy or ordering principle, make it impossible to settle on a definitive reading, and indeed that is precisely the point: the specific aim of this type of theatre is to disrupt and destabilise our conventional ways of seeing. Ultimately, it is not in any of the individual signs that meaning is to be found, nor in their harmonious integration. Rather like a jigsaw puzzle that has too many pieces, it is in the conflict and disjunctions produced by the overload that any kind of reading must be sought; the sum is greater than its many parts:

> [Foreman] once described how much he loves watching the first ten minutes of a film – any film, regardless of its quality. During those minutes, nothing is clear. He doesn't know who's who, where the characters are, or how they are tangled up in each other's lives. The characters don't have a visible past, and their future is as yet unknown. He can't decide who will be a major character and who, after this scene, will end up a mere bystander. As the actors speak in fragments, he can't always tell what they are referring to, or evaluate the importance of the information. Faced with so many unsolved mysteries, he hangs on every word and scrutinizes every frame, piecing elements together, hoping for a story to take shape. In his own theater, Foreman tries to stretch the charged atmosphere of these ten minutes over an entire evening.[13]

And rather like film, Foreman's theatre has a capacity to burn certain images on to the brain, which remain long after the impact made by the extravagant profusion of signs has begun to fade. This particular production has come in for some criticism, as well as praise, for its conscious references to the contemporary political scene. This is untypical of Foreman: usually, he contrives to maintain a creative gap between the discourse of the plays and that of the surrounding social and political realities.[14] In the light of what has been said already about his scenographic practice, however, it should come as no surprise that such political references as do slip through the cracks and insinuate themselves into the world of *King Cowboy Rufus*, still tend to be rather oblique and obscure.

However, at a certain point in the action, a number of dolls, about ten or twelve of them perhaps, are lowered from a hidden space above the grid. They are identically swaddled in black cloth, decorated with beads and bangles, and suspended upside-down above the characters' heads. Watching the play in the aftermath of the invasion of Iraq, and conscious of Foreman's programme note describing King Cowboy Rufus as someone who, "dreams of becoming an imitation George Bush", it is difficult to read these vaguely Middle Eastern-looking babies as denoting anything other than the many hundreds of children maimed and killed during that conflict.[15] Perhaps, after all, it is only possible to hold the signs at bay for so long: even in this theatre of phenomenological overload, they will ultimately reclaim their right to mediate meaning and 'useful' semantic content.

NOTES

1. Foreman interviewed by Kriszta Doczy, *Foreman Planet*, DVD, Contemporary Arts Media, 2003.
2. States, B. O., *Great Reckonings in Little Rooms: On the Phenomenology of Theater*, Berkeley & London: University of California Press, 1985, p.37.
3. Foreman, R., 'Foundations for a Theater', *Unbalancing Acts*, New York: Theatre Communications Group, 1993, pp.4–5.
4. Foreman, R., *Reverberation Machines: the later plays and essays*, Barrytown: Station Hill Press Inc., 1985, pp.226–227.
5. Shklovsky, V., in Bert O. States, *Great Reckonings in Little Rooms*, p.21.
6. Foreman interviewed by Kriszta Doczy, *Foreman Planet*.
7. Ibid.
8. Ibid.
9. Schlemmer, O., Moholy-Nagy, L. and Molnár, F., *The Theater of the Bauhaus*, London: Eyre Methuen, 1961, pp.92–95.
10. Foreman interviewed by Kriszta Doczy, *Foreman Planet*.
11. States, B. O. *Great Reckonings in Little Rooms*, 8. See also States' essay 'The Phenomenological Attitude' in Reinelt, J. G. & Roach, J. R., *Critical Theory and Performance*, Ann Arbor: University of Michigan Press, 1992, pp.369–379.
12. Ibid., pp.29–36.
13. Foreman, R., *My Head Was A Sledgehammer: Six Plays*, New York: Overlook Press, 1995, ii.
14. One other notable exception to this general trend is the play *Symphony of Rats*, 1987, which portrays an American president, who believes that he is receiving telepathic messages from outer space.
15. Richard Foreman in a programme note for *King Cowboy Rufus Rules the Universe*, Ontological at St. Mark's Church, New York, 8th January 18th April 18, 2004.

Spatial Practices

The Wooster Group's Rhode Island Trilogy

Johan Callens

The Wooster Group, the New York-based experimental performance company directed by Elizabeth LeCompte, is perhaps best known for their complex inter-medial stage productions, incorporating almost from its inception canonical texts. Yet, despite the company's wholehearted inscription into the televisual culture, prepared for by LeCompte's fine arts studies at Skidmore College, their productions show a marked architectonic awareness. This goes back to the company's emergence in 1975 out of Richard Schechner's Performance Group, whose working space, the Performing Garage, LeCompte took over. Even if the Wooster Group has distanced itself from his theatre, it is the shared environmental emphasis, which remains noticeable, an emphasis always conducive to perceptual reconfigurations and the critical participation of the spectators. Without actually keeping them on their feet LeCompte insists on dividing the spectators' attention between simultaneous, non-hierarchical actions on different areas of the stage. Drawing on Michel de Certeau's distinction between place and space,[1] we could say that realism's spatial practices enhance the illusion of spatial stability and order, whereas the Wooster Group's very much undermine that illusion.[2] Their complex scenographic strategies admit contradictory and simultaneous positions and orientations, which places normally exclude as unique physical locations. In the Rhode Island Trilogy, 1975–9, theatrical space was tectonically layered: a literal landscape traversed by an emotional geography, an imagistic and fluid dreamscape, structured by Spalding Gray's childhood recollections and private fantasies, and travelled through on the rhythms of their artificial evocation. What further held together the pieces was LeCompte's self-styled painterly "portrait"[3] of Gray's emerging artistic persona, a creative process which he himself, with the other company members and the spectators, self-consciously took part in. The result, said Gray, was an exploration of the "self as other," a study of, "one who sees himself seeing himself."[4] It would eventually become an ongoing "life-study", since Gray turned this self-absorption into the means and matter of the dramatic monologues written after he left the Wooster Group. To the point that he repeatedly wondered whether his life was not lived for the sake of his art. In any case, the epilogue to the Rhode Island Trilogy was a farewell for Spalding, the character. In subsequent productions he would only be present as a voice or occasional performer.[5]

SAKONNET POINT

The first Wooster Group production, *Sakonnet Point*, 1975 used as a 'found' environment the set for the Performance Group's concurrent *Mother Courage*. It had the spectators seated on platforms of various heights surrounding the performing space on three sides.[6] That space was dominated, beacon-like, by an elevated red-domed tent from which a tarpaulin sloped down and sheets were hung on clothes line, both sculpting the space and occasionally hiding the performers from view. On the floor masking tape created triangular vectors of energy, apart from suggesting architectural outlines. LeCompte has compared these to Cézanne's pictorial grid patterns[7] but Richard Foreman's strings articulating theatrical space and guiding perception were not too far off, nor was Michael Kirby's *Sculpture as a Visual Instrument*.[8] The performers included, besides a boy and Gray, LeCompte's sister, Ellen, whose feet early in the production dangled from a trapdoor in the Garage's ceiling and who later lay down beneath the opening as if having suffered a lethal fall. The invoked realities were both the apartment above the performance space and a surreal third realm between boyhood and adolescence, past reality and present evocation, actor and character, between normality and abnormality, too. Given the boy's mock strangulation and a woman's scream emitted from the domed tent towards the end, it was a realm increasingly dominated by the suicide of Gray's manic-depressive mother after a seemingly successful stay at a sanatorium involving electric shock treatment. That was the faltering heart of a production bathed in Tchaikovsky's First Piano Concerto, hymns, and the sounds of nature, an almost wordless choreography in reaction to the dominance of narrative in Schechner's work and the discursiveness of the adult world in general.[9]

RUMSTICK ROAD

In the trilogy's second instalment, *Rumstick Road*, 1977,[10] the frame-breaking and perspective play of *Sakonnet Point* became more outspoken, if also more disciplinarian as when a massage demonstration on a woman turned into molestation. This discipline was in keeping with the production's alignment of the voyeuristic and objectifying gaze of theatre spectators and doctors, whether treating patients privately or publicly lecturing on them in anatomical theatres. LeCompte has acknowledged using Renaissance illustrations of such lectures,[11] though the scenic situation of *Rumstick Road* also resonates with T. S. Eliot's *The Cocktail Party*, the play that featured already in rehearsals but only surfaced in the subsequent Wooster Group production. More particularly, the lecture-demonstration set-up evoked that tragic-comic moment in which people stretched on a surgeon's table become, "a piece of furniture in a repair shop" for the "masked actors" surrounding them.[12] For the rest, the performance area staked out by the plywood set resembled a funnel, with the lights above it diminishing in size, the further they were removed from the audience. The stage picture thus conveyed the inaccessibility of the past dwelt on, the evanescence of the human and theatrical projects already slipping in the act of material representation. That private documents from Gray's past had been used made no difference, insofar as these, too, remain partial and selective.

At the same time the set or stage 'house' was divided into two identically shaped sides, with the left-hand projection screen mirroring the right-hand window, 'artistic' perception counterbalanced by 'natural' perception. The stage actions possibly made for a further differentiation, with the left side at times suggesting a more feminine, familial perspective through the collectively viewed slides, and the right a more masculine and paternal one during Gray's interviews of his father, Rockwell, even if the phone call with the psychiatrist took place on the left and the tent, which tended to be associated with the mother, figured on the right. As a prolonging of the contrast which the predominantly silent *Sakonnet Point* established between the child's imaginary or pre-discursive realm and the adult's symbolic one, *Rumstick Road* also distinguished between, on the one hand, a feminine-gendered objectification, non-verbal screams of hysteria, bodily expression and emotion in The Woman's Dance to a Bach Partita for solo violin, and on the other hand, a masculine-gendered subjectivity and "transitiveness," as well as a logo-centric and analytical control.[13] Short of localising these gender differences in specific zones of the brain, the 'bi-cameral' set evoked the two cerebral hemispheres or eye sockets, sundered by a wedge-shaped technician's booth. This slightly elevated control centre hid an upstage passage, whose side doors, opening onto the public, had been covered with Mylar mirrors, indirectly revealing what went on inside. The backlights silhouetting Gray in his opening address and blinding the spectators, together with their occasional reflections in the booth's mirrored side doors, spelled the inversion of stage and the spectators' 'house', as evidenced in the production's ground plan, which was shaped like an hourglass. Audience and performers were now equally subject to scrutiny, and in an ongoing process, as the changing angle of the mirrored doors kept changing the reflections. And the spectators, as if operating a stereoscope, had to re-connect stage actions spatially separated by the operator's booth, which stood for technology, art, and disjointed perception, much as Gray, who strongly identified with his mother, in the theatrical process came to appreciate his father's perspective, too. Following the same logic, that is, that of an unstable, composite perceptual reality, LeCompte's more secure documentary reliance on family slides, letters, and audiotapes, of Gray's maternal grandmother, of him and his father or the psychiatrist who treated Bette Gray, was complemented by the deceptive presentation of the toy house from *Sakonnet Point* as part of the exterior seen from afar through the window in the set's right-hand back wall. When the domed tent, large enough to hide two adult performers, was moved into the same tunnel-like space behind the window, the laws of Newtonian physics and Euclidean space no longer held, just as when Libby Howes, standing in front of the projected image of Gray's house on *Rumstick Road*, touched its rooftop.

Rumstick Road's different mediations thus resulted once more in a third realm, by juxtaposing, montage-like, inner and outer, the distant and the close-by, artistic and natural reality, memory and dream, stage and house, each threatening to destabilise the other. It was a paradoxical theatrical realm at times as surreal as Alice's narrative or René Magritte's pictorial wonderland. Gray's appearances covered by a white sheet, invoked canvases like *Les amants*, *la ruse symétrique*,

L'invention de la vie, and *L'histoire centrale*. All these works were painted in 1928, the year in which Magritte's father died, though they purportedly deal with his mother's suicide by drowning, in 1912, when René was 14, since her nightdress was wrapped around her head when her body was retrieved from the river Sambre. If I here take the liberty of briefly establishing a parallel with Magritte, it is because LeCompte wants her material to generate a freewheeling, personal response in the interpreters. "[P]laying with images" is positively encouraged.[14] Magritte's paintings, however, tend to defy the viewer in finding the dreams behind the image, dreams whose distensions and compressions resist the anchoring of the referential process, all too often required by psychiatrists and academics. Against such anchoring Magritte's *Les deux mystères*, 1966 explicitly agitates by recycling his famous, *La trahison des images*, 1926 on a blackboard, placed on a painter's easel, below another, larger pipe, appearing on the back wall. As Michel Foucault has argued:

> Everything is solidly anchored within a pedagogic space. [...] a drawing that 'shows' the form of a pipe; a text written by a zealous instructor [...]. We do not see the teacher's pointer, but it rules throughout – precisely like his voice, in the act of articulating – very clearly [...] From painting to image, from image to text, from text to voice, a sort of imaginary pointer indicates, shows, fixes, locates, imposes a system of references, tries to stabilize a unique space.

Still, any effort at stabilizing meaning founders in the welter of negations: "This is not a pipe, but a drawing of a pipe," [...] "This is not a pipe but a sentence saying that this is not a pipe,"[16] [...] "In the sentence 'this is not a pipe,' *this* is not a pipe: the painting, written sentence, drawing of a pipe – all this is not a pipe." Even the pipe-like 'vapor' 'floating' above the blackboard frame, amidst the confusion, is not a pipe.

By jumping the frame of *La trahison des images*, Magritte loosened the image from the words, protected it from being reduced to any singular, trivializing interpretation. Here lies one incentive for LeCompte's early quarrel with Schechner and her ongoing dispute with other academics, over "who owns history",[17] art, knowledge and the concomitant power. Hence, the company's appropriations, a cultural "guerilla"[18] whose mobility and ill-assorted spoil undermine property and the Euclidean properness of place, breach the mutual imposition of signifier and signified, in order to set both afloat. Hence, Ron Vawter's parody of the medical school lecture in *Rumstick Road*, a persona or mask, informed by his having been a military instructor prior to joining the Wooster Group and by the professorship in English at Washington University at St. Louis of Gray's brother, Rockwell Jr.

NAYATT SCHOOL

LeCompte's refusal to anchor the signification process also explains her reframing of the instructor's persona in the third production of the Rhode Island Trilogy. *Nayatt School*, 1978, evolved from Gray's exegesis of *The Cocktail Party*, his first extended monologue. This was a dramaturgical dissection made literal in the clinical examinations around which some of the work's subsequent sections were built, 'A Day at the Dentist' and 'The Chicken Heart', two radio horror skits from Arch Oboler's *Drop Dead*, and Jim Strah's 'The Breast Examination', much as Eliot's play is built around several psychiatrist-patient interviews and has the kind of intricate structure he used to expound with chalk on a blackboard.[19] Refusing to leave it at that, LeCompte had the mock instructor subsequently reappear in *Route 1 & 9 (The Last Act)*, 1981, where Vawter mimicked Clifton Fadiman's scholarly lecture on Thornton Wilder's *Our Town*. A further offshoot of the first trilogy, ever extending its iconography and issues, was Dafoe's playing the male lead in *Tom and Viv* in 1994, Brian Gilbert's movie adaptation of Michael Hastings's 1984 bio drama, based on the disastrous marriage of the Anglophile poet from St. Louis, Missouri, to the British aristocrat Vivien Haigh-Wood, who was interned during the last years of her life, 1938–1947, partly upon Eliot's instigation.[20]

Insofar as Celia Coplestone in *The Cocktail Party*, 1949, is informed by Vivien, *Nayatt School* mapped her character onto that of the mentally unstable Bette Gray, the figure haunting *Rumstick Road* and by extension the Rhode Island Trilogy as a whole. That Bette Gray's mother, Dorothy Spalding 'Wood,' shared her name with Eliot's first wife is one of those coincidences the Wooster Group's method invites and readily exploits. Similarly, Dorothy Wood's Christian Science ideals added context to Bette Gray's religious aspirations and experiences, for example, her allegedly having been visited by Christ, or having floated to the ceiling of the Providence orchestra hall. These in turn resonated with Eliot's conversion to Anglo-Catholicism, with Vawter's time spent in a Franciscan seminary because he wanted to become a military chaplain, and with Celia's joining an austere nursing order, a spiritual sanatorium of sorts. 'Coplestone' actually means 'cornerstone' and is a metaphor of Christ in Mark 12:10.[21] To this associative chain could be added Sir Henry Harcourt Reilly's paternalistic farewell to his patients, "go in peace",[22] a stock phrase in Catholic ritual, accompanying the absolution at the end of confession and Mass.

That the characters' talk of nervous breakdowns and sanatoria was rooted in Eliot's and Vivien's personal experiences, which may seem obvious. Yet, the blatant overlap between an ongoing life and work, is at odds with the modernist sense of closure and Eliot's theory about the objective impersonality of art. Granted, his Flaubertian belief that "The world of a great poetic dramatist is a world in which the creator is everywhere present, and everywhere hidden", from his 1953 lecture "The Three Voices of Poetry", acknowledges life's impact and only shies away from its explicitness in his "acutely personal" art.[23] For LeCompte, who would eventually stage Flaubert's unstageable *tentation de St.Antoine*, biographies form an outspoken and upfront creative mainstay, those of the writers taken an interest in and of her performers, whose personalities are never obliterated by any characters. Thus, Eliot's *The Cocktail Party* also featured prominently in *Nayatt School*, the first canonical text to do so in a Wooster Group production, because Gray acted in the play as a college student and fledgling professional actor, not to mention the prismatic refractions of his mother's plight through Celia and Vivien, diffusing the loss. In addition Eliot's imagination, like LeCompte's, is strongly visual, influenced as he was by paintings like Piero della Francesca's *The Baptism of Christ*, 1448–50, Giovanni Bellini's *The Agony in the Garden,* 1459, and Turner's *The Slave Ship*, 1840.[24] As a student Vawter incidentally read Bernard Berenson's essay on Piero della Francesca, *The Ineloquent in Art*, 1954, and was much impressed by its insistence on being rather than on representing.[25] The Rhode Island Trilogy thereby effected a double displacement, of life 'and' art, each putting the other into perspective, taking turns to 'mask' and expose the other in a game of hide-and-seek, literally so, when a slide of Gray's dead mother was projected onto Libby Howes's face.

Dramatically speaking *The Cocktail Party* presents four characters, the married couple Lavinia and Edward Chamberlayne, and their unacknowledged lovers, Celia and Peter, an aspiring writer and film-maker, at a crossroads in their lives, a notion Eliot derived from Taoism. Ultimately, the paths taken are interrelated and exclusive, as they: "Are only pieces of a total situation […] The single patient\ Who is ill by himself, is rather the exception."[26] In the words of Edith Sitwell, a poetess influenced by Eliot, to the point of conversion, and one from whose *Facade* poems of 1922 Gray recited: "At some point in their marriage Tom went mad, and promptly certified his wife."[27] Eliot's madness was more than figurative, since he had been interned with Vivien on at least two occasions, in Malmaison and Divonne-les-Bains, France. Indirectly, he acknowledges his responsibility for Vivien through one of Celia's lines, read on stage during *Nayatt School* and visually repeated in Ken Kobland's pre-recorded video registration of the staged sequence: "I should really *like* to think there's something wrong with me – Because, if there isn't, then there's something wrong […] With the world itself – and that's much more frightening!"[28]

Celia's tenuous balancing of viewpoints like LeCompte's pairing of live action with its video registration, may well be crucial to grasp the Wooster Group's scenographically induced perspective play, apart from Eliot's interest in Piero della Francesca, author of *On Perspective in Painting*, 1474–1482, and *On the Five Regular Bodies*, a treatise on proportion written after 1482. Throughout *The Cocktail Party*, never "seeing oneself through the eyes of other people"[29] proves problematical, though "to reverse the propositions"[30] either triggers comedy, as during the marital bickering, or opens up tragic vistas, as in Celia's death, an effect of western colonialism. To Edward, her tragedy is a total waste, to Peter the only meaningful event of his stay abroad.[31] Eliot, however, underscores the necessary double perspective and tragicomic interdependence of his characters' plights, only to clinch the plot's conservative resolution. Celia's religious vocation and subsequent crucifixion by the natives of Kinkanja become the precondition for Edward and Lavinia's marital compromise, just as earlier Celia had accepted being his mistress because a divorce would have ruined his career. Even Eliot's own subsequent return to normality, by Reilly's standards a relative state, seems implicated. Ten years after Vivien's death, he surprised everyone by marrying his secretary Valerie Fletcher, as if he were still following his model for *The Cocktail Party*, Euripides' *Alcestis*, 438 BC. There the imminent sacrifice of the eponymous heroine is transformed into a happy end, when Hercules outwrestles Death at the gates of hell and saves the only one willing to die instead of her husband, King Admetus.

The scenography of *Nayatt School* obviated the self-evidence of female victimisation as the condition for social restoration.[32] This tragic if also Christian idea of redemption through sacrifice paradoxically underlies Eliot's comedy of manners and masks a class motif in Celia's relative disenfranchisement, the political unconscious disguised by the mythical archetype, acknowledged through Reilly's song.[33] After all, Celia's parents cannot afford a place in town and she shares a London flat with a cousin, so she is the outsider among the smart set.[34] The Wooster Group therefore exposed the relativity of the characters' respective fates, as laid down by Eliot and already intuited by Gray's exploration of the "self as other".[35] Much like *Rumstick Road*, *Nayatt School* made the spectators aware of their respective positions. Eliot's characters see each other as wish-fulfilling projections. Shifting the ground from psychology to religion, Julia's and Reilly's biblical 'one-eyedness' warns the partygoers to pluck out their sinful eye,[36] that is, to abandon their secular waywardness and love of appearances and go for a more "truthful," religious vision. By analogy the occasional family slide in *Rumstick Road* had been projected upside down making for an erroneous vision.[37] Such vision is not necessarily wrong, no more than any other representation. As with Peter's excursion into Hollywood, Celia's into Africa, and Lavinia's temporary abandonment of her husband, the slide's dislocation was meant to open up new insights. To the same effect *Rumstick Road*'s right-hand trapezoidal room seemed shifted to the left for *Nayatt School*, the room's window now facing forward. In addition, the Performing Garage's division into several disjointed planes, now exploiting the space's full width, had broken up the narrowing perspective of the disciplining set. In the back was the lowest playing area, featuring the skeletal room, its floor raked and tiered by a trough, its roof transparent plexiglas, the red-domed tent, and protruding from it, a long table as if for panel discussions. Closer by, more elevated, stood a second such table behind which the performers could also sit. Several feet higher began the audience bleachers, their tilt, like that of the stage room, defying gravity.

The whole configuration resulted in a strong sense of spatial disproportion and repetition. The implication, for example, that the oversized table might have fitted into the tent again substantiated LeCompte's collapsing of scales or tampering with the laws of Newtonian physics. The same directorial principles governed the condensed re-enactment of *The Cocktail Party*'s final scene, following plain summaries of the dramatic action and selective staged readings. By conflating scales and violating the traditional principle of identity, that scene offered an analogue or parody of the Christian doctrine of transubstantiation underlying the crucifixion and cannibalizing of Celia, as well as followed principles of quantum physics where matter can be particle and wave, simultaneously. Child performers dressed up in adult costumes, doubled the adult performers, appearing diminished when using the trough in the room, just as *Sakonnet Point* had juxtaposed Spalding-the-actor with Spalding-the-boy played by Erik Moskovitz. The unsettling effect was compounded by 'doubled props' such as the long table, disembodied amplified voices coming from the soundproof room and textual images of cancerous growths, natural in an instructional record on breast cancer, and the product of male scientific experiments à la Frankenstein in Oboler's 'Chicken Heart' skit.

Crucial, however, was the inter-medial reproduction of Eliot's text, read and enacted live, heard as pre-recorded by Sir Alec Guinness, and fragmentarily visualised in the subtitles of Kobland's video. The choice of Guinness's performance followed from Gray's former reliance on it as an aspiring actor to study the part of Alex. The Guinness album also extended the Chamberlaynes' argument over the uses of their "good records,"[39] escapism, love of music, not to mention cultural status in an upper-class home regularly becoming the setting for much talked of social events. In fact, the 1949 premiere of *The Cocktail Party* at the Edinburgh Festival, then in its third year, was a celebration of high culture, drawing the beau monde to the Lyceum theatre in order to acclaim a writer who had been awarded the Nobel Prize in November 1948 and an actor whom Harold Hobson in his review compared to Gielgud, Olivier and Richardson.[40] To that extent the proliferation of Eliot's text in *Nayatt School* materialised the authorial oppressiveness of the playwright's words and of acting models like Guinness, besides conveying the endless dissemination and mediation of cultural products in general.

Granted the irony of Gray's subsequent career as a monologist, *Nayatt School*'s logorrhea became a symptom of the patriarchal logo-centrism founding the canonised drama around which the production revolved. The traditional performer, identifying with the character, and the priest transmitting the 'Word of God', are both authorised by speaking the prescribed words. Recognising all too well the dangers of Reilly's ordainment, Vawter insisted on limiting the performative investiture to a "stand-in".[40] In Lyotard's terminology of "lieutenancy" it nonetheless retains its military connotations of empowerment.[41] Aptly so, for these found, if not excuse, the sacrifice of Alcestis and the scapegoating of Celia, so the order at home and abroad can be restored. At the same time, *Nayatt School*'s logorrhea disrupted Eliot's logo-centrism. Taking advantage of Eliot's intuition that certain experiences, "can only be hinted at in myths and images",[42] LeCompte followed the deconstructionists' method of seeking out the texts' weaknesses, the fissures in its argument. The logorrhea thus complemented the scenographic refraction of a singular and continuous centralising perspective, installing and supporting an omniscient, authoritative view. Ironically, Eliot defended the return to verse drama on the grounds that poetry multiplies the interpretative possibilities, allowing each spectator to take from it whatever s/he pleases, to the point even of utter disagreement. "[B]ecause if you read an explanation by a literary critic and entirely agree, the thing is finished. One should never entirely agree with any literary critic." Eliot also freely revised his dramatic work upon suggestions by Martin Browne.[43]

POINT JUDITH – AN EPILOGUE

LeCompte's self-conscious participation in this process of perspective and cultural dispersal also transpired in *Point Judith*, 1979,[44] the epilogue to the Rhode Island Trilogy. The slide projections in *Rumstick Road* had been very much confined to the back wall of one inner room, its side door occasionally refracting the images. In *Nayatt School* the filmic refractions were doubled and deflected onto the back wall of the theatre. But in *Point Judith* the images were sent into orbit through the Performing Garage, lighting up above the, now roofless, frame house and against the upstage wall for Kobland's colour video, *By the Sea*, or downstage on a hand-held screen for the black-and-white home movie of the nuns in Kobland's video. Textually, *Point Judith* parodied Eugene O'Neill's *Long Day's Journey into Night*, a highly autobiographical play resounding with echoes of Irish folk legends and several literary classics. Like *The Cocktail Party*, *Long Day's Journey* is a play Gray appeared in, notably as Edmund, in 1966, and like Eliot's text, O'Neill's reconfigures and develops central concerns of the Rhode Island Trilogy such as, hereditary illness, sacrifice, religious and artistic transcendence, perception. Of course, the very idea of a theatrical trilogy with an epilogue ever recycling texts, figures, and themes, already implies a visual and dramatic recursive nature. The composite portrait of Gray ended up resembling a triptych encompassing his biographical and theatrical families, whose members were shown to harbour different identities, refracted over time and space. Finally, the posthumous release in 1956 of this 1941 play in which O'Neill, going by the epigraph, managed, "to face [his] dead at last"[45] provides a somewhat specious substantiation of the postmodern 'death of the author.' The playwright even named his dramatic alter ego, Edmund, after his dead infant brother, and reserved his own name, Eugene, for the play's deceased.

Still, *Long Day's Journey* is as good a case of logo-centrism as *The Cocktail Party*. A picture of Shakespeare, as the epi-centre of the western canon, takes pride of place in the Tyrones' living room and Lao Tzu's 'Ching', or classic, to some even 'sacred' text, inspired the major image of O'Neill's title.[46] Equally important is the logo-centric alignment of Edmund's, O'Neill's, and the spectators' views,[47] their joint conscription on this personally liberating journey finished in 'Tao' House. And as in *The Cocktail Party*, liberation comes at a considerable cost. On this journey the male trinity of James Tyrone Sr., Jamie and Edmund assumes the position of omniscient observer, unceasingly keeping its eyes on Mary, ever watchful for signs of her renewed narcotic tripping. Even beyond their purview, in the upstairs spare room, she imagines herself observed, objectified by their transcendent or "panoptic intuition",[48] their "seeing" without seeing or being seen. Once Mary has relapsed and exposed herself by the physical effects of the morphine injections showing in her eyes, she is given up. Instead of being freed by not being looked at censoriously, she now lacks any existence at all.

As often happens in realist American drama, each of these characters' sidetracked lives is tied to the notion of place. The tension between rootedness and exile, or imprisonment and escape, makes for what Una Chaudhuri has called the characters' geopathology. Important in this regard is the seaside setting of this play invaded by the past. O'Neill wrote *Long Day's Journey* in the mountain-enclosed Tao House, Danville, California. Yet, the liminality of the Tyrones' house within view of the harbour and waterfront recalls that of the abandoned coast guard station on Peaked Hill Bar,[49] Provincetown, where, from 1919 onwards, O'Neill worked during the summers, his writing there an analogue for "heaving anchor."[50] After O'Neill had given the house to his son, Eugene Jr., it was literally reclaimed by the encroaching sea 10th January 1931.[51] Of course, The Wharf Theatre, Provincetown, the former fish house where O'Neill's career as a performed playwright had begun in 1916 with *Bound East for Cardiff*, stood in the water. To the extent that its makeshift structure threatened to be washed away with each high tide it was a perfect emblem of the theatre's evanescence, if also of the shiftlessness of O'Neill Sr. and his son's subsequent careers, or the vicissitudes of the Wooster Group ever searching for sponsors, losing company members, being threatened by censorship.

For all that, performance may well "succeed[s], where addiction fails." Says Chaudhuri: "A muted metatheatricality runs like a fault line through the plays of [...] O'Neill [...] sending tremors up and down the otherwise solidly mimetic edifice of realism."[52] In Michael Selmon's analysis, too, Mary's re-appropriation of Tyrone's theatrics in the 'mad-Ophelia' scene may well signify a re-empowerment.[53] Too bad if, with O'Neill's self-reflexive turn, the realist notion of a singular, well-delineated character joins that of the traditional author in an inter-textual, performative limbo. There, the spectator's gaze will keep the fragmentary and ghostly figures of O'Neill's composite portrait alive, as long as it is a mobile gaze, anything but the transfixing, panoptic one. Within the theatre, the building's spatial configuration or the director and scenographers' choices must safeguard the gaze's mobility, to avoid a renewed victimisation like that implied by the disciplining, stereoscopic set of *Rumstick Road*. Otherwise, Gray's study of "one who sees himself, seeing himself" would only have duplicated the panoptic structure of "watchers-being-watched", which *Long Day's Journey* is.[54] Hence, in the Wooster Group's parody of any central authority, Gray travestied Tyrone, the father figure, and a twelve-year-old boy, Edmund. Selmon's belief that any explicit enactment of the private surveillance of O'Neill's play in the public realm of the theatre already "countermands" its "panoptic force" seems overly optimistic.[55] The mutation of the disciplinarian paradigm into the performative one as documented by McKenzie, indicates as much.[56] Selmon has granted the present day survival of the panoptic mechanism. That Selmon reappraises O'Neill Sr.'s melodrama, rather than praising his son for transcending that tradition and its stereotypical portrayals of women, fits Eliot's and LeCompte's drawing inspiration from the popular theatre, as evidenced in Reilly's drinking song[57] and the two skits from Oboler used in *Nayatt School*. Selmon's interpretation also underscores the performative challenge Mary issues to her husband in his own melodramatic terms. Behind her theatrical mask Mary briefly escapes the panopticon, and affects an absenting trick, self-controlled, this time, and to her own advantage, since she manages to escape to the spring of her senior year when she was happily in love. In character Mary can be anywhere and nowhere, defy the laws of physics, like Edmund on the square-rigger's bowsprit.

Following Mary's example, LeCompte in *Point Judith* re-appropriated O'Neill's classic as the last of four party pieces, disrupting the routine of four workers on an oil rig. The setting is supposed to be the Gulf of Mexico, though Point Judith, like the trilogy's other titles, is a place in Rhode Island on the Sound's mouth, opposite Sakonnet Point. In addition, the title evokes the biblical character whose apocryphal story Cathleen, the maid, reads in the show's predominantly silent, final section. Judith is the Jewish heroine who saved the Israelis by secretly conveying herself to the tent of the Assyrian general Holofernes, to seduce and behead him. As such the story supports Mary's final empowerment by means of performance. It also forms an analogue to LeCompte's directorial prerogatives with regard to the male playwrights recycled and her becoming the organisational, if not experiential centre within the Wooster Group after Gray's departure. By self-consciously exploiting O'Neill's meta-theatricality, LeCompte further dismantled the illusionary realist edifice, as well as exposed melodrama's gendered discrimination and sentimental pieties, such as faith and family, both pertaining to Eliot and Gray, too. The Wooster Group thereby maintained the momentum of the "infinite regress of performance and counterperformance" in O'Neill's play, finding, as with *The Cocktail Party*, an answer to the staging in the text itself.[58]

The set of *Point Judith* recycled the skeletal room from *Nayatt School* though initially it was kept hidden behind a curtain, which limited the playing area to the foreground for the opening card game among the rig workers. The subsequent fifteen-minute travesty of O'Neill's long-winded family drama with manically speeded-up actions hardly burst the spatial confines of the room. The selected lines heard on audio tracks were drowned by Berlioz's *Requiem* and the story, narrated by Stew, the foreman (Gray), and mimed by him and his crew, was viciously terminated when Tyrone (doubled by Gray) shot his entire family, just as in the cocktail party ending of *Nayatt School* Edward shot Peter, and the children doubling the adults one by one died. The temporal and textual reduction, the parody style, and the revised end, all radically contained the traditional impact and significance of *Long Day's Journey*. So did the frame. The production's opening section was taken up entirely by the card game and by the first three party pieces, songs by the Kid (Hansell), BB (Dafoe) and Dan (Vawter). The closing section consisted of Kobland's *By the Sea*. Cued by Mary Tyrone's religious candidature and Gray's one-time performance of *The Cocktail Party* in a nunnery in upstate New York, the video recreated the daily routine of a religious order, as set down in *The Book of Hours*. For this purpose the stage room had been set on stilts, like a rig, amidst the waves of the Long Island Sound. It was as if the Wharf Theatre in Provincetown had merged with the life station on Peaked Hill Bar and floated down the sea of time. The cultural flotsam and jetsam even included Giotto's *Annunciation to St. Anne*, 1305, for the stage room, now with bed and sheet curtain, a stage within the stage, had been modelled after this fresco in the Arena Chapel, Padua. The set's anachronistic antenna piercing the sky, however, reprised the strange incident from Bette Gray's life of a partridge crashing through two windows and a curtain, before knocking over the television aerial and dropping dead on the table, as if anticipating its more down-to-earth fate as a Saturday night dinner.[59] The idea of Revelation, finally, had fed Vawter's former dream of being parachuted into Cambodia or the Dominican Republic to "dispense spiritual gifts" as a "green beret chaplain".[60]

Apart from activating a plurality of associations, Kobland's video re-established the spatial recursive and perspective play of *Nayatt School*. By taking the plywood set into the open the Wooster Group first inverted realist art's "fundamental dislocation," which "makes of nature", that is, external reality, "a mere setting – scenery".[61] The company then doubled back on its tracks by projecting the cinematographic recreation of that excursion within the artificial surroundings of the theatre performance, a countermove to the male performers' exit onto Wooster Street after their theatrical romp, leaving Cathleen to clean up the mess during the finale. More recently, Kobland's video resurfaced in *Half Air*, the exhibition of paintings, drawings, video, and photography by avant-garde artists, curated by the Wooster Group member Clay Hapaz, together with Elisabeth Ivers and Jay Sanders, and running at Marianne Boesky's Gallery, New York, from 8th July – 29th August 2003. Short of halting the endless recursive reflections of art and life as in opposite mirrors, the art world's conspicuous institutional framework would seem to have clinched the Wooster Group's systematic attack on the illusionism of realist theatre.

In the process, O'Neill's naturalistic concept of character and environment as immutable fate sustained heavy damages, too. Given Mary's isolation within the male-dominated household, the gender distribution of *Rumstick Road*'s stereoscopic set had become more marked in *Point Judith*, possibly compounded by O'Neill's melodrama. After all, O'Neill's men either idealise women or denigrate them when the reality strays from the projection. In both cases the men turn the women into fascinating objects, whether of piety as with Mary or perversion with the character of Fat Violet, ascribing them Medusa-like powers as an excuse for their panoptic imprisonment. Accordingly the sexist, all-male card game of the opening, whose antagonisms prefigured those in O'Neill's family, and were further transposed in Stew's rowdy 'Party Piece', was paired off with the ritually composed, all female activities of the convent, albeit performed by the men 'rigged' out in drag. Going by LeCompte's own comments, the oil rig and convent played off fantasies of male and female isolation.[62] As such they constituted biased extremes of gender-based identities whose metaphorical representations are determined by place. Still, the meditative video, in which the camera like a lighthouse scanned the seashore, with far off, the cooling tower of a nuclear power plant, provided an outlet for the rig workers' aggressiveness and O'Neill's accusatory family quarrels, as filtered through the coarse performance of the men. These had to shout down their own taped voices, simultaneously played back at high volume, thus precluding any identification with the parts. In the material and bodily emphasis of these riotous moments, the discrete, objective presence or visibility of the props, lawnmower, garden hose, vacuum cleaner were also asserted, their refusal to be regimented into an overarching fiction. But no matter how overwhelming Stew's Party Piece may have been for actors and spectators alike, the hectic style of the abridged O'Neill play functioned as a precondition for the hard won, provisional composure of the end sequence.

The technique of pitting the performers' voices against loud music had already been used in *Nayatt School*, where a disco tune *Love in C Minor* cheapened and undermined the peace Reilly (Gray) wished Celia (Joan Jonas) at the end of the staged reading of their private encounter. And in keeping with Eliot's evocation of that moment when human beings join the material realm,[63] LeCompte also had the concluding cocktail party erupt into an improvised chaos. Instead of objectively documenting Bette Gray's madness, as in *Rumstick Road*, the mourning of her death now became a riotous celebration.[64] The child performers screamed, danced, and knocked over plastic glasses, while the adults finally desecrated the records, chopping, smashing, and burning them, even penetrating them with electric drills and faking masturbation with the fanolas's arms to the overwhelming sound of a hymn. Presumably Eliot would have considered the outrage in tasteless excess of its composite objective correlative, Edward's personal hatred of his wife's records, the repressions of the upper class, and Eliot and Guinness' canonical status. But, then at Harvard, Eliot also wrote pornographic poetry and the storm-scape in his beloved *Slave Ship* radically contrasts with the measured Albertian perspective of Piero's *Baptism of Christ* or the serene composition of Giotto's *Annunciation*. In *Nayatt School*, however, the mayhem was concluded by composure equally ambiguous as that in *Point Judith*. From the seclusion of the plywood room Gray lost himself in Bach's Partita for solo violin, while thirty feet above his head, on a narrow ledge, standing in for his parents, a half-naked Vawter and Howes were skirting the back wall of the Performing Garage. To Vawter the scene visually evoked Masaccio's *Expulsion from the Garden of Eden*, 1426–7, but the mood may have been closer to that of a flight from the production's madness, as well as from the pretenses and consequences of Eliot's theological realm.[65] The scene thus prefigured the geo-pathological broiling of exile and escape, marking the epilogue to the Rhode Island Trilogy.

CODA: LIFE, ART – UNDONE

Spalding Gray, born 1941 was twenty-six when his mother was asphyxiated in her car. Increasingly he developed her symptoms of manic-depression, for which his collective work with the Wooster Group and his subsequent monologues became a form of therapy. Nevertheless, he made attempts on his life and had to be hospitalised for depression. On 10th January 2004, he was reported missing after finishing a run of *Life Interrupted* at P.S.122. This was a reworking of *Black Spot*, the monologue in which he had tried to come to terms with a debilitating car accident but which had to be cancelled after another suicide attempt. On Sunday, 7th March 2004 Gray's body was dragged from the East River near Greenpoint, Brooklyn.[66] It is believed he jumped off the Staten Island Ferry. In the retrospective light of the Rhode Island Trilogy the manner and place of Gray's final crossing assume the deeper significance of an environmental staging of sorts, another confrontation with himself. To paraphrase the *Four Quartets*,[67] used in rehearsals of *Nayatt School* and as motto for Gray's monologue, *Morning, Noon, and Night*.[68] 1999, in the end was his beginning. Or to close with Gray's own words, framing *Impossible Vacation*,[69] 1992, he had, "half dreamed and half remembered [his] Mom's never-ending passion for the sea" and, "At last [must have felt] driving home," "to Gram's summer house in Sakonnet, Rhode Island," "driving straight for the Atlantic Ocean."

Notes

1. de Certeau, M., *The Practice of Everyday Life*, Berkeley: California University Press, 1984, p.117.
2. LeCompte, E., 'An Introduction', *Performing Arts Journal*, 3.2, fall 1978, pp.81–86.
3. Bierman, J., 'Three Places in Rhode Island', *The Drama Review*, 23.1, T81, March 1979, pp.13–30.
4. Gray, S., 'About Three Places in Rhode Island,' *The Drama Review*, 23.2, T81, March 1979, pp.34–35.
5. Savran, D., *Breaking the Rules: The Wooster Group*, New York: Theatre Communications Group, 1988 [1986], p.61, p.133, p.157.
6. Stills of the Rhode Island Trilogy productions can be found in the archive section of the performance company's website at .
7. Savran, *Breaking the Rules: The Wooster Group*, p.59.
8. Kirby, M., *The Art of Time: Essays on the Avant-Garde*, New York: Dutton, 1969, pp.225–233.
9. Schechner, R., 'Six Axioms for Environmental Theatre', *The Drama Review*, 12, spring 1968, pp.41–64.
10. Wooster Group, The, 'Rumstick Road', *Performing Arts Journal*, 3.2, fall 1978, pp.92–115.
11. Savran, *Breaking the Rules: The Wooster Group*, p.75.
12. Eliot, T. S., *The Cocktail Party*, London: Faber, 1950, p.35.
13. Savran, *Breaking the Rules: The Wooster Group*, p.87.
14. Gray, S., 'Playwright's Notes', *Performing Arts Journal*, 3.2, fall 1978, pp.87–91, p.88, p.91.
15. Foucault, M., *This Is Not a Pipe*, edited, introduced and translated by Harkness, J., Berkeley: California University Press, 1982 [1973, 1968], pp. 29–30.
16. Ibid., p.30.
17. LeCompte, E., 'Who Owns History?', *Performing Arts Journal*, 6.1, 16, 1981, pp.50–53.
18. Savran, *Breaking the Rules: The Wooster Group*, p.157.
19. Ackroyd, P., *T. S. Eliot*, London: Hamish Hamilton, 1984, p. 244 and figure 57.
20. Seymour-Jones, C., *Painted Shadow*, London: Constable, 2001.
21. McCarthy, J. A., 'T. S. Eliot and Logocentrism in a Post-Conversion Work: *The Cocktail Party*,' *Yeats Eliot Review* 13.1–2, summer 1994, pp.37–41, p.40.
22. Eliot, T. S., *The Cocktail Party*, London: Faber, 1950, p.126, p.142.
23. Schuchard, R., *Eliot's Dark Angel: Intersections of Life and Art,* New York: Oxford University Press, 1999, p.3.
24. Spender, S., *Eliot*, Glasgow: Fontana, 1977 [1975], p. vii, pp.128–9.
25. Berenson, B., *The Ineloquent in Art*, London: Chapman & Hall, New York: Macmillan, 1954, p.40 in Savran, *Breaking the Rules: The Wooster Grou*p, p.53.
26. Eliot, *The Cocktail Party*, p.114.
27. Hastings, M., *Tom and Viv*, Harmondsworth: Penguin, 1985 [1984], p.11.
28. Eliot, *The Cocktail Party*, p.130.
29. Ibid., p. 97.
30. Ibid., p.123.
31. Ibid., p.170.
32. Gray, S., 'About Three Places in Rhode Island', *The Drama Review*, 23.2, p.42.
33. Eliot, *The Cocktail Party*, p.38 in Browne, M., *The Making of T. S. Eliot's Plays*, Cambridge: Cambridge University Press, 1969, p.174.
34. Browne, M., *The Making of T. S. Eliot's Plays*, p.131.
35. Gray, S., 1979, p.35.
36. Matthew 18:9.

37. McCarthy, 'T. S. Eliot and Logocentrism in a Post-Conversion Work: *The Cocktail Party*', *Yeats Eliot Review* 13.1–2, p.38.

38. Eliot, *The Cocktail Party*, p.97.

39. Browne, *The Making of T. S. Eliot's Plays*, p.241.

40. Savran, *Breaking the Rules: The Wooster Group*, p.114.

41. Lyotard, J-F., 'The Tooth, The Palm', translated by Anne Knap and Michel Benamou, *Sub-Stance* 15, (1976), pp.105–110, p.110.

42. Eliot, *The Cocktail Party*, p.175.

43. Browne, M., *The Making of T. S. Eliot's Plays*, pp.236–7.

44. Wooster Group, The, 'Point Judith', *Zone* 7, spring 1981, pp.14–27.

45. O'Neill, E., *Complete Plays 1932–1943*, Bogard, T., (ed.), New York: Library of America, 1988, p.714.

46. Floyd, V., 'Eugene O'Neill's *Tao Te Ching*: The Spiritual Evolution of a Mystic', pp.3–12, in Liu, H., and Swortzell, L., (eds), *Eugene O'Neill in China*, Westport: Greenwood Press, 1992, p.3; also see Robinson, J. A, 'Iceman and Journey, Yin and Yang: Taoist Rhythm and O'Neill's Late Tragedies' in, Liu and Swortzell, pp. 21–27, p.21.

47. Schmitt, N. C., *Actors and Onlookers, Theater and Twentieth-Century Scientific Views of Nature*, Evanston: Northwestern University Press, 1990, pp. 57–59.

48. McDonald, D., 'The Phenomenology of the Glance in *Long Day's Journey into Night*', *Theatre Journal* 31, 1979, pp.343–356, p.348.

49. O'Neill, E., *Complete Plays 1932–1943*, Bogard, T., (ed.), New York: Library of America, 1988, p.717.

50. Gelb, A. and B., *O'Neill*, NY: Harper and Row, 1973 [1962], p.393.

51. Ibid., pp.552–3.

52. Ibid., p.58.

53. Selmon, M., '"Like…So Many Small Theatres': The Panoptic and the Theatric in *Long Day's Journey into Night*," *Modern Drama*, 40.4, winter 1997, pp.526–39.

54. McDonald, p.343.

55. Selmon, p.527.

56. McKenzie, J., *Perform or Else: From Discipline to Performance*, London: Routledge, 2001.

57. Schuchard, R., Eliot's Dark Angel: Intersections of Life and Art, New York: Oxford University Press, 1999, p.117.

58. Orr, J., in Chaudhuri, U., *Staging Place: The Geography of Modern Drama*, Ann Arbor: Michigan University Press, 1995, p.275, n12.

59. Savran, *Breaking the Rules: The Wooster Group*, p.100.

60. Ibid., p.128.

61. Chaudhuri, *Staging Place: The Geography of Modern Drama*, p.55.

62. Savran, *Breaking the Rules: The Wooster Group*, p.138.

63. Eliot, *The Cocktail Party*, pp.34–35.

64. Savran, *Breaking the Rules: The Wooster Group*, p.102.

65. Ibid., Savran, D., *Breaking the Rules: The Wooster Group*, p.132.

66. McKinley, J., 'Spalding Gray, 62, Actor and Monologuist, Is Confirmed Dead', *New York Times* 8th March, 2004.

67. Eliot, T. S., *Four Quartets*, NY: Harcourt, Brace and World, 1971 [1943].

68. Gray, S., *Morning, Noon and Night*, New York: Farrar, Straus and Giroux, 1999.

69. Gray, S., *Impossible Vacation: A Novel*, New York: Knopf, 1992.

PHYSICALITY AND VIRTUALITY
MEMORY, SPACE AND ACTOR ON THE MEDIATED STAGE

Thea Brejzek

The focus in both my practical work as an opera director working with electronic media on the stage and my academic research lies on the discourse between actor and technology and the integration of electronic media in the stage, both within the classical repertoire and in transdisciplinary projects. With recourse to some recent productions, an analysis of the practical and theoretical reformulation of the theatrical body and space representations on the mediated stage is suggested. With Deleuze it will be shown that the central characteristics of the mediated stage lie in the conceptualization and design of the coalescence between actuality and virtuality, between materiality and immateriality and between physicality and virtuality. Deleuze's notion of the crystal image that contains the ever alternating image between actuality and virtuality that is located in the mirror, is central to the idea brought forward, of the mediated stage as an infinitely folded space of possibilities.

"In a mediated world there are no longer places in the sense we once knew them."

Peter Eisenman.

"sont liés dans une affinité turbulente et insistente: ces deux expériences ne privilègent-elles pas une certaine autorité de la présence et de la visibilité?...Mais si, depuis toujours l'invisible travaille le visible, si par exemple la visibilité du visible – ce qui rend visible la chose visible – n'est pas visible, alors une certaine nuit vient creuser d'abîme la présentation même du visible. Elle vient laisser place, dans la représentation de soi, à cette parole par essence invisible, venue du dessous du visible."

Jacques Derrida.

"Doch zwischen dem Theater und der Alchemie besteht eine noch höhere Ähnlichkeit, die in metaphysischer Hinsicht sehr viel weiter führt. Die Alchemie wie das Theater sind nämlich sozusagen virtuelle Künste, die ihren Sinn und ihre Wirklichkeit nicht in sich selbst tragen."

Antonin Artaud.

On the basis of five media stage productions between 1996 and 2004 directed by the author, directing concepts and design processes are introduced that contrast the physical stage with a virtual space or, rather, that inscribe a virtual space onto the physical one. Starting from Deleuze's localisation of the crystal image as a receptacle of the mutual image between actuality and virtuality in the 'mobile' mirror,[1] the central role of physical and virtual mirrors in four music theatre productions and one interactive mobile robotic installation are understood as a conceptual development in the interplay between music; time/memory, performer; physicality/memory and space; virtuality/memory. The central concern of this chapter is in regards to the mediated stage which is developed through in the concept and design of the coalescence between actuality and virtuality, between physicality and disembodiment and between materiality and immateriality.

From the physical mirrors in Verdi's *Rigoletto,* Wellington 1996, to the production of Richard Strauss' *Ariadne auf Naxos*, Sydney 1997 and 2002, that was inspired by the notion of baroque virtuality, to the mirrored memory space in the world premiere of Peter Eötvös' *As I Crossed a Bridge of Dreams*, Donaueschingen 1999, Paris 2000, and from the vocal interactivity of the music-performance-installation *Memoria Futura Bacon*, Vienna 2001, to the interactive robotic mobile

Figure 31. Performance still, Ariadne auf Naxos, Opera Australia 2002

installation *ExpoRobots*, Expo2000 Hannover, Hammamatsu, Japan 2004, through this range of mixed-media stage productions discussed here, we can see their common concern is found in the extension of the physical stage towards a virtual space: where the use of physical mirrors and/or the utilization of digital media, memory is visualised on the mediated stage.

Each stage director knows well the impetus to reflect on one's own artistic projects in regard to conceptual and visual 'leitmotifs'. In the daily run of rehearsals, however, the distance necessary for such a critical view is not existent, if it was present, it would disturb the intense communication between director, creative team and performers. After opening night the director's eye is already focussed towards the next production. The retrospective view of one's own work thus seems to be desired, but is impossible in reality, destructive even as it implies the director's distancing from practice. For the author, however, the reading of *Time-Image. Cinema 2* by the French philosopher Gilles Deleuze in the years 1998/99 meant a rising consciousness in regard to her own 'line' of directing.[2]

Whilst being busy with the first conceptual sketches for Donaueschingen New Music Festival 1999, that involved complex mirror/space constellations, Deleuze's analysis of the relationship between mirror, mirror image and the space within the mirror, opened a theoretical space that enabled the retrospective view, to productions before 1998, and ahead, towards productions in planning, as it seemed to describe the meaning of mirrors for the time-space structure in a mediated theatrical space. Meanwhile, the production of Verdi's *Rigoletto* for Wellington State Opera, 1996, utilizes the classical semi-transparent theatre mirror as a psychological projection surface and in this context media selection and design happen on the grounds of the individual psychology of the character of Rigoletto.

Richard Strauss' *Ariadne auf Naxos*, 1997, 2002, a production for Opera Australia in the Sydney Opera House follows the slogan, 'Baroque meets Techno', and the choice of media, motorised

Figure 32.Visualisation, As I Crossed a Bridge of Dreams, *Donaueschingen 1999, Paris 2000*

Figure 33.Video Still, ExpoRobots, *Hammamatsu, 2004*

mirrors, large-scale video and slide projection, are to be understood as contemporary analogies of baroque stage virtuality complete with reflections, apparitions and flying machines.

The quotational character of the opera and its ironic refractions meet their analogy in the conscious quotational character of set and costumes.[3]

In the world premiere of Peter Eötvös' sound theatre piece *As I Crossed a Bridge of Dreams*, Donaueschingen 1999, and Paris 2000, semi-transparent mirror, video projection and transparent gauzes serve as media for the reconstruction of the protagonist's memory, a court lady from eleventh-century Japan.

The interactive mobile robotic installation *ExpoRobots*, realised for Expo2000 Hannover and for Pacific Flora, Hammamatsu 2004, deals thematically with bionic structures and their technological equivalents.

Especially the model of the natural bird swarm, seen as a highly complex, de-centrally and non-hierarchically organised network, which opens the space towards the equally de-centrally organised communication and knowledge navigation system of the Internet. There are 72 robotic objects following a complex software programme which moved both singularly and in de-centrally organised swarms through a darkened space of approximately 3000 square metres. They react in their paths with each other as well as with the audience that is moving freely through the space. Onto the inner skin of the semi-transparent fibre glass objects, video sequences are projected that deal artistically with the themes of communication technology and bionics. These video sequences, again, are supported through a twelve-channel programme swarm behaviour and interactivity programme. Through interactivity and audience participation acts, the inherent visual memory of the robots is activated, forming multiples of collective recollections throughout the large space.

Memoria Futura Bacon, Lopes/Brejzek, first staged in 2001, in the open space of the Schauspielhaus Vienna, describes an interactive performance installation with live mix 3D video projection and live mix sound. In a reversal of the traditional stage-audience geography, the four actors and two singers are placed on pedestals within a media space and thus exposed to the voyeurism of an audience, which is free to move around the space. In *Memoria Futura Bacon*, a reflection on Francis Bacon's technoid fantasy *New Atlantis*, first published in 1624, a virtual and interactive musical space is inscribed onto the media stage, evoked by interactive vocal loops by the six singer-performers.

THE PRACTICE AND THEORY OF THE MEDIATED STAGE

Each of the five projects discussed above takes as its central themes the mental concepts of 'memory' and 'recollection', be it in the form of an individual's memory (Rigoletto, Ariadne, Japanese court lady), be it in the form of a collective memory as in an interactive real-time composition as in *Memoria Futura Bacon*, or as in the case of the *ExpoRobots*, with the inherent visual memory of mobile robotic objects. The visualisation or vocalisation of memory has been designed utilizing both 'old' and 'new' media: from the classical semi-transparent theatre mirror in *Rigoletto* and *As I Crossed a Bridge of Dreams*, to digitally constructed large-scale video projections in *Ariadne*, to interactively navigated vocalisations in *Memoria Futura Bacon* and interactively and motion-controlled video sequences for the *ExpoRobots*.

Independently from the utilized analogue, digital or digital-interactive media a virtual space opens up in the mirror, in the mirrored video image, or in the semi-transparent skin of a robotic object that contrasts with the actual space surrounding it. Any virtual space corresponding with the actual space is a dynamic and a constantly renewing space in which multiple performative processes occur. These serve to temporarily invent all the parameters of the perception of time and space: presence, past, future and proprioception – that is, the perception of one's own body and of the bodies of others in the stage environment. In the collaboration of director and media artist on the mediated stage the qualities of performativity, namely the constructed, the made and the provisory nature of the stage event, are emphasized.

In contrast to the classical, built theatre space the mediated theatre space, is liberated from a linear time axis: it is competent in the communication and visualisation of the temporal structures of simultaneity, of anticipation and of recollection. Thus, the virtual space constitutes a space in which parallel to the actual action, to the actual set constellation and to the actual lighting state, inner psychological processes of one or more protagonists can be visualised explicitly. Such alternative processes or states may be dreams, moments of recollection and memory, wishes, anticipations or emotions, which are contrasted with the actual emotions on the stage.

Popular notions of virtuality and the construction and reception of mediated theatrical spaces associate these directly with digital, as supposed to analogue, media and with interactive constellations. 'Unorthodox' opinions, however, are much more useful for an analysis of any mediated theatrical practice by placing it within historical and contemporary continuities. Such an 'unorthodox' point of view defines as 'interactive' not only digital and computer-based installations with participatory character, but emphasizes the inherent characteristics of interactivity. This refers primarily to the dialogue character of an artwork but also, in more general terms, to a psychological interactivity as the conceptual basis of a painting, a sculpture, an installation, of theatre, cinema and photography:

> When we use the concept of 'interactive media' exclusively in relation to computer-based media, there is a danger that we interpret, 'interaction' literally, equating it with physical interaction between a user and a media object (pressing a button, choosing a link, moving the body), at the sake of psychological interaction. The psychological processes of filling-in, hypothesis forming, recall and identification, which are required for us to comprehend any text or image at all, are mistakenly identified with an objectively existing structure of interactive links.[4]

Lev Manovich differentiates an implicit interactivity in the sense of a mental dialogue between artwork and viewer, and an explicit interactivity that is based on audience participation, essentially from an interactive man-machine-dialogue. In the theatre context this means that even in an analogue/digital and non-interactive stage situation, interactive strategies and principles may be both formally and aesthetically effective. This is valid in particular for the principle of immersion that denotes the 'diving' of actor or viewer/participant into virtual spaces as seen in *Ariadne*, and *Memoria Futura Bacon*, and the principle of disembodiment resulting from the tension between the three-dimensional figure of the performer and his two-dimensional portrait in a physical or virtual mirror, as in *Rigoletto*, and *As I Crossed A Bridge of Dreams*.

VIRTUALITY AND ACTUALITY: THE MEDIATED STAGE BETWEEN PHYSICALITY AND DISEMBODIMENT

Independently from a man-machine-dialogue that may open up a virtual space by binary decisions, and in which the participant may navigate with a joystick, a data helmet or glove, the virtual space in the stage productions introduced, is located within a physical mirror or 'flows' through specific design and media solutions into the immersively designed, three-dimensional media space of the proscenium stage. The term 'virtuality' is used here following Bergson's and Deleuzes' systematic and primarily philosophically coined notions of time and space.[5] Alliez describes Deleuze's philosophical oeuvre as an "ontology of the virtual", or as a "materialism of the virtual."[6] With recourse to Bergson's notion of the duration, Deleuze understands the virtual space as constantly referring to an actual space.[7] The memory or the mirror describe the bridge between them and constitute at the same time the receptacle of the virtual image. Deleuze localises the virtual image in the mirror itself, as the receptacle of the crystal image that denotes 'the pure' memory or recollection. The real object, 'the actor', is reflected in the mirror image and in the virtual image, the mapping or the image in the mirror, while the virtual object at the same time surrounds and reflects the real object.

Thus, there exists a coalescence between the real and the virtual object. Embedded in the notion of coalescence is the notion of the psychological localisation or the meta-body of the protagonist. Both concept and design of the Deleuzian coalescence are in this sense the main areas of innovation on the mediated stage.

"The transformation of the body by the means of mirrors and projections towards a two-dimensionality contains the dematerialisation and thus a development towards a meta-physical body that reflects the relationship between body and consciousness."[8] In the simultaneous employment of physical and disembodied representations the extension of the performer's body by a virtual or imaginary dimension is inscribed. What lies at the centre of the tension between actuality and virtuality in the workings of the mediated stage, however, is the construction of the virtual, of the 'potential' body, the 'other' in the mirror.

Whether the performer in *As I Crossed a Bridge of Dreams* is communicating with her alter ego, the trombonist, through the semi-transparent mirror, whether Rigoletto with his dead daughter at his feet is constructing an ideal daughter in a virtual mirror scenario, or whether Ariadne's fragmented, reflected body cannot be separated anymore from her projected places of memory, each time the coalescence between the actual and the virtual body on the stage has been constructed in such a way that the virtual body enables the protagonist on the stage to continue to live, as in *Rigoletto*, to continue to communicate as in *As I Crossed a Bridge of Dreams* or to remember as in *Ariadne*. Thus, actuality and virtuality are inseparably connected in a field of tension and the two sides of the image are completely reversible. The virtual can become actual by referring to the actual and the actual can become virtual by referring to the virtual. Following Deleuze, this reversibility occurs through mirrors, especially through such mirrors that distort, break and multiply the person's mirror image. "The indiscernibility of the real and the imaginary, or of the present and the past, of the actual and the virtual, is definitely not produced in the head or the mind, it is the objective characteristic of certain existing images which are by nature double."[9] The cycle of the mirror is thus at the same time an exchange in the sense of a change of sides. The image and even the mutual and reciprocal image holds an irreducible relationship to itself. Actuality and virtuality exist at the same time indiscernably and distinctly in the 'crystal image' that describes a state of balance in which perception and memory determine each other.[10] "(Time) is the virtual element which we invade to find within the pure recollection that becomes actual in a memory-image."[11] Accordingly, there can be no virtuality without actuality and vice versa. For the performer's physicality it follows that there will always be her actual presence and actual absence as well as her virtual presence and virtual absence.

A NETWORK OF TEMPORALITIES: MEDIATISATION AND VIRTUALISATION OF THE STAGE

Those representative aspects of the body, absence vs presence, and the space-time relationship, towards delinearity and simultaneity of spaces and action levels, that have been changed by the mediatisation of theatre, evolve as central issues in the concept and design of the coalescence. In the discussion about materiality and technology, the earlier discussed concept of the importance of the design of the coalescence, the interface between the actual and the virtual, appears as the central concern of the mediated stage. Deleuze localises the 'in-between', the digitally constructed interface between absence and presence of the performer body or between body and representation on the mediated stage, in the mobile mirror. The crystal image, in the mirror, acts as the focus of actuality, in front of the mirror, and virtuality, within/behind the mirror. The field of tension between body and disembodiment, between physicality and virtuality finds its dissolution in the crystal image; in memory and in the (re)construction of memory. The virtualisation of the stage creates primarily the dynamisation of an, until then predictable, Aristotelic and linear body, space and time concept. In analogy to the virtual permeation of the world, the virtualisation of the theatre stands for the breaking up of a linear temporal structure and unity of space towards the 'infinite' simultaneity of spaces as well as the simultaneity and de-linear narrativity of actual and virtual levels of plot lines and time. The linking of temporally and geographically distant situations that has become possible on the mediated stage extends the stage towards an open system with multiple entrances and exits, beginning and end points. Borges' description of the 'Garden of forking paths', "(He believed) in an infinite series of times, in a growing dizzying net of divergent, convergent and parallel times. The network of times which approached one another, forked, broke off, or were unaware of one another for centuries, embraces ALL possibilities of time," describes such an open system without inside, interior or outside, exterior, without centre or periphery: a network of temporalities.[12]

THE 'BECOMING BAROQUE' OF THE STAGE

The inherent property of the mediated stage, to split open the unity of time and space, produces an up until now unknown 'maximisation' of stage volume through simultaneous and parallel programmed time-space-layers. Such a 'maximization' of stage volume, technologically supported by the enormous capacities of electronic storage media and the high speed of real-time manipulations and calculations, enables the theatrical visualisation of complex dramaturgical de-linear structures and processes. It is thus possible to store 'imaginary' memory contents of one or more protagonists in the 'crystal image' of the mediated stage and to reproduce these identically, in non-interactive and non-identically, in interactive situations. In regard to the artistic and technological potential of the mediated stage to store and reproduce infinite amounts of visual material, Deleuze's definition of the baroque as the fold, towards inifinity, opens up a theoretical space in which to describe the infinite process of design as the folding from form towards expressive form. The infinite process of folding cannot be thought without the simultaneously happening process of virtualisation at the touching line of idea and materiality. Taken away from the specific historical period of the baroque, Deleuze illuminates what is valid for the mediated stage per se, the virtualisation of the stage, both as a theoretical model and on the actual theatre stage is never completed and the process of virtualisation inevitably leads towards the infinite. The extension of time and space towards simultaneous and de-linear time and action 'modules' and towards equally simultaneous, possibly alogical, layered and imaginary spaces, as well as the detachment of the body from its mirror image to its mediated portrait, are the central characteristics of the mediated stage. In the context of the live and mediated performer on the mediated stage, body and space oscillate between absence and presence, between actuality and virtuality. The design of the mediality in regard to the chosen materials and technologies is dependent on the respective and respectively specific coalescence between the actual and the virtual. Following Wölfflin, Deleuze quotes the material qualities of the baroque, "the formation of a whirl form, nourished from ever new turbulences and ending like the mane of a horse or the spray of a wave; the tendency of matter to overboard the space, to couple with the liquid, while at the same time the waters divide as masses."[13] This short text describes unwillingly two central parameters of the mediated stage, namely the 'interactive' principle of immersion and the 'formal and aesthetic' principle of perception, namely of performativity. The notion of immersion, defined as the desire to dive into three-dimensional worlds or, with Wölfflin, as the "tendency of matter to overboard the space", also denotes the property of the mediated stage to condense spatial volume and store an infinite amount of constantly moving imagery.[14] Deleuzes' and Wölfflin's vivid philosophical images come very close to the specific aesthetic and technical qualities of the moving electronic image in the mediated space. The often described liquidity of the electronic image, the constant formation and transformation of miniscule digital elements, that is pixels or the time-space extension of the traditional stage with its embrace of digital worlds and complex de-linear narrative structures can absolutely be described with the Deleuzian image of the ever-devouring and ever-transforming wave, which again is closely related to the infinite fold. While in painting, sculpture and architecture the fold has hardened and solidified in the materialities of canvas and marble, the process of folding and of design, in the mediated theatre space proceeds towards the infinite. Characterised by the constant cycle of actuality and virtuality, of body and disembodiment, the mediated stage corresponds with the Deleuzian notion of the baroque in its constant folding of space towards the infinite. Thus, the transformation towards infinity lies at the centre of the materiality of the mediated stage. By definition then, the mediated theatre space is not completed but manifests itself on the contrary as an infinite space of possibilities. And just as a processual, emerging and transformative character is central to the mediated space between actuality and virtuality, it is closely connected with the notion of performativity in the sense of, "the event temporality of aesthetic perception."[15]

'BAROQUE MEETS TECHNO': THE IMMATERIAL STAGE

'Baroque meets Techno' was the term applied in 1997 in Sydney as the director's conceptual slogan for the multidisciplinary team of set designer, costume designer, media artist and lighting designer. Using high-tech projections on the stage and synthetic textiles and materials for the costumes, as well as utilizing digital post-production and video technologies, Richard Strauss' *Ariadne auf Naxos* was put onto the twenty-first-century stage as a techno-baroque spectacle. The digital set design with computer generated video sequences can be understood as a contemporary analogy to baroque theatre illusions and effects such as apparitions, water, fire, flying machines and mirrors.[16] The visualisation of Ariadne's streams of memory is manifest in the digitally constructed projection and mirror spaces of the Sydney stage. Embedded into the both shrill and opulent aesthetics, sets and costumes of a 'techno-baroque', opera buffa and opera seria elements constrasted with Ariadne's hypnotic mediated memory space. It belongs to Ariadne's lamento in the second act and in analogy to the self-reflexion, mirroring, of the genre 'opera', the stage protagonist Ariadne is reflected in the mobile mirror blades of her subjectively constructed memory theatre, whereas right at the end, the audience is reflected upon the stage.[17] The very same audience that had taken part in an "analytical demonstration", a dramatic deconstruction and a distanced and quotational reconstruction of a historical genre now sees itself applauding in the motorised reflectors on the stage. The visualisation of the central aesthetic and musical mechanism in the collaboration between Hofmannsthal and Strauss, namely 'deconstruction' and 'reconstruction', occurs in Sydney with three different reflective techniques. First of all with the fragmented reflection of the stage figure onto mobile mirrors, secondly, with the reconstruction of the figure in mirror blades that have been inserted horizontally into the video projection screens and finally in the reflection of the protagonist into the digital landscape of their memories, into the video projection itself. In *Ariadne*, Hofmannsthal realises for the first time the principle of transformation, a motif that he would be concerned with all throughout his life. Hofmannsthal wrote to Richard Strauss:

> Verwandlung ist Leben des Lebens, ist das eigentliche Mysterium der schöpfenden Natur; Beharren ist Erstarren und Tod. Wer leben will, der muss über sich selbst hinwegkommen, muß sich verwandeln: er muß vergessen. Und dennoch ist ans Beharren, ans Nichtvergessen, alle menschliche Würde geknüpft. Das ist einer von den abgrundtiefen Widersprüchen, über denen das Dasein aufgebaut ist, wie der delphische Tempel über seinem bodenlosen Erdspalt.[18]

To the 'insisting' to the 'nonforgetting', as Hofmannsthal paraphrases memory, the 'dignity', or in psychological terms, the 'personality' of an individual is related. Cognitive psychology regards the connection between personality and memory as characterised by such knowledge and values that constitute the individual and social status of a person.[19] Thus the individuality of a person and, in a more abstract sense that of a stage figure lies in that which they remember: they are characterised by the contents of their memory. Ariadne's autobiographical memory is staged in Sydney as a memory theatre, according to the notion that was expressed by Matussek, that the contents of memory are not statically stored objects but actors in constantly changing productions.[20]

Ariadne's memory theatre houses the concrete spaces of her childhood as well as imaginary spaces of love, of solitude and of death. These are ever-changing, they 'morph' into each other and in this they belong closely to Hofmannsthal's motif of 'transformation' as it is present throughout his work. Relationships transform; music transforms, spaces are constantly in motion. What is shown transforms in the same way in which the viewer's perspective changes. Thus, perspective and object are subject to individual personal selection. The principle of the subjective memory of one or more protagonists can be visualised on the mediated stage with the projected electronic image. The finest changes of the digital pixels that constitute each singular frame enable a visual metamorphosis that corresponds structurally to the non-linear fabric of human memory.[21] The images that have been constructed, that are projected and integrated into the built set, constitute Ariadne's memory theatre. The place of her memory is that of her childhood in the palace. She appears as a baroque princess in the Sydney production, and thus her childhood palace is not Greek but instead the baroque palais in which according to Strauss and Hofmannsthal, the prologue is set. Both new and historical photographs of the baroque New Palais in Sans Souci, Potsdam form the visual base for

Ariadne's memory places. The early video sequences of the opera seria section in Act II speak of the baroque princess' desire for the representative spaces of her past. With her growing melancholy and desire for death, these spaces are filled with water. Water floods her memory spaces, the interiors drown in water and sink down into the digital tides, out of which finally, as if re-newed the heads of the heroes and gods that determine Ariadne's existence, Theseus, Bacchus and Hermes, appear. Ariadne's memorial images form an autobiographical and spatial memory. Three childhood locations, the palais, the park and the grotto, comprise the opera seria sections and are composed from photographic stills. With digital post-production, with flame and inferno using silicon graphics software, manipulated in colour, dynamics and rhythm are brought into motion, digitally constructed water streams flow around the images of baroque court architecture and dissolves them in the overflowing of the spaces. Each static memory is flooded by the present, by the isolation of Ariadne's existence on the deserted island of Naxos, surrounded only by water. Visual layers overlap each other in the same way in which images of memory can cross, displace or overlay one another. The origin of the images, however, is a photographic still, a kind of frozen memory that only in the act of remembrance in combination with other static images can create novel, formerly experienced or imaginary sequences of moving images:

> Through dreams, the various dwelling-places in our lives co-penetrate and retain the treasures of former days. And after we are in the new house, when memories of other places we have lived in come back to us, we travel to the land of Motionless Childhood, motionless the way all Immemorial things are. We live fixations, fixations of happiness. We comfort ourselves by reliving memories of protection. Something closed must retain our memories, while leaving them their original value as images.[22]

Bachelard, versed both in Jung's phenomenology and Bergson's notion of time and duration, attempts to understand the dynamics of memory and its specific function. By bringing static, not moving, childhood images close to us, we try to interrupt the dynamic course of a sometimes frightening presence and thus we insist on the illusion of time standing still. Forgetting, however, is, as is remembering, a process or a mental activity. With Hofmannsthal, Ariadne's acts of forgetting, the man, the pain, the solitude, can only occur through transformation, "The fateful groom: Bacchus. Crossing of mythical motifs. The mutual transformation. The allomorphic element."[23] The visualisation of Hofmannsthal's allomatic transformation as a kind of alchemical principle occurs in Sydney not with a traditional technical scenery change, but as a dynamic visualisation in an immaterial projected and digital set. The immateriality of the projected moving images and the set constructed from projection screens allows for the visualisation of memory, forgetting and allomatic transformation.

THE CONSTRUCTION OF A DIGITAL SPATIAL AUTOBIOGRAPHY

With the continuous changing of one pixel into another in the digitally manipulated video image, constant and mutual transformation occurs. The liquid video sequences and their disruption, fragmentation, splintering and multiplication by mobile mirror blades, correspond with the immaterial and non-linear stream of Ariadne's memories. The digital images themselves appear liquid and flowing:

First of all we ascertain the essentially 'flowing' character of this image type, that had Frederic Jameson say, the notion of a total fluxus was the only framework in which to sensibly discuss video. Flowing as water, but also fiery flaming, cloudy or fluffy, diffused and soft, or imbalanced and fragmented, at any rate elementary, just think of the lack of clarity of this image type, its essential fuzziness – and of the difficulty of its theoretical formulation, referring to pure light matter, a constantly vibrating flow of electrons that dissolves the linearity of the visible in a continuous process of explosion – implosion.[24]

It is the central task of the Sydney production video to create in conjunction with the mobile mirror blades the crystal image after Deleuze. In the crystal image, occurs the continuous exchange between memory and perception, between actual and virtual image. While Ariadne moves in her subjective memory space, the mirror blades double her physical presence and project her figure into her memory images. The video environment of Ariadne is immersive in its character, as it simulates the performer's complete 'dive' into digitally created worlds. "Immersive is a term that refers to the degree in which a virtual environment submerges the perceptual system of the user in computer-generated stimuli. The more the system captivates the senses and blocks out stimuli from the physical world, the more the system is considered immersive."[25] The image of the three nymphs that float in the digital set and who seem, similar to avatars, to navigate within an immersive environment, can be seen as exemplary for an artistic project in which the utilization of interactive strategies negates any questions as to the nature of the format actually used. The mobile mirror blades weave Ariadne's memory processes into the dramatic and musical future, presence and past. "The crystal always lives at the limit, it is itself the 'vanishing' limit between the immediate past which is already no longer and the immediate future which is not yet…mobile mirror which endlessly reflects perception in recollection."[26]

ExpoRobots Interactive mobile robotic installation

In the projects discussed, the interactive robotic installation *ExpoRobots* holds a special status, as an example of mediated scenography. This form of conceptual extension of the stage towards a multifunctional, mediated scenic space is primarily found in exhibitions, trade fairs and events rather than in a more traditional theatrical context. Within the large world exhibition *Expo2000 Hannover*, the theme park *Knowledge* is meant to stage the ever more complex life environment of man in the twenty-first century, as an immersive information environment. With a size of 5.500 square meters, the exhibition's central themes of *Knowledge Information Communication* are a major part of the theme park with exhibitions relating to *The Future of Work* or *Sustainability*.

Seventy-two mobile bionic objects, designed between a natural and a technical form, move in six swarms of twelve objects each through the hall that is dimly lit in blue. The objects are programmed with a navigational and position recognition system and react in their movements to each other and to the audience that is freely moving through the large space.

The ZKM Centre for Art and Media Technology, Karlsruhe under the then director of the ZKM media museum, Hans Peter Schwarz, was commissioned by the Expo to realise the scenography for the show *Knowledge Information Communication*. Two teams were chosen to realise scenography and interactive media production, respectively. The ZKM Team Hannover with Olaf Arndt[27] and members of the artists' group BBM were responsible for the overall design concept, and producer Lawrence Wallen with the three directors, Thea Brejzek, Lillevän Pobjoy and Zahi Chalem, were responsible for the interactive media production and implementation. Fraunhofer Institut Dortmund developed the navigation software and media connect Augsburg the position recognition system.

TECHNOLOGY MOVEMENT SOUND

The 'eggs', the 'potatoes' or even the 'eggheads', as the objects are named by the press and the public, quickly become the audiences' favourite at *Expo 2000*. Thematically they deal with bionic structures and their technological equivalents. "This [the robots] is possibly the only scenario of the whole Expo that is immediately overwhelming that renders you speechless and makes you think hard. Here one is confronted closely with seemingly artificial intelligences in strange bodies and one finds mutual approaches and rejections of real and artificial bodies in the space to be approximately even."[28]

Each robotic capsule is equipped with its own audio system creating atmospheric sound. The surround sound of composer Hartmut Bruckner constantly changes its orientation, volume and dynamics. The viewers move freely through the space and influence through their paths movement, image and sound the movement of the robots. With a sensoric programme, the 'knowbots', as project leader Stefan Iglhaut calls them, check their surroundings and react autonomously to obstacles. There is a programmed preference for the robots to stay within their own swarm. If they do join another swarm, with a short time delay they take on the media sequence of this swarm. Equipped with MPEG (Motion Pictures Experts Group)-players, sound systems and video projectors, each mobile object owns the totality of all audio-visual information. The individual knowledge storage contrasts with the social behaviour of the objects in the swarm. This is comparable to the de-centrally and non-hierarchically functions of a swarm of birds or fish, the objects behave as 'super organisms' whose specific qualities become visible only in their communal acting as a group.

THE SWARM: CHOREOGRAPHY AND DE-LINEAR NARRATION

In the network of complexity and self-organizing systems the image of the robot swarm is both metaphor and leit motif. "Swarms are networks without central control."[29] The video sequences projected from within the robots constitute the visual memory of the bionic objects and their respective visual 'utterance' is activated by the movement of one or more objects within the swarm. Deleuze's virtual space, housing the crystal image corresponds here with the spatial interactivity and visual storage, MPEG-player and video projector, of the bionic objects.[30]

During the twenty-minute show all the produced image sequences are shown. Their chronological sequence, however, differs from show to show as it is dependent on the audience's activity. Part of a three-dimensional sound and image space, the viewer moves within a playful artificial world and while his/her movements influence the robots' movements and video behaviour, their inherent visual memory functions autonomously. It is influenced in swarm orientation and image chronology but remains a coherent behaviour in relation to each other while the viewer becomes part of the sensoric and tactile world of the robot swarms.

THE FUTURE OF THE MEDIATED STAGE

While the mediated stage contributes to the blurring of borders between performing arts, media and visual arts genres, and indeed fosters the emergence of new theatrical forms, there is no such thing as an identifiable 'system' of the mediated stage or stage practice.

Responsible for this, in part, is the lack of experimentation possibilities for theatre practitioners in collaboration with media artists, composers and technology experts wishing to concentrate on practice as research in the areas of aesthetics, stage technology and dramaturgy. Subsequently, we see a multitude of singular works and the impossibility of a continuously extending pool of knowledge and experience that can be accessed by practitioners and theorists alike. What is needed, therefore, is a transdisciplinary laboratory open for research without immediate deadlines for production or publication. However, the physical location of such a laboratory naturally defines its research perspective. An opera and technology laboratory within an opera house will disturb and disrupt the smooth functioning of the repertory, while a technology institution housing such a laboratory will mostly be lacking performance-specific prerequisites and conditions.

"Innovation is inefficient. More often than not, it is undisciplined, contrarian, and iconoclastic; and it nourishes itself with confusion and contradiction. In short, being innovative flies in the face of what almost all parents want for their children, most CEOs want for their companies, and heads of states want for their countries. And innovative people are a pain in the ass."[31] The statement of Nicholas Negroponte is as provocative as it is fitting, and it flatly outlines the dilemma of practice as research outside clearly defined genres and outside a necessarily consensual dialogue. Only in an independent performance and media laboratory can theatre practitioners, theorists and technology experts aim to develop innovative technology applications, stage architectures and dramaturgy, text, and music models for the mediated stage in mutual provocation.

NOTES

1. Deleuze, G., *Das Zeit-Bild. Kino 2*, 2nd edition, Suhrkamp Verlag, Frankfurt a.M., 1999.
2. Ibid.
3. Ernst, A., 'Reflections, Refractions and Schroedinger's Cat: Ariadne on Naxos and Art about Art', Programme Book, Opera Australia, Sydney, 1997.
4. Manovich, L., *The Language of New* Media, MIT Press, 2002.
5. Bergson, H., *Materie und Gedächtnis: eine Abhandlung über die Beziehungen zwischen Körper und Geist*, Felix Meiner-Verlag, Hamburg, 1991.
6. Alliez, É., 'Deleuze, Bergson, und das Virtuelle' in Samsonow von, E. and Alliez, É., (eds.) *Telenoia. Kritik der virtuellen Bilder*, Turia + Kant, Wien, 1999.
7. Deleuze, G., *Das Zeit-Bild. Kino 2*, 1999.
8. Gehse, K., *Medien-Theater. Der Einsatz von Medien im zeitgenössischen Theater*, Deutscher Wissenschafts-Verlag, Diss., University of Bonn, 2001.
9. Deleuze, G., *Das Zeit-Bild. Kino 2*, 1999.
10. Ibid.

11. Ibid.

12. Borges, J. L., *Labyrinths. Selected Stories & Other Writings*, A New Directions Book, New York, 1964.

13. Wölfflin, H., in Deleuze, *Die Falte. Leibniz und der Barock*, Suhrkamp Verlag, Frankfurt a.M., 2000.

14. Ibid.

15. Roselt, J., 'Kulturen des Performativen als Denkfigur zur Analyse von Theater und Kultur im ausgehenden 20 Jahrhundert', in Schade, S., (ed.), *Konfigurationen: Zwischen Kunst und Medien,* Fink Verlag, München, 1999.

16. Treppmann, E., *Besuche aus dem Jenseits. Geistererscheinungen auf dem deutschen Theater im Barock*, UVK Universitätsverlag, Konstanz, 1999.

17. Kunze, S., 'Die ästhetische Rekonstruktion der Oper. Anmerkungen zur "Ariadne auf Naxos"' in Mauser, W., (ed.), *Hofmannsthal und das Theater. Die Vorträge des Hofmannsthal Symposiums Wien 1979*, Verlag Karl M. Halosar, Wien, 1979.

18. Hofmannsthal, H. von, *Sämtliche Werke*, (ed.) Freies Deutsches Hochstift, 37 Volumes, Frankfurt a.M., 1975– ; *Richard Strauss – Hugo von Hofmannsthal, Briefwechsel,* Schuh, W., (ed.), Atlantis Verlag, Zürich, 1952.

19. Klix, F., 'Gedächtnis' in *Handwörterbuch Psychologie*, Asanger, R., Weininger, G., (eds.), Psychologie Verlags Union, Weinsheim 1999.

20. Matussek, P., 2001.

21. Klix, F., 'Gedächtnis', 1999.

22. Bachelard, G., *The Poetics of Space*, Beacon Press, Boston, 1994.

23. Hofmannsthal, H. von, (ed.), *Sämtliche Werke*, Freies Deutsches Hochstift, 37 Volumes, Frankfurt a.M., 1975–, W22.226; A 218.

24. Alliez, É., Deleuze, G., Bergson, H., 'und das Virtuelle' 1999.

25. Biocca, F. and Delaney, B., *Immersive virtual reality technology*, Hillsdale, NJ. Lawrence-Erlbaum, 1995.

26. Deleuze, G., *Water and Dreams: an essay on the imagination of* matter, The Bachelard Translations, The Pegasus Foundation, The Dallas Institute of Humanities and Culture, Dallas, 1983.

27. Arndt, O., (ed) *Hyperorganismen*, Internationalismus Verlag Berlin, 2000.

28. Werner, *Expo2000*, publicity material, 2000.

29. Kelly, K., *Das Ende der Kontrolle. Die biologische Wende in Wirtschaft, Technik und Gesellschaft*, DtV Verlag, Mannheim, 1997.

30. Deleuze, G., 1983.

31. Negroponte, N., 'Creating a culture of ideas', *Technology Review*, Cambridge, Massachusetts, cited, *Herald Tribune*, 24th January 2003.

SELECTED BIBLIOGRAPHY

Ackroyd, P., *T. S. Eliot*, London: Hamish Hamilton, 1984.

Arndt, O., (editor), *Hyperorganismen*, Internationalismus, Berlin: Verlag, 2000.

Ayer, A. J., *Language, Truth and Logic*, London: Victor Gollancz, 1964.

Bachelard, G., *Water and Dreams: An Essay on the Imagination of Matter*, The Bachelard Translations, The Pegasus Foundation, The Dallas Institute of Humanities and Culture, Dallas, 1983.

Bachelard, G., *The Poetics of Space*, Boston: Beacon Press, 1994.

Beckman. J., (editor), *The Virtual Dimension: architecture, representation and crash culture*, 1st edition, New York, Princeton: Architectural Press, 1998.

Bergson, H., *Materie und Gedächtnis: eine Abhandlung über die Beziehungen zwischen Körper und Geist*, Felix Meiner-Verlag, Hamburg, 1991.

Berenson, B., *The Ineloquent in Art*, London: Chapman & Hall, New York: Macmillan, 1954.

Biocca, F. & Delaney, B., *Immersive virtual reality technology*, Hillsdale, NJ. Lawrence-Erlbaum, 1995.

Birringer, J., *Media & Performance along the border*, The Johns Hopkins University Press, Baltimore, 1988.

Birringer, J., *Theatre, Theory, Postmodernism*, Bloomington, Indiana University Press, 1991.

Borges, Jorge Luis, *Labyrinths. Selected Stories & Other Writings*, A New Directions Book: New York, 1964.

Candy, L. and Edmonds, E., *Explorations in Art and Technology,* London: Springer-Verlag, 2002.

Carver, G. and Bearden, C., (editors), *New Visions in Performance: The Impact of Digital Technologies* Lisse, Netherlands, Swets & Zeitlinger Publishers, 2004.

Chaudhuri, Una, *Staging Place: The Geography of Modern Drama*, Ann Arbor: Michigan University Press, 1995.

Costello, P., *James Joyce: the years of growth 1882–1915*, London: Random House, 1993.

de Certeau, Michel, *The Practice of Everyday Life*, translated, Steven Rendall, Berkeley: University of California Press, 1984.

Deleuze, G., *Water and Dreams: an essay on the imagination of* matter, The Bachelard Translations, The Pegasus Foundation, The Dallas Institute of Humanities and Culture, Dallas, 1983.

Deleuze, G., *Das Zeit-Bild. Kino 2*, 2nd edition, Suhrkamp Verlag, Frankfurt a.M., 1999.

Deleuze, G., *Differenz undWiederholung,* 2nd edition, Wilhelm Fink Verlag, München, 1997.

Deleuze, G., *Die Falte. Leibniz und der Barock*, Suhrkamp Verlag, Frankfurt a.M., 2000.

Donnell, A. & Polkey, P., (eds), *Representing Lives, women and auto/biography*, London: Macmillan Press Ltd., 2000.

Eynat-Confino, I. and Sormova, E., (editors), *Space and the Postmodern Stage*, Prague, CzechTheatre Institute, 2000.

Foreman, R., *Unbalancing Acts: foundations for a theatre*, NewYork:Theatre Communications Group, 1993.

Foreman, R., *Reverberation Machines: the later plays and essays*, Barrytown: Station Hill Press Inc., 1985.

Foucault, M., *This Is Not a Pipe*, edited, introduced and translated by James Harkness, Berkeley: California University Press, 1982.

Gehse, K., *Medien-Theater, Der Einsatz von Medien im zeitgenössischen Theater*, Deutscher Wissenschafts-Verlag, Diss., University of Bonn, 2001.

Gelb, A. and B., *O'Neill*, NY: Harper and Row, 1973.

The Citizens' Company 1979–1985, Glasgow Citizens Theatre.

Grau, O., *Virtual Art: from Illusion to Immersion*, Cambridge, MA: MIT Press, 2003.

Hamon-Sirejols, C. and Surgers, A. *Espace Sonore, EspaceVisuel* edited by Presses Universitaires de Lyon, Lyon, 2003.

Henderson, M. C., *Mielziner: Master of Modern Stage Design*, Back Stage Books, 2001.

Howard, P.,*What is Scenography?* Routledge, 2002.

Kelly, K., *Das Ende der Kontrolle, Die biologischeWende in Wirtschaft, Technik und Gesellschaft*, DtV Verlag, Mannheim, 1997.

Kintz, L., *The Subject's Tragedy*, Ann Arbor, University of Michigan Press, 1992.

Kirby, Michael, (editor), *Futurist Performance: with manifestos and playscripts*, translated by Victoria Nes Kirby, NewYork: PAJ Publications, 1971.

Kirby, Michael, *The Art ofTime: Essays on the Avant-Garde*, NY: Dutton, 1969.

Kustow, M., *Theatre@risk*, Methuen, London, 2000.

Laurel, B., *Computers asTheatre*, Reading MA: Addison-Wesley, 1991.

McAuley, G., *Space in Performance: making meaning in the theatre*, University of Michigan Press, Ann Arbor, 1999.

McLuhan, M., *Understanding Media*, Routledge, 2001.

McKenzie, J., *Perform or Else: From Discipline to Performance*, London: Routledge, 2001.

Nicholl, A., *The Development of theTheatre*, Harrap, 3rd edition, 1946.

Oddey, A., *Devising Theatre*, Routledge London, 1994.

O'Neill, Eugene, *Complete Plays 1932–1943*, (editor) Travis Bogard, NY: Library of America, 1988.

Reinelt, J. G. & Roach, J. R., *Critical Theory and Performance*, Ann Arbor: University of Michigan Press, 1992.

Russell Brown, J., *EffectiveTheatre: a study with documentation*, Heinemann, London, 1969.

Samsonow von, E. and Alliez, É., (editors), *Telenoia, Kritik der virtuellen Bilder*, Turia + Kant, Wien, 1999.

Savran, D., *Breaking the Rules:TheWooster Group*, NY: TCG, 1988.

Schade, Sigrid, (editor), *Konfigurationen: Zwischen Kunst und Medien*, Fink Verlag, München, 1999.

Schlemmer, O., Moholy-Nagy, L. and Molnár, F., *The Theater of the Bauhaus*, London: Eyre Methuen, 1961.

Schmitt, N. C., *Actors and Onlookers, Theater and Twentieth-Century Scientific Views of Nature*, Evanston: Northwestern University Press, 1990.

Schuchard, R., *Eliot's Dark Angel: Intersections of Life and Art*, NY: Oxford University Press, 1999.

Schuh, W., (editor), Richard Strauss – Hugo von Hofmannsthal, *Briefwechsel*, complete edition, Atlantis Verlag, Zürich, 1952.

Seymour-Jones, C., *Painted Shadow*, London: Constable, 2001.

Sherman, R. S. and Craig, B. A., *Understanding Virtual Reality: interface, application, and design*, USA, Morgan Kaufmann Publishers, 2003.

Simonson, L., *On the Ideas of Adolph Appia*, from *The Stage is Set*, Harcourt Brace & Co., 1932, reprint Theatre Art Books, New York, 1963.

Smith, S. and Watson, J., *Reading Autobiography: A Guide for Interpreting Life Narratives*, Minneapolis, The University of Minnesota Press, 2001.

Sollors, W., (editor), *The Adrienne Kennedy Reader*, Minneapolis, The University of Minnesota Press, 2001.

Spender, S., *Eliot*, Glasgow: Fontana, 1977.

States, B. O., *Great Reckonings in Little Rooms: On the Phenomenology of Theater*, Berkeley & London: University of California Press, 1985.

Styan, J. L., *Modern Drama in Theory and Practice 2, Symbolism, Surrealism and the Absurd*, Cambridge University Press, 1981.

Svoboda, J., *The Secret of Theatrical Space*, translated and edited by Burian, J. M., Applause Theatre Books, New York, 1993.

Todd, A. and Lecat, J.-G., *The Open Circle: Peter Brook's Theatre Environments*, Faber and Faber, 2003.

Treppmann, E., *Besuche aus dem Jenseits. Geistererscheinungen auf dem deutschen Theater im Barock*, UVK Universitätsverlag, Konstanz, 1999.

Tschumi, B., *The Manhattan Transcripts*, 1st edition, New York, 1981.

Ursic, G. U., (editor), *Josef Svoboda Scenographer*, Union des Théâtres d'Europe, 1998.

Vidler, A., *Warped Space: art, architecture and anxiety in modern culture*, Cambridge, MA: MIT Press, 2001.

Wagner, R., *The Artwork of the Future*, 1849, translation Ellis, W. A., 1895, Kegan Paul, Trenchy, Trubner & Co., Ltd.

Weishar, P., *Digital Space: designing virtual environments*, New York: McGraw Hill, 1998.

White, C. A., Carver, G., *Computer Visualizations: 3D modelling for theatre designers*, Focal Press, 2003.

BIOGRAPHIES OF AUTHORS

Dr Thea Brejzek is a stage director. Her work is concerned with the relationship between audience, performer and technological systems in the context of mediated environments and the integration of interactive media in the classical opera repertoire and newly commissioned works. Besides her opera work, she is a lecturer in Mediated Scenography/Music Theatre in the Postgraduate Scenography Programme at the University for Design and Art, Zürich (HGK Z Zürich).

Dr Johan Callens teaches at the Vrije Universiteit Brussels (VUB) and is the author of *Double Binds: Existentialist Inspiration and Generic Experimentation in the Early Work of Jack Richardson*, (Rodopi), *Acte(s) de Présence* (VUBPress), and *From Middleton and Rowley's "Changeling" to Sam Shepard's "Bodyguard": A Contemporary Appropriation of a Renaissance Drama* (Edwin Mellen). More recently he has edited two special issues on Sam Shepard for *Contemporary Theatre Review* (Routledge) and one on intermediality for the journal *Degrés* (2000), besides a collection of essays, *The Wooster Group and Its Traditions* (P.I.E. – Peter Lang) and an essay "Dislocating the Canon in the Wooster Group's Rhode Island Trilogy", which extends the research here in *Reading Without Maps: Cultural Landmarks in a Post-Canonical Age*, ed. Christopher Den Tandt, Comparative Poetics Series, (Brussels & Bern: P.I.E. – Peter Lang)

Professor Lesley Ferris is Chair of the Department of Theatre at The Ohio State University. Her books include *Crossing the Stage: Controversies on Cross-Dressing* (Routledge) and *Acting Women: Images of Women in Theatre* (Macmillan). She is the author of numerous essays including "The Mask in Western Theatre: Transformation and Doubling" (in *Masks: Faces of Culture* Harry N. Abrams). Other recent essays include "Cooking Up the Self: Bobby Baker and Blondell Cummings 'Do' the Kitchen" in *Interfaces: Women/ Autobiography/ Image/ Performance* (University of Michigan Press) and "Horse and Bamboo's *Company of Angels*" (Theatre Forum). She has directed over 50 productions in the USA and the UK, one of the most recent being Adrienne and Adam P. Kennedy's *Sleep Deprivation Chamber* at Ohio State which experimented with digital animation, interactive computer interfaces, and real-time visual effects (2003). Her current research focuses on Notting Hill Carnival in London and in October 2004 she was invited to give a lecture by the British Society of Theatre Research on "Carnival as/is Theatre." She has spearheaded several international initiatives including the London Theatre Program, the Contemporary Performance and Culture in Cuba course, and an exchange with theatre artists in the Czech Republic. For her work supporting international education she was given an Outstanding Faculty Award by the Office of International Education in 2002.

Professor Pamela Howard FRSA is Professor Emeritus, Scenography at University of the Arts London, Visiting Professor Royal Holloway College University of London and University of the Arts Belgrade. She is a freelance director and designer, educator, curator and writer. Pamela Howard has worked as a stage designer in the UK, Europe and USA since 1960, and has realised over 200 productions. She has worked at all the major national and regional theatres, including the creation of several large-scale site-specific works with the late John McGrath. Currently the Director/Designer for the Greek premiere of *The Greek Passion: the opera* by Bohuslav Martinu & Nikos Kazantzakis for the opera of Thessaloniki, to be performed in the old Byzantine citadel. As writer, director and visual artist *The New Jerusalem*—a story of Evangelism in Britain in 1811. Productions as part of teaching assignments in 2005 for the National Theatre school in Copenhagen, *Why do you always wear Black ?* and for University of the Arts Belgrade *Please take a Seat! – a memory play*. Pamela Howard is active in the world of International Scenography and was the organiser of SCENOFEST at the Prague Quadriennal in 2003. She is the author of *What is Scenography ?* (Routledge) and in preparation *Designing Nothing* (Nick Hern Books). She has curated exhibitions for the British Council, and is currently preparing for a large exhibition of paintings and drawings in Chichester at the end of 2006.

Professor Alison Oddey is Professor of Contemporary Performance & Theatre Studies at Loughborough University. She is a performer, writer, broadcaster and teacher. Her forthcoming publication, *Shifting Directions: a new kind of theatre-making in the twenty-first century*, (MUP), is essentially concerned with a twenty-first-century vision of arts making, and the director's role as creator and maker of performance. Other book publications include *Devising Theatre*, (Routledge); *Performing Women: Stand-ups, Strumpets and Itinerants* (Macmillan Press) and the forthcoming second edition of *Performing Women* (Palgrave), due to be launched at the Royal National Theatre, London. She presented the BBC Radio 4 series of six half-hour programmes, *Stand-ups and Strumpets*, which were broadcast in 2001 and 2003, and were based on her book. She has been Guest Editor for *Contemporary Theatre Review*, for a special issue on 'Practice as Research' in 2002. Her next piece of performance is for the performance installation, *Flying Free*, in 2006. This project is linked to the Science Research Initiative Funding of the *Scenography & Performance Laboratory*, designed to develop work in areas of performance, technologies for performance and visual arts, live and recorded media, as well as exhibition and installation. Alison has guest lectured and taught workshops on devising theatre at the universities of Amsterdam and Utrecht, Holland, and Antwerp, Belgium. She is co-convenor of the *Different Directions* International Symposia (2000–07), involving practitioners and academics from the Creative and Performing Arts and Visual Media worldwide in varying collaborations. She is an independent evaluator for the Arts and Humanities Research Council (AHRC) and is a member of the AHRC Peer Review College for Performance and Live Art, Contemporary and 20th Century, UK, Ireland, Western Europe and North America.

Scott Palmer is currently the programme co-ordinator of the Performance Design degree in the School of Performance and Cultural Industries at the University of Leeds, UK. He has been involved in a wide range of theatre production work since the mid-1980s fulfilling a variety of roles from production and technical manager. He has directed productions at the Edinburgh Fringe Festival and designed shows at venues such as Warwick Arts Centre, Grange Arts Centre, Oldham and Project Arts Centre, Dublin, where *Eurodans* was staged in autumn 2002. He undertook the video production for the UK National Design Schools Exhibit for the Society of British Theatre Designers' UK Tour and subsequent presentation at the Prague Quadrennial: *The Labryrinth of the World and Paradise of the Theatre*, in June 2003. Scott has worked for a number of government organisations, national awarding bodies and as an educational consultant, trainer and principal moderator for vocational qualifications in the Performing Arts and Media sectors. Scott's research interests lie within the field of scenography, principally in lighting design and in the interaction between technology and performance. Current collaborative research with KMA Creative Technologies has contributed to projection work for *Eng-er-land*, a piece presented by Phoenix Dance Company as part of its '*inter vivos*' UK tour in 2005. Scott's publications include *Essential Guide to Stage Management Lighting and Sound*, (Hodder & Stoughton); 'Creating Common Ground: Dialogues Between Performance and Digital Technologies' (with Dr Sita Popat) in *International Journal of Performance Arts & Digital*, 2005; 'Making Light Work – Lighting Design in Contemporary British Theatre' in *Theatre; Espace Sonore, Espace Visuel* edited by Hamon-Sirejols, C and Surgers, A Presses Universitaires de Lyon; 'Virtual Light – Using Digital Technologies in the Process of Lighting Design' in *Tradition and Innovation in Theatre Design*, Jagiellonian University, Cracow and 'Technology and Scenography – Teaching Lighting for Performance' in *Lighting 2000*, (CIBSE (ed.) The Chameleon Press Ltd).

Roma Patel is a scenographer, and her practice is rooted in collaborative and multidisciplinary forms of productions. Her work includes set and projection designs for theatre, art direction, set visualisation for film, and digital installation art. She has been interested in the potential of digital technology within performance space itself, and has conducted research in the scalability of virtual reality and immersive interactivity. Roma's design work seeks to exploit the almost infinite possibilities of the digital realm in order to subvert the clean, generic norms that brand and limit digital art. She has most recently worked with the London International Festival of Theatre, Manchester Library Theatre and Desperate Optimists. She is also a visiting lecturer on the theatre courses at Central St Martins College of Art and Design, Rose Bruford College, Nottingham Trent University and Loughborough University. She has presented papers on interactivity and theatre in Britain and Germany.

Professor Natalie Rewa is the author of *Scenography in Canada: Selected Designers* (University of Toronto Press). She served on the jury of the Siminovitch Prize (for design, 2003). She edited *Canadian Theatre Review* between 1987 and 1993 and her work has appeared in *Australasian Drama Studies*, *Canadian Theatre Review* and *Tessera*. She was a contributing editor to *Sources of Dramatic Theory*, volume 2 (Cambridge University Press). Natalie Rewa is Professor in the Department of Drama at Queen's University in Canada.

Dr Neal Swettenham lectures in drama at Loughborough University. His interest in Richard Foreman's unusual theatre texts grew out of a wider study of narrative in performance. He has visited New York on a number of occasions (once supported by AHRC funding) to interview Foreman and his actors, watch rehearsals, and view work. He is establishing a Richard Foreman research archive at Loughborough, which will contain, amongst other things, rare recordings of a number of Foreman's productions. Recent and forthcoming publications include "An opportunity to get hit by a car: Richard Foreman at work", in Studies in Theatre and Performance Volume, 22.1, a new study of "The actor's problem: performing the plays of Richard Foreman", and "Categories and Catcalls: cognitive dissonance in The Playboy of the Western World", (Routledge) in an anthology of essays entitled *Performance and Cognition* edited by Bruce McConachie and F. Elizabeth Hart.

Dr Christine White is Senior Lecturer in Drama and Theatre Studies at Loughborough University. She has lectured in lighting, sound and multimedia theatre. Her book *Technical Theatre* (Arnold Press) documents productions from the 1990s, which have shaped her professional career, and she has worked for a variety of UK companies and events in the arts. She was Exhibition Designer & Lighting Designer 'Under Construction', *The Gallery of the Future*, April 1998, a multimedia and interactive gallery experience. She has developed the MA in *Making Performance and Multi-Media Texts* and her book with co-author Gavin Carver, *Computer Visualisations: 3D Modelling for Theatre Designers*, (Focal Press), is a key text for this research study programme. Her next book develops from her research in scenography and new media, *Pictures, Images, and Pixels: The Synaesthetics of Scenography*. She has written papers on lighting and sound in performance and is currently developing product designs for intelligent lighting, supported by the Art and Humanities Research Council. She is editor of *Scenography International*, www.sceno-international.com. She has been the convenor for the International Federation for Theatre Research for the Scenography Working Group and organised a number of international conferences and symposia. She is a member of the AHRC Peer Review College for Scenography and Performance.

Katie Whitlock is currently teaching at Ohio State University in the Department of Theatre and the Advanced Computing Center for the Arts and Design. She received a B.F.A. from the University of Arizona in stage and arts management, an M.F.A. from the University of Memphis, Tennessee in theatrical sound design, and her Ph.D. from Ohio State University in theatre history, literature, and criticism. Her dissertation entitled *Theatre and the Video Game: Beauty and the Beast* examines a variety of games genres in relation to a range of theatre theorists including Aristotle, Bertolt Brecht, Antonin Artaud, Augusto Boal, and others. This combination of popular culture and art is particularly appealing to her as a commentary on the future of performance whether onstage or in a game. She teaches classes ranging from theatre to animation, covering both practice and scholarship. As an artist, her career has taken her from performing to directing to designing in traditional theatre, as well as exploring interactivity and multimedia in performance.

Nick Wood studied at Oxford University and then worked in the theatre as an assistant director at the Royal Court, London. As a writer his early plays were produced by BBC Radio, the Kings Head, the Orange Tree, Richmond, and Hampstead theatre. He has directed new work for the

Orange Tree, and an Arts Council of England tour of the UK. In 1983, he was a founder member of the Equality Group, which performed at the ICA, London. For the last ten years, he has worked at the Central School of Speech and Drama, where he is Course Leader of the MA in Advanced Theatre Practice. This programme attracts students from around the world, and is a multidiscipline course, which enables students to work together in collaborative companies to create an integrated language of theatre. Graduates of the course include the performance group Shunt, whose latest work *Tropicana* is part of the Royal National Theatre's current season. He has contributed articles to *Artscribe* and *The Independent*, and is an editor of *Dramaturgy Forum* (dramforum.net).

INDEX